IN THE WILDERNESS

Ex dono Dr RCS Walker
socii
2001

IN THE WILDERNESS

The Doctrine of Defilement in
the Book of Numbers

Mary Douglas

OXFORD
UNIVERSITY PRESS

OXFORD

UNIVERSITY PRESS

Great Clarendon Street, Oxford OX2 6DP

Oxford University Press is a department of the University of Oxford.
It furthers the University's objective of excellence in research, scholarship,
and education by publishing worldwide in

Oxford New York

Athens Auckland Bangkok Bogotá Buenos Aires Cape Town
Chennai Dar es Salaam Delhi Florence Hong Kong Istanbul Karachi
Kolkata Kuala Lumpur Madrid Melbourne Mexico City Mumbai Nairobi
Paris São Paulo Shanghai Singapore Taipei Tokyo Toronto Warsaw
and associated companies in Berlin Ibadan

Oxford is a registered trade mark of Oxford University Press
in the UK and in certain other countries

Published in the United States
by Oxford University Press Inc., New York

© Sheffield Academic Press 1993

The moral rights of the author have been asserted
Database right Oxford University Press (maker)

First published in paperback 2001

British Library Cataloguing in Publication Data

Data available

Library of Congress Cataloging in Publication Data

Data available

ISBN 0-19-924541-X

1 3 5 7 9 10 8 6 4 2

Printed in Great Britain
on acid-free paper by
Antony Rowe Ltd,
Chippenham, Wiltshire

In the Wilderness . . . In the Days of Her Youth

'These are the statutes which the Lord commanded Moses, as between a man and his wife, and between a father and his daughter, while in her youth, in her father's house' (Num. 30.16).

'Thus says, the Lord,
I remember the devotion of your youth, your love as a bride, how you followed me in the wilderness, in a land not sown' (Jer. 2.2).

'Therefore, behold, I will allure her, and bring her into the wilderness, and speak tenderly to her . . . and there she shall answer as in the days of her youth and as at the time when she came up out of the land of Egypt . . . And I will betroth you to me forever; yea, I will betroth you to me in righteousness and in justice, and in steadfast love, and in mercy. I will betroth you to me in faithfulness, and you shall know the Lord' (Hos. 2.14–20).

CONTENTS

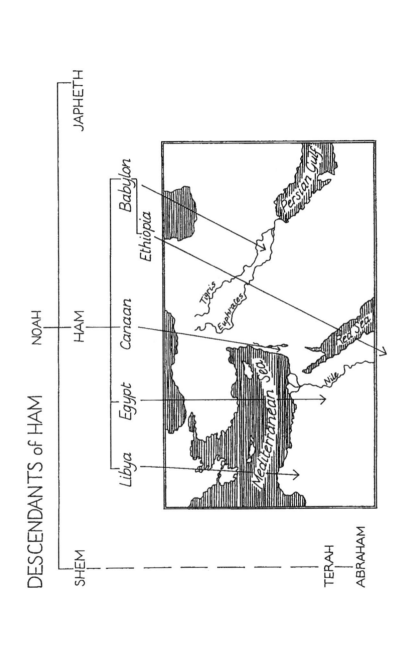

DESCENDANTS of HAM

SHEM — NOAH — JAPHETH

HAM

Libya   Egypt   Canaan   Ethiopia   Babylon

TERAH
ABRAHAM

Mediterranean Sea

Tigris
Euphrates

Persian Gulf

Red Sea

Nile

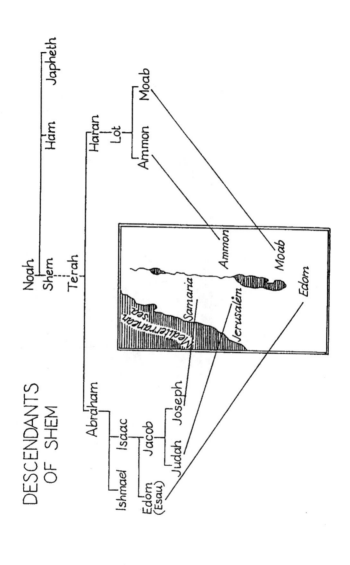

DESCENDANTS OF SHEM

Noah
Shem — Ham — Japheth

Terah
Haran
Lot
Ammon — Moab

Abraham
Ishmael — Isaac
Edom (Esau) — Jacob
Judah — Joseph

Mediterranean Sea
Samaria
Jerusalem
Ammon
Moab
Edom

Preparing a new edition, a friend told me, is like 'confession with a firm purpose of amendment'. This paperback edition of *In the Wilderness* is not a new edition in the full sense; the original book has not been revised, no new bits added or old bits suppressed. In default, an extended preface gives me a chance to confess my errors and thank my critics. There are also points of disagreement, on which I will try to make my views more persuasive.

First I must thank Oxford University Press for bringing out a paperback edition of this book on Numbers (which was originally published by Sheffield Academic Press) at the same time as a paperback of *Leviticus as Literature*.[1] It is good that they should be together since Leviticus and the book of Numbers are already a pair, assumed to have been edited by the same person/persons, or at least to stem from the same priestly milieu, and at about the same time. My two books on them are also a pair; the second depends on the first. The work I had done earlier on Numbers is the foundation for how I approached Leviticus. For example, I naturally carried over to Leviticus the prejudice in favour of the priestly editor that I had formed while studying Numbers.

I start with an absurd mistake that was passed over by most of the reviewers in charitable silence. It is like saying left instead of right, or east instead of west; there is no defending it, only confession. On p. 100 a diagram made Abraham look like the ancestor of Noah (p. 101). What I had in mind is explained correctly on the previous page. I had been struck with the thought that Numbers takes up themes of fraternal rivalry from Genesis, and produces developments or commentaries on them, but in reverse order. For example, at the beginning of Genesis Canaan is cursed by Noah, his grandfather (9.25), and the curse has its effect at the end of Numbers when the armies of Israel

---

[1] Mary Douglas, *In the Wilderness: The Doctrine of Defilement in the Book of Numbers* (Sheffield Academic Press, 1993); Mary Douglas, *Leviticus as Literature* (Oxford University Press, 1999).

defeat the Canaanites (31). At the end of Genesis the dying Joseph foretells that God will bring the sons of Israel to the land he has promised
them (50.24), which links directly to the beginning of Numbers where
the arms-bearing men of Israel are numbered in readiness to fight for the
land. It would have been much simpler to show it as a ring, one side of
which is the Genesis sequence, taken up chiastically by the Numbers
sequence. The other criticisms are more important.

Who was the Priestly Editor?

There has been some discussion about whether it is acceptable for me
to treat Leviticus and Numbers as two separate books. True, they are
more like major sections of one vaster work, the Pentateuch, and no
one could seriously dispute their elaborate intermeshing with each
other and with the other 'books', nor do we want to quibble about the
word 'book'. I could use the word 'composition' quite comfortably,
but I am impressed by the compositional differences, by the independence from each other of the two literary patterns, and by the completeness of their execution. It is worth insisting on these differences
and it seems to be unlikely that the same editor (philosopher or poet)
could have achieved two equally splendid and equally polished compositions in one lifetime. It is possible, but it would be a stupendous
achievement. There are many differences between what I am calling
two books because one is centred on the tabernacle, the other an epic
journey and war history. As far as theology and the cult are concerned,
their agreement is close. There certainly could have been one priestly
editor, or a school of priestly editors who used the same linguistic
resources and stock of ideas, and whose members may have taken up
the task at different times.

The priestly editor is called P in the context of the documentary
hypothesis which stratifies the Pentateuch into different authorial
periods based on putative documents, identified as J, E, P and D. The
immensely learned philological debate about P is very technical. The
general questions which underlie it are somewhat like those debated in
Homeric scholarship at the beginning of the twentieth century. Two
conversations were running along parallel lines, taking little notice of
each other. Who was Homer? Who was P? What was he like? Was he
one person or several? How could one poet alone be responsible for
such an enormous achievement? Was Homer literate? Did he write
down the *Iliad* himself? Are the repetitions in P evidence of an oral
tradition?

Homer never lacked admiration, but P used to have many detractors. It is distressing to see how unkindly he has been treated by important biblical scholars. Wellhausen started with an assumption about how religion would develop. He saw it as originally spontaneous and direct, but moving inevitably towards bureaucratization and meaningless rituals with its ministers passionless and remote from the congregation. This chimed with the passage in Isaiah and Psalms in which God rejects sacrifice and demands a humble and contrite heart; and it chimes with our own denominational history. The effect was that the priestly books were all too lightly dismissed by prejudiced scholarship; and not so long ago.

Writing as late as the 1960s Martin Noth, a great Bible scholar, saw Leviticus as a codex of regulations, 'mostly concerned with daily life and its different circumstances and activities. In its transmitted form, this codex is indeed remarkably diverse and disordered. Even the apparently capricious and random alternations between second person singular and third plural . . . show that the whole probably took shape as part of a fairly long and complicated process . . . The different departments of life were arranged very much at random.[2] He was similarly convinced that the book of Numbers was an incoherent jumble: 'There can be no question of the unity of the Book of Numbers, nor of its originating from the hand of a single author. This is already clear from the confusion and lack of order in its contents.'[3] He regarded Numbers as 'a multiplicity of texts' that had been quite carelessly put together. Conformably with the practice of source critics, even though he felt unable to assign its parts among the recognized Pentateuchal sources, his main effort was to assign primary and secondary character to individual bits. This is the practice that, for a long time, has stopped the book from being read as a whole.

The obscurities in the law books seems to have given free rein to nineteenth century imperial prejudices against primitive mentality, culture and magic, and to the anticlerical prejudices of our own nonconformist tradition against dark superstition and the dead hand of hierarchy. To my mind the biggest insult to the priestly editors was to expect their texts would not make sense. Many would still agree with Lester Grabbe who starts his book on Leviticus saying: 'No other book of the Bible is less appealing, at first sight, to the modem student of theology than Leviticus.[4]

[2] Martin Noth, *Leviticus*, The Old Testament Library (London: SCM Press, 1965).
[3] Martin Noth, *Numbers: A Commentary* (London: SCM Press, 1968), 4.
[4] Lester L. Grabbe, *Leviticus*, Old Testament Guides (Sheffield: Sheffield Academic Press, 1993).

Dating and History

Many reviews of *In the Wilderness* made criticisms of the kind that a writer must humbly accept. These were mostly in the domain of history. I could never develop or defend an independent conclusion about the probable dating of Numbers or Leviticus. My principal mentor, Jacob Milgrom, takes a complex view of the dating issues: some parts of Leviticus and Numbers are very, very old, perhaps even premonarchical, and, at the same time, their editing into the literary form we know could have been very late: in the sixth century BCE, exilic, or post-exilic. From this I have taken licence to focus only on the final versions, and so indulged my desire to read the book as a whole.

The really mysterious thing is that the production of the Pentateuch would have been the most important event of the epoch, world-shaking, and yet nothing is said about it in the contemporary sources. Perhaps the work started during the exile in Babylon, and perhaps it was finished in the period of the second temple community, but, if a learned reviewer[5] says that I am 'making some leaps of faith' in dating Numbers to this period, so be it. The scholars are divided; what can I say? The matter is still very technical. So little is known about the tabernacle at Shiloh and the premonarchical society living at the earliest date attributed to the sources for Numbers and Leviticus that it would be difficult to perform the anthropological exercise of relating a text to its historical context for the earliest date. This may be why I find myself leaning towards the later date, the post-exilic community.

In any case, if there was a consensus it had started to crack before I started. Vast new resources on the ancient Near East were available, documentary and archaeological. New vistas were presented on every side. The liberating spirit of the 1960s opened topics that had been closed; a new tolerance flourished in the schools. According to David Noel Freedman the spirit of renewal infected the San Francisco Theological Seminary and the Graduate Theological Union, where he and Jacob Milgrom first met in 1965. From that 'momentous and portentous time' they have been 'associated as companions-in-arms in the mighty battles of the Bible, the very serious work of expounding and

---

[5] Ronald Hendel, 'In the Wilderness: the Doctrine of Defilement in the Book of Numbers', *The Bible Review* 11.3 (1995).

interpreting the Torah and Tanakh'.[6] Mighty battles! What a far cry from regarding Leviticus as boring. A completely justified criticism is that I know too little about post-exilic Israel. Yes, too true. At the time of writing I thought that Samaria was the main danger recognized by the governors of Judah. Since then, of course, I have been trying to read that complex history. I realize that the province of Judah itself was full of foreign settlements, refugees, merchants, farmers and labourers. The histrionics of Ezra and Nehemiah made me suspect them of paranoia, but I find that historians agree with their assessment of the perils surrounding Judah while they were returning from exile. Israel's political integrity, its very existence, was really at grave risk from the nations playing out the great game of international politics. So Samaria was not the only or main problem, as I imply in this book. At least we can agree that, if the redaction process is dated to the postexilic period, it was a troubled time indeed, and it would have been hard to keep out of politics.

We do not know whether the priestly editors were left in the land of Judah when the others were taken into exile. If they had remained they would have been out of sympathy with the returning exiles. The latter, living within closed ranks in their own small enclaves in Babylon, among many other exiled ethnic groups, would be inclined to think of themselves as the elect in a world of saints and sinners; sectarian in the sense that all issues were moral issues, and moral issues all seen in black and white. They would be more suspicious of outsiders. By contrast, the priestly families of pre-exilic times had been leading members of a rich temple community. They would remember the far-reaching contacts with wealthy and influential foreigners that they had enjoyed and knew how much the prosperity of Judah depended on friendly interaction. They would have had deep misgivings about the exclusionary views of the returnees.

Moral and Political Concerns

The above pre-empts the criticism of several reviewers who rebuked my belief in the Numbers editor's strong political bias. It is an interesting point. Some reviewers regard it as sacrilege to attempt to give

---

[6] D. N. Freedman, Preface to David P. Wright, David Noel Freedman, and Avi Hurvitz (eds.), *Pomegranates and Golden Bells, Studies in Biblical, Jewish, and Near Eastern Ritual, Law, and Literature in Honour of Jacob Milgrom* (Winona Lake, Ind.: Eisenbrauns, 1995), p. ix.

historical context to sacred books which have a timeless vision. It is as if historicizing the priestly editor would besmirch his integrity. To place him in history gives scope for attributing to him motives born of local conflicts and so impugns his divinely inspired insights. I would like to persuade these critics that no harm would come of trying the historical interpretation. The difference between us may come from professional bias. An anthropologist considers that knowledge of the community for whom a text has been composed enhances understanding of its message. Knowing the context is essential for interpretation and detracts not one jot from the authority of the writer. I would still say that politics are the framework for the theological issues of the book of Numbers. Furthermore, I consider the price of refraining from historical interpretation is too high if it means accepting the denigration of the priestly editors.

Numbers starts with Moses being told to count the children of Israel, and he does so. The number of the 'father's houses' or tribes descended from the sons of Jacob, is twelve. There are other countings in the course of the story, and each time there are always twelve tribes. Attributing the book to the second temple period has the advantage of providing a plausible reason for reckoning the twelve tribes, over and over, so prominently. By that time there was only Judah and a remnant of Benjamin. The rest had disappeared into mythology, except for the Josephites (represented by Ephraim) who had been located in Samaria: the remnants of the Northern Kingdom of Israel. Politically, Samaria and Judah confronted each other; rival peoples with a common ancestor. It is not safe to jump from the beginnings of the first return to Judah from Babylon in 538 to the return of Ezra in 455. But one can assume that, to a large extent, the problems faced by returning exiles concerning the local populations would have been much the same from the start: problems about land, intermarriage and inheritance.

When the Assyrian king defeated Samaria and deported her inhabitants he drafted in thousands of miscellaneous deportees from other conquered lands to replace them. Ezra and Nehemiah seem to have understood that Samaria was now inhabited only by foreign idolaters and refused to have anything to do with them. They made the equivalent assumption that in Judah there were no Judeans or other people of Israel; apart from those who had returned from Babylon the inhabitants were all foreign idolaters. For these leaders the full responsibility for keeping the covenant with God now lay solely with Israel. As they defined her, Israel consisted of the returnees from Babylon inhab-

iting Judah: a province in great danger, surrounded by idolatrous enemies. But the definition of Israel was too narrow. There would have
been numerous heirs to the covenant still living around; many of them
in Judah itself, or in the bordering countries.

Rather than supposing that he was not involved in politics it was
more likely the Numbers editor was making a major political statement against the Persian-backed governors of Judah. Numbers makes
sense as an attack on their policy against intermarriage, and particularly as a rebuke to the definition of Israel as consisting only of those
who had been to Babylon. In that political climate it would have been
bold for these priests to say outright to their congregations, 'Look,
these surrounding peoples (whom our governor tells us to reject) are
our brothers. We must cherish them.' Many passages in the book read
as a covert plea on behalf of the other people living in Judah, 'sons of
Jacob, but not Jews', as Rolf Rendtorff puts it.[7] The book insists
overtly that the *ger*, the stranger, is entitled to share in the cult (Num.
5.14–16). He has the right to offer sacrifice and he can have atonement
made for his unintentional sins (Num. 22–30). It follows that the rules
of ritual uncleanness must apply to him because he is entitled to
approach the tabernacle.

It is fair to read the priestly editor as protesting against the appro-
priation of the Covenant for a small section of the descendants of
Jacob. It was certainly very much his duty as a priest. In this light the
Numbers' stories of wars fought by the armies of Israel against the
Canaanites, sometimes viewed askance as a glorification of violence
and bloodshed, carry another implication. The war stories (19–21)
show God's people fighting together, against terrible odds; all twelve
tribes marshalled against common enemies. The point is reinforced
when the armies of Reuben and Gad, who seem prepared to opt out,
are speedily brought back into line (32). If my reading of the political
context is right, recalling the wars celebrates the common military past
of all these, now scattered, peoples. They have fought together, shoulder to shoulder, and shared in losses and victories; they should stand
together and succour each other now.

However ancient their sources, there would have been a reason for
composing the whole book around these numberings. If it was edited
in the tempestuous days of the second temple period, it was probably

---

[7] Rolf Rendtorff, 'The *ger* in the Priestly Laws of the Pentateuch', *Ethnicity in the Bible* (forthcoming); Mary Douglas, 'The Stranger in the Bible', *Archives Europ. Soc.* 35 (1994), 283–298.

a brave thing to insist that all of Jacob's twelve sons were heirs to God's promises to Israel.

Enclavism

Another criticism that I willingly accept concerns the typology of religions that fills the first three chapters of my book.[8] The reviewer is quite right in pointing out that I have drawn too sharp a line between the culture of hierarchies and the culture of sectarian religions. This has been borne home to me by two workshops on the culture of the enclave organized subsequently in London.[9] Several Jewish friends have told me that Chapter 2, on enclave religion, reminded them vividly of their childhood in a kibbutz, particularly the concern to prevent defection, especially defection of the young, and the attempt to censor information. When they ask how I got the experience of a sectarian culture, I confess it was not from studying the anthropology of a kibbutz, but from my childhood in the Catholic culture of England in the 1930s. The members of what outsiders take to be a confident, well-entrenched, hierarchical system may actually be very sectarian in their values. It is my own belief that these categories, which are useful for talking about religious organization, apply to quite ephemeral forms. The boundary round an enclave, for all the anxious wishes of its leaders, is a wavering line, a fact which is fully in accord with the theory that cultural bias is a response to a particular type of organization.

The Catholic Church in France, beleaguered by the philosophical rationalism prevailing since the eighteenth century,[10] and the Catholic Church in England, a minority almost submerged by waves of scientific western secularism, are good examples of how easily a form of organization that could be expected to be open and liberal, can develop an exclusionary, defensive culture. It then changes its own organization to fit its ideology. Recently, for another example, the *Irish Times* reported the formal request for forgiveness made by Dr W. Walsh, Catholic bishop of Killaloe for the 1908 decree on mixed marriages, and the opinion of the Church of Ireland archbishop that the

---

[8] J. W. Rogerson, 'Enclave in Judah', *Times Literary Supplement*, 12 Aug.1994, p.28.

[9] The first, 'Withdrawal, Control and Terror', sponsored by the ESRC, convened by Gerald Mars and Mary Douglas, in Jan.1999. The second, 'In and Out of the Enclave: The Jewish Experience', sponsored by the Jewish Studies Department, University College London, convened by A. Baumgarten, in March 2000.

[10] R. Griffiths, *The Reactionary Revolution: The Catholic Revival in French Literature, 1570–1914* (London: Constable, 1966).

decree had been 'one of the most painful issues facing church of Ireland communities'.[11] With these instances in mind of sectarianism recurring in hierarchical places it is easy to acknowledge the force of the criticism that the line in Chapter 2 is drawn too sharply.

Aniconic Religion

The same reviewer made another point: it is a mistake to associate aniconic behaviour with sectarian religion. He cites a recent source which suggests that King Josiah's religious reforms in 622 BCE caused the seals of ruling families to become aniconic; so here the rejection of images begins with the royal court. This is very interesting, and the point I have just conceded about the fluidity of cultural bias and the ease with which sectarian attitudes can arise, prepares the ground for bowing to the criticism.

Since working on *In the Wilderness* I have been trying to read more about aniconic religion. Outstanding is Moshe Barasch's *Icon*.[12] It is a classic introduction to theories of representation which reviews, among other topics, ancient arguments about imaging the invisible. The same profound questions about artistic representation of the divine have been aired from antiquity through the Renaissance to modern times. It was for me an eye opener to learn that aniconic doctrines were being argued, won and lost throughout antiquity, like sectarianism. Aniconic religion was evidently not introduced to the world by the Bible. The perfect partner to this book is Lionel Kochan's *Beyond the Graven Image*[13] which sets Jewish views in a broad context. He makes it obvious that images are bound to have attracted philosphical suspicion at all times. Aniconism is always with us; it may not always surface, but tension between the work of art and the philosophy of perception is at the heart of aesthetic experience. In Jewish cultural history a discourse on the falsity of the icon carries overtones from the discourse against idolatry. As the title suggests, Kochan goes far beyond the Bible, but it is salutary for the Bible students to recognize these themes in their own history. Distance is reduced; the

11 The 1908 decree obliged both partners to a mixed marriage to give a written undertaking that all children of the union would be brought up as Roman Catholics, *Irish Times*, 8 May 1997. Admittedly this was a response to a history of exclusionary behaviour on the part of the established Church.

12 Moshe Barasch, *Icon: Studies in the History of an Idea* (New York: NYU Press, 1992).

13 Lionel Kochan, *Beyond the Graven Image: A Jewish View* (London: Macmillan, 1997).

biblical command against graven images is less alien. So well does he turn the tables on our preconceptions that we want to reverse our original question: not when, or why, are icons rejected, but the other way round; when and how far are they ever acceptable?

Pondering these things I fortunately talked to Margaret Barker who directed me to T. Mettinger's article synthesizing sources on ancient Near Eastern aniconism.[14] In surveying archaeological evidence for aniconic cults in the ancient Semitic world, he finds that, prior to the biblical prohibitions of graven images, there was a long-standing tradition of aniconism, and cites evidence of the decline of anthropomorphism in Israelite art from Iron Age I. He concludes his survey with: 'Some of the West Semitic cultures, the Arabic, the Nabatean, the Israelite and the Phoenician ones, fostered a type of aniconism of their own with the cultic role of standing stones as the characteristic feature. Secondly, it should be clear that Israelite aniconism is by no means a late, isolated phenomenon, due to some internal Israelite development' (p. 176); it was intrinsic to Israelite religion.

So aniconism is normal, always lurking, ready to come out and take over in favourable circumstances. In response to my critic, I would venture to suggest that the shifting of a population into a sectarian organization, seeking to restore more austere approaches to the divine, would provide just the right conditions for a renewed attack on images. Another conclusion is that Bible studies are coming out of any protective academic enclave they might have sheltered in. They are showing tremendous enthusiasm, taking up old themes such as aniconism in a broad, interdisciplinary sweep. There is a renewed interest in rhetorical conventions in the literatures of the region.[15]

The Structure of Numbers

Most of the reviewers have noted the novel account of Numbers' composition in a ring. I still think that the main interest of *In the Wilderness* is the finding that Numbers conforms unexpectedly to a well-known literary convention. To conform the work must be composed of recog-

[14] T. Mettinger, 'Aniconism: A Western Context for the Israelite Phenomenon', in Walter Dietrich and Martin Klopfenstein (eds.), *Ein Gott Allein?*, Kolloquium der Schweizerischen Akademie der Geistes, 13 (1993), 159–173.

[15] D. Luciani, 'Soyez saints, car je suis saint . . . un commentaire de Lévitique 19', *Nouvelle Revue Théologique de Louvain,* 114.2 (1992), 212–236; 'Le Jubilé dans Lévitique 25', *Nouvelle Revue Théologique,* 30.4 (1999) 456-486. In these two recent articles, D. Luciani has used chiastic structures to defend Leviticus against the charges of confusion and randomness levelled by Noth.

nizably distinct units in parallel pairs, the pairing so organized that the last one matches the first and arranged so that the ending comes back to the beginning. Most of *In the Wilderness* discusses and illustrates this genre. I am sorry that it imposes hard work on the reader who tries to read Numbers synoptically across matching pairs of text. In the case of Numbers, section 2 starts the series of laws and matches to 12, which concludes it; the stories in 3 correspond to those in 11; the laws in 4 correspond to those in 10, and so on. The result is that the whole of Numbers is constructed in a huge ring formed of alternating stories and laws set in parallel with each other, twelve in all.

We are so used to linear writing that it is a shock at first to imagine a whole law book or epic constructed as if it were a sonnet with a very definite rhyming system. But the sonnet is a good example to have in mind because, when it comes to metre or rhymed line endings, there is no scope for disagreeing about the sounds of the consonants and vowels or the length of the metre. It can be conclusively shown that either the pattern is abba abba cc, or it is another pattern. There is nothing subjective about it. Everything depends on how clearly the units of the structure are identified. A different kind of patterning makes semantic structures in mythology, (or in my feeble attempt on pp. 100–1 to show a chiastic relation between Numbers and Genesis, apologized for on the first page above). Semantic structures give a great deal of scope for arbitrary and subjective patternings. Classicists, trying to decided how the *Iliad* was originally divided up, cannot come to any firm agreement because they are not looking for objective building blocks of the structure.[16] Bible scholars are much stricter: when one of them claims to have found a complex chiastic patterning the critics will not be convinced unless the alleged parallelism is supported by verbal evidence, such as marking the structural units by the exact repetitions which had led earlier students to suppose the editor was nodding.

The Numbers poet meets this strict test by having selected a clear set of cues to mark the switch between one section and the next, so making the principle of alternation unmistakable: first a narrative section, with a very clear beginning and ending, then a legal section, then alternating narrative and law all the way to the end. To check on my claims for Numbers it is helpful to hold the Bible in one hand and my analysis in the other and read them simultaneously. The reviewer who thought I was basing the structure on semantic similarities had not

---

[16] M. S. Jensen, 'Dividing Homer, When and How were the *Iliad* and the *Odyssey* divided into Songs?', *Symbolae Osloenses* 74, 1999, 5–91.

noticed the account of what was objectively there for anyone to see, nor appreciated David Goodman's careful notes on the Hebrew text expressly included to keep me from cheating.

The result is to give the whole book a surprisingly different set of meanings. It is a challenge, not just to readers of the Pentateuch, but to the accepted reading of many ancient sacred texts in other cultures. Heroic poetry was often composed on a principle of alternation whether of alternating male and female voices, of prose and verse, or of scene shifts. It seems very probable that the alternation of nights and days in the *Iliad* is a similar automatic indicator of how the poem is divided.[17] The sceptical reviewer predicted that I would be able to find the structure in any text that I cared to examine. But however hard I might try, Leviticus is not amenable to that patterning as it has only two stories. It does turn out to be arranged in a consummately beautiful but quite different pattern of parallels. It helps to understand the structure of each of the books by comparing one with the other.

There is nothing very rare about parallelism; in fact it is a widely dispersed literary form. Roman Jakobson maintained that it is a form of expression as hardwired to our brain as the capacity for grammar.[18] The anthropologist, James Fox, has recorded native parallel poetry in widely scattered parts of the globe,[19] and the Zoroastrian scholars have found it far back in time.[20] I would hope that finding a chiastic structure governing the whole composition of Numbers, and quite another governing the composition of Leviticus, will be helpful to classicists and others trying to find the original joints in an antique literary work. Ring composition is based on analogies; discovering that one story has been matched to another sharpens the satisfaction of reading; there is wit in finding that a and a[i] have been selected for something in common, and that together they point to a meaning deeper than either. The wit and daring in a non-verbal way are captured by David Noel Freedman when he draws a comparison between the author of Psalm 119 and a master juggler:

What fascinates is the way in which the poet manages to establish and maintain the underlying and overarching patterns and at the same time seems to

---

[17] Mary Douglas, 'The Glorious Book of Numbers', *Jewish Studies Quarterly*, 1.3 (1993–4), 193–216.

[18] Roman Jacobson and Krystyna Pomorska, *Dialogues between Roman Jacobson and Krystyna Pomorska*, (Cambridge University Press, 1983)

[19] James Fox, 'Roman Jacobson and the Comparative Study of Parallelism', *Roman Jacobson: Echoes of his Scholarship* (Lisse: Peter de Ridder Press, 1997).

[20] Martin Schwarts, 'The Ties that Bind: On the Form and Content of Zarathrustra's Mysticism', in F. Vejifdor (ed.), *New Approaches to the Interpretation of the Gathas*, Proceedings of the Tint Gatha Colloquium (London: W.Z.O., 1998).

lose his grip and wander off the defined limits; but in fact everything balances out and we can only applaud the artist and his finished work. . . . we may think of a master juggler, who having started with the usual hoops and balls, manages to keep adding more and more objects to his repertoire and at the same time climbs on a chair that is balanced on one leg, juggles with different parts of his body: arms, legs, head; seems on the point of losing everything, then miraculously collects everything piece by piece, including the chair, makes his bow, and departs to sustained applause, while people wonder how he did it. The same is true of this poet and his poem.[21]

The Numbers editor is no psalmist, but certainly a master of balance.

October 2000   Mary Douglas

---

[21] David Noel Freedman, 'The Structure of Psalm 119', in Wright, Freedman and Hurvitz (eds.) *Pomegranates and Golden Bells*, 727.

PREFACE

My first thanks must go to the University of Edinburgh for inviting me to give the Gifford Lectures in 1989 and to Graeme Auld and James Mackey who, with the members of the Divinity School, hosted me so kindly there and encouraged me to continue my sojourn in the territory of biblical studies.

Since almost any work in the field of social anthropology would seem suitable for meeting the desire of the founder of the Gifford Lectures, that they promote the study of 'natural religion', I was casting round widely for a topic when Katherine Sakenfeld asked me to drop into the Princeton Seminary to talk to her students about Chapter 19 in the book of Numbers. This is about the so-called sacrifice of the red heifer for the purification for the people of Israel. I read the chapter for the first time, and though puzzled, I went readily to talk to the class, feeling confident that there was sure to be something helpful that an anthropologist could contribute to the study of ritual defilement and purification. I was quite mistaken: there was nothing I could tell those student that they did not already know.

The text was so thick with problems that I was reminded of the late Professor Stein's correction of my draft chapter on Leviticus for *Purity and Danger*. I had written that the Levitical list of forbidden birds was the hoariest puzzle in the Bible, but in the margin he wrote, No, and explained afterwards that the Bible is so full of hoary puzzles that it would be arbitrary to privilege one. I thank Katherine Sakenfeld for making me read the book of Numbers and starting me on the most absorbing quest for understanding that anyone could hope for.

I am specially grateful to the faculty of the Department of Religious Studies in Princeton for their stimulus and interest. This study would have progressed more rapidly on a surer route if I had started serious work on the Bible in their company, but before it had got very far I retired to London. Fortunately I was able to benefit from an affiliation to the Religious Studies Department in Lancaster, whose staff I also thank for their patient support. I must thank the Trustees of the

Rockefeller Centre in the Villa Serbelloni at Bellagio for a pampered month in idyllic circumstances in 1989.

Trying to enter a new field of study when professionally in retirement has special problems which I would not have been able to overcome but for generous grants towards research assistance. I am extremely grateful to the Nuffield foundation for a grant which enabled me to engage Richard Lim and Mark Pegg for short periods in 1988, and to the Spencer Foundation for a grant towards help from Ronald Hendel in 1989. These historians' critical support was invaluable for helping me to formulate my research problems. Thanks to a grant from the British Academy in 1991 I engaged David Goodman to work with me on the Hebrew text of Numbers. It is a rare privilege to collaborate with an erudite, sensitive and enthusiastic scholar and I owe David Goodman much gratitude for his guidance, and for the notes on key Hebrew words that are appended to chapters in the book.

The Community of Bible scholars has been extraordinarily supportive and generous with time and criticism. The towering figure in the interpretation of the priestly work is Jacob Milgrom, who has been my friend for more than twenty years. During this time he was preparing a major commentary on Numbers which finally appeared in 1990, and was quickly followed by the first volume of an even bigger commentary on Leviticus. It has to be confessed that the priestly work is not a high favourite with students of the Bible, and so Milgrom's magisterial commentaries are landmarks for everyone in a sparse terrain. My overwhelming personal indebtedness shows in the large file of careful notes that I have received from him, some from work, some written while packing for a holiday, some, alas, from a hispital bed. Academics do not normally take such pains for ignorant enquirers, and I sense that I have been the beneficiary of a kind of pastoral concern. Perhaps it comes from an extended rabbinical tradition, for Ihave had remarkably kind attention from Jacob Neusner in the past and from Baruch Levine, whom I consulted more recently about defilement in Leviticus.

I have to apologize to Bible scholars. In poor return for their courtesy and help I fear I have produced a kind of 'smart Alec' statement, which suggests (as a friend remarked) that since the year one we have 'all been marching out of step, except our Mary'. The unfortunate effect is partly due to a newcomer's brashness and partly to my conviction that the priestly editors have been neglected and misinterpreted. I find them often contrasted unfavourably with the prophets, and charged implicitly with cherishing the trappings and neglecting the substance of religion. It is almost as if the interpretation of Judaism has to do with two religions, one of compassion and the other of rules. It has taken me a long time to realize that the prophets and priests were one religious community, and the religion a whole; and that the first words of Numbers, 'In the Wilderness', are pregnant for its meaning.

So many Bible scholars have shown me what I should be doing, the most valuable of course being those who disagree with me profoundly and so forced me to think harder. I cannot name them all. Professor Talmon encouraged me to apply the model of the beleaguered enclave society to the postexilic community. Those who encouraged me to study the literary form of Numbers must be acknowledged gratefully. I thank Wolfgang Roth for demonstrating the synoptic reading of one book of the bible through another; Rolf Rendtorff for supporing the hypothesis that numbers is a structured composition, even if I have not identified the correct structure; Peter Schäfer for asking bluntly if the book has a structure what difference that makes to the reading; Benjamin Harshav I thank for advice about Hebrew poetry and Yiddish literature; Robert Littman for revealing to me that the structure that I had found in Numbers was similar to literary forms well-known in the Mediterranean region from the eighth to fifth centuries; Michael Goulder for the demonstration of how to read a book of the Bible in its historical context; the ISISSS class of 1991 for brilliant stimulus.

I specially want to thank a numbeR of people who taught me about literary structures in other cultures: Milena Dolezelova on thirteenth-century Chinese novels, John Van Sickle on first-century Latin poetry, Conrad Leyser on synecdoche in Vergil, Arthur Hatto on epic styles, Aditya Behl on ring composition in Persian poetry, Miriam Hansen on early film techniques of montage, Wendy Doniger on Hindu mythology. I will always be grateful to Klaus Reichert for the glimpse I had of his linguistic and Renaissance scholarship.

Another group of people on whose work this study draws directly, Michael Thompson, Steve Rayner, Gerald Mars, and Aaron Wildavsky, have revealed the cosmological underpinnings of contemporary society with respect to perception of risk. Marcel Calvez opened up new depths by discovering the contemporary populist appeal of pollution ideas about handicap and contagion. Emmanuel Sivan's original work on enclave culture and fundamentalism gives me confidence in the usefulness of the analytic framework I have used in this volume. I will not forget that Kate Cooper warned me that when interpreting documents on governance in Late Antiquity she found it is misleading to take references to women and womanhood literally; or Noriko Ouchi who corrected me on the idea of hierarchy in traditional Japan. My thanks also to Mark Pegg for many exhilarating discussions about medieval ideas of insidious danger.

I know that as a freelance without any defined place in the academic system I have made specially taxing demands on my colleagues in London. At Heythrop College, where the library has been an invaluable resource, Jenny Dines and Robert Murray gave constant encouragement as well as irreplaceable bibliographic help. I also thank Louis Jacobs and Christopher Holdsworth, Marjorie Reeves and other members of the London Society for the Study of Religion. In the University of London I have benefitted from the patient criticism of Mark Geller, Lin Fox Hall, Chimen Abramsky and Michael Weitzman, who so kindly read and commented on parts of the text. Richard Coggins also worked on the chapter on Balaam and has my special thanks for making available to me his knowledge of the postexilic period.

Among anthropologists Adam Kuper deserves special gratitude for poring over the lists of Jacob's sons with me and updating me on kinship. For analysis of archaic literary sources I thank Bernadette Bucher, Douglas Lewis, James Fox, Rodney Needham, and also Richard Fardon who read the whole of the penultimate version and advised major changes which I have tried to adopt. Thanks do not give responsibility, and I suspect that none of these scholars agree with what is said in these pages.

I thank Pat Novy for the diagrams. Times have changed, and where formerly a secretary might have taken the strains of producing a book, it is the technical staff who now allay an author's feverish anxieties. I humbly thank Lee Drew in the Computer Advisory Services for awesome technical skills and heroic rescues, and further thank Edith hall for her calm control of the formidable machinery in the Copying Room of University College.

Mary Douglas
February 1993

MAPS AND DIAGRAMS

ABBREVIATIONS

HUCA	*Hebrew College Annual*
JAAR	*Journal of the American Academy of Religion*
JCS	*Journal of Cuneeiform Studies*
JSS	*Journal of Semantic Studies*
NCB	New Century Bible
VT	*Vetus Testamentum*
WBC	World Biblical Commentary

Kindly note that the text of this book starts on page 21 and not page 1 as is normally found.

Chapter 1

THE BOOK OF NUMBERS IN THE CONTEXT
OF COMPARATIVE RELIGION

1. *Defilement*

The object of this study is to open a place for a new reading of the book of Numbers. Trying to apply the practice of anthropology to Numbers produces several surprises. For one, the interpretation of defilement in the Bible turns out to be quite different from religious defilement as understood elsewhere. Another is the unexpectedly complex and elegant rhetorical structure of the book. Then the political implications of Numbers turn out to be more universalist, open, and anti-separatist than usually credited. This introduction will first explain some fundamental things about defilement and magic from an anthropologist's point of view.

From a religious perspective defilement is not merely a symbol of something else, or even the balance on which ideas of virtue and sin are weighed, but the basic condition of all reality. That the idea is ontological is difficult for modern readers of the Bible to appreciate. A secular vocabulary has no way to denote religious reality and so no way of understanding a vocabulary of cosmic danger from transgression. We have trouble understanding the word because changes in our own usage have destroyed the possibility of direct translation. For us purity is completely absorbed into the vocabulary of hygiene, a word to do with household detergents and pure foods, cut off from any religious sense of divine action in the universe[1]. In most religions

---

1. Wittgenstein protested against Frazer's trivializing of the ancient fire-festivals: 'What narrowness of spiritual life we find in Frazer! And as a result: how impossible for him to understand a different way of life from the English one of his time!' (*Remarks on Frazer's Golden Bough* [ed. R. Rhees; New Jersey: Humanities Press, 1979], p. 5e).

there is some such word, like Polynesian *mana*, or Arabian *baraka*, meaning positive power, whose complementary opposite is something equivalent to the idea of defilement, in the same way as curse and blessing, or sin and grace, are complementary. Without a contrast set of words to oppose divine energy with its contaminating danger, the language of religious impurity is undecipherable.

For this reason it is a mistake in reading a religious text to keep curses and blessings (which we understand fairly easily) in a separate compartment from defilements and purifications (with which we have difficulty). Many times a biblical passage on avoidance of corpses, or avoidance of other defilements, presents a stumbling block: given the emptiness of our idea of purity, God's violent reaction to impurity seems overdone. To meet the problem a Mesopotamian scholar has suggested that a quite alien word, the Polynesian word 'taboo', would make a better translation now than 'defilement'. It is good advice to use the word taboo to make a clean break with our preconceptions. According to Mark Geller the Mesopotamian equivalent to impurity is a rule of separation which if breached will unleash automatic disaster.[1] Taboo is part of a complex of forces which includes oaths, vows, blessings and curses. It is not a semantic matter but part of the theory of existence. A power as inescapable as the force of gravity is built into the constitution of the universe, everything works through it, and nothing can work against it. It cannot be stopped from having its effect. Even the Mesopotamian gods are subject to it. Each god or goddess has certain taboos which have to be observed by the worshippers and whose effect he or she cannot mitigate: again our grammatical usage impedes translation—the taboo is not something that a god 'has' so much as an intrinsic part of his being, what he is.

While the priests of Israel were carefully separating what should be said about the God of Israel from what was being said in the region about the false gods, they would be amending the theory of existence to fit their vision, and in that vision defilement would have had a necessary place. Oaths have taboo effect, because words are implicated in this complex of energy: not all words, but certain words, and especially names, and especially names of gods. The dire effects of a broken oath cannot be averted. In the Bible all the various causes of disaster—from broken oaths to curses, trespass into holy places, lying,

---

1. M. Geller, 'The Šurpu Incantations and Lev. V.1-5', *JSS* 25.2 (1980), p. 183.

stealing, false witness, all the misdeeds which we tend to treat separately—come under the heading of impurity. One may think of it like a rift in existence: on the one side there is God and everything he establishes, on the other side, inevitably and necessarily, there is impurity. For the Bible, and in the whole region, the destructive effect of impurity is physical, like a lightning bolt or a disease. Nothing less than divinely instituted rites of purification will defend against it. The underlying principle is that death and life are opposed, corpses cannot be in the presence of the Lord, nor any unpurified persons who have been in contact with a corpse, nor sinners. The rule is as inexorable as if God had taken an oath or vow against corpse contact, but no oath is necessary, it is in the nature of the Lord to be in command of death and to be in contradiction of it. The same for murder, lies and cheating, and all the sins bracketed together as breaking faith: impurity is a taboo of God, and liable to have dire results.[1] The practice of religion is to make it possible for humans to relate to the dread source of power, and to enjoy the benefits of the relations without suffering from unwanted dangerous effects.

Knowing this we can adjust our usual interpretation of oaths and vows. They are not the same as the words which have judicial implications in our courts of justice: these biblical oaths trigger the power that drives the universe. Invoking God is conditional, used to back a promise or to support an intention, with terrible effect if the condition is not met. A person who makes a vow is held to it, not by any one else's intention, but by the inherent nature of vows. Human persons make vows and are compelled to keep them or to suffer the consequences, and in the same way, God's taboos are like vows for God. The nearest equivalent that can bring this idea closer to our experience is the notion of honour among the Vikings, or in medieval Europe, or honour still to this day around the shores of the Mediterranean. Bad consequences, real disaster, will finish the life of one who breaks a vow. A lie, a broken promise, an unfulfilled vow or oath denied are all defiling.

This means that it is blasphemous to doubt God's promises, for the covenants he made with Noah, Abraham, Isaac and Jacob are his

---

1.   Jacob Milgrom in a personal communication rightly demurs against using the one word 'taboo' to combine the rule and the effects of its breach, but this convenient verbal slackness is normal usage in anthropological writing, and I ask to be forgiven for continuing it here.

vows. As humans have their honour to defend, God's honour is at stake. Noah's blessings and curses on his sons, and Jacob's dying blessings on his twelve sons, which will figure largely in this reading of Numbers, have the same force. They must come true. Nothing can be done to stop them. A vow, a curse, or a blessing commits the future.

In all previous civilizations the religion defines reality and the concept of impurity shapes the world. For us a long scientific liberal tradition has made our culture secular and pluralist. The effort of tolerance so needful for living in a plural society leads us to repudiate the drawing of moral lines and social boundaries but it is of the essence of impurity to draw sharp lines. This may be why comparative religion starts with a prejudice against impurity and finds defilement difficult to understand.

One of the peculiarities of biblical defilement is the logical clarity with which the concept is developed. It is a highly cerebral philosophy of existence, much more systematically expressed than most taboo ideas. The biblical idea of purity is simple and coherent. The nature of the living God is in opposition to dead bodies. Total incompatibility holds between God's presence and bodily corruption. God is living, life is his. Other gods belong to death and the contagion of decay.[1] Blood is the very locus of the opposition: living blood is his, poured out for atonement; dead blood, torn bleeding bodies, cadavers with blood in them, are the sign of the false gods. The other gods are not only dead, but their worship is conducted in graveyards and tombs, by necromancy, consultation with ghosts, magic performed upon the bodies of necrophagous animals, bats, bugs, and worms. Humans are subject to normal processes of physiological decay, but woe to the human person who does not take immediate steps to be purified after contact with death, and woe again to the person who touches or eats animals which feed on carrion or take blood into the body for nourishment. Defilement is lethally contagious.

For anthropologists there is something extraordinary about biblical defilement. Defilement is never just a doctrine in the abstract. A system of purity rules is like a net spread to isolate expected sources

---

1. M. Smith (*Palestinian Parties and Politics that Shaped the Old Testament* [London: SCM Press, 1971]) suggests (pp. 83-84) that the association of defilement with idolatry is an innovative ruling of the 'Yahweh-alone party', as found in Hag. 2.13.

of contamination, and especially particular categories of persons who present a danger of contamination. To understand it, we always need to know who is issuing accusations of defilement and who is the accused. The answer fits a map of social classifications into the theory of existence. Unless we can trace which categories of social life are being kept apart, how they are ranked and who is being excluded, the usual analysis of defilement is blocked.

On the traditional reading of Leviticus and Numbers the defiler is taken to be the outsider: the thrust of the doctrine is thought to be exclusionary. It is a reasonable reading, since this is the normal use of defilement as a weapon of exclusion anywhere in the world. On this reading, the laws of purity would be the mechanism by which Judaism was turned away from the nations. Max Weber's position summarizes the generally accepted view:

> The negative attitude of the Jews themselves was rather the decisive factor for anti-semitism in antiquity, the increasingly rigid rejection of community with non-Jews.[1]

Weber makes the inference that the priests, as the framers of the purity code, were the prime agents of this turning away. However, close attention to the laws of defilement in Numbers and Leviticus gives a very different slant.

These books never use the principle of ritual purity to separate classes or races, foreigners or natives. This is very remarkable. In Leviticus and Numbers certain bodily conditions, idolatry, and transgressions against keeping faith with God are defiling. However much isolated bits of the text may have been quoted to support contrary views, in the biblical creed defilement is not caused by contact with other people; it comes out of the body, or it comes out of moral failure. Everybody is liable to be defiled or to defile. This should be totally unexpected to the anthropologist used to purity codes in other religions.

It is difficult to exaggerate the immense difference it makes to the interpretation of Numbers and Leviticus. The biblical purity code tells the people of Israel that impurity comes out of their own bodies and their own transgressions. Impurity is universal. The purity law does not encourage them to believe that defilement comes from where they might like to look for it: biblical defilement is *not* from contact with

---

1. M. Weber, *Ancient Judaism* (New York: Free Press, 1952), p. 417.

foreigners or from lower classes. It is not used for keeping them out-side or in lower ranks. As to dealing with the stranger, Leviticus teaches the congregation, 'Love the stranger as thyself' (Lev. 19.34).

In the pages that follow the idea will be proposed that the priestly doctrine of purity was designed as an antidote to popular theories of defilement aimed against immigrant labourers or foreigners settled in the region. The priestly doctrine which universalizes the causes of defilement and only allows it to be used to protect the sanctuary would also be part of a programme of rationalizing and organizing the philosophy of Judaism. Hence its abstract completeness and the absence of information about social discrimination. The highly abstract and coherent form of the laws of purity encourages us to persevere in the over-intellectualist bias in our traditions of comparative religion.

2. *The Intellectualist Bias*

Historians of religion sometimes betray the assumption that religion is a stable factor, carried in the heads of the people, and only likely to shift when the people travel and take it with them. When they move, bits of other people's religions rub off on to theirs as a result of con-tact, but essentially theirs remains recognizably their original religion, plus some accretions. The people of Israel, on this immigration model, would have always had their own, unique, monotheistic reli-gion. After all, this is what they said themselves. Contagion from immigrants carrying Canaanite or Assyrian religion, or from settlers belonging to cults of the north or the south, are the usual explanations of the diversity of cults found in the Bible. The rejection of these foreign elements is treated by scholars as a process for protecting from adulteration an original Israelite religion, very old and quite unlike the religions of Egypt, Babylon, Phoenicia, Assyria and Canaan. The Bible's claim that Abraham came from afar with a new religion fits the intellectualist view according to which a religion is a normally stable pattern of thought, only altered by foreign influence. This view has to deal with the contradiction between the Israelites' own tradition of having entered and forcibly conquered the region, and the absence of evidence that they were not there continuously.[1] If they had always been living in Canaan, the intellectualist approach has

1. J.A. Soggin, *A History of Israel, from the Beginnings to the Bar Kochba Revolt, A.D. 135* (London: SCM Press, 1984), chs. 6 and 7.

a puzzle about the difference between Israelite and Canaanite religions. We know so little about the Canaanites we cannot be sure that they did not also have monotheistic moments, complex pantheons which at times held together under the authority of a single rational, moral God, and at other times dissolved into warring local deities.

Part of the puzzle derives from the over-concretization of the idea of a religion as if it were something inherently resistant to change, held together by the logic of its thoughts. So Israel's religion would always have been what it is said by its adherents to be, essentially opposed to its neighbours' religions. Antiquated ideas about the difficulty of achieving monotheism have created the rest of the puzzle. Monotheism, often said to be the highest achievement of Judaism, is not difficult, nor rare. Many versions of monotheism could have been possible. It is not the invention of monotheism in a region where a plurality of gods abounded that is the true originality of Judaism, but the invention of an aniconic God, who could not be imaged, who tolerated no other gods, in whose name an exhaustive purity code was enforced.

Writing the Bible is one thing; inventing a new religion and writing it down is quite another. It is widely agreed that the main editorial work was put in hand by priests and scribes during the exile in Babylon,[1] and probably completed during the postexilic period. This only gives fifty to a hundred years for producing a new religious synthesis. It seems to be short for a brand new form of religion. There would have had to be prior agreement among the scholars, priests, lawyers and poets engaged in the task. They could hardly have patched up severe disagreements on theological or political matters in so little time without more seams showing in the writing. The written synthesis of the Bible could only be so strong if the synthesis of the religion was already well in hand at the level of practice, and not mainly created out of learned discussion between historians and theoreticians.

A congregation would have been performing the ceremonies together and applying their religious ideas to their common lot. Their leaders would have to be competing for the congregations' approval, mixing with secular political problems and taking sides on contemporary issues. The religion would be made to accommodate many disparate interests in the life of its congregation; it would need

---

1. Between 586 BCE, the destruction of the first temple, and 538, the edict of Cyrus allowing the remnant to return (Ezra 1.2-4; 6.2-5).

to be complex in its ritual and its philosophy. Complexity takes time to develop. The close fit between the theology of the book of Numbers and the rest of the Pentateuch implies that Numbers draws upon an existing religious synthesis. Its theology is not a purely intellectual invention. It uses much that is spelt out at length elsewhere in the Bible, without sermonizing, philosophizing or belabouring. The connection between false gods and plague, leprosy and all forms of bodily defect and rot is explained fully in Leviticus; the central importance of oaths and punishments is well understood. For Numbers to present its grand themes so compactly most of the religious synthesis would have been present in regular practice. This statement from anthropology about the nature of religion does not detract from the achievement of the writers of the Bible: the laws and the story of a religion are the tip of the iceberg, the action is the thing.

By contrast, our secular civilization takes religion to be essentially a kind of thought, an intellectually distinctive attitude, a philosophy or theory rather than a way of living. The intellectualist prejudice is an Enlightenment heritage. The first edition of the *Encyclopaedia Britannica* in 1771 describes three kinds of religion in antiquity, of which only metaphysical speculation earned the respect of the encyclopaedists:

> First, that of the philosophers, who treated metaphysically of the nature, the attributes, and of the works of the Supreme Being. They endeavoured to discover the true God, and the manner in which he ought to be worshipped. It is not wonderful, that these men of exalted genius should in some degree ridicule, in their works, the two other positive religions, and those gods on whom they were founded; at the same time that they outwardly professed the established religion, in order to preserve the peace of society, and to avoid the persecutions of the legislature, and the insults of the populace. For in fact, was it possible for them to believe the pagan fables?[1]

1. 'Myth', *Encyclopaedia Britannica* (1st edn, 1771), III, pp. 355-57. The quotation goes on with the splendid confidence of the encyclopaedists:

> Must they not foresee that their religion would one day give place to another, while their own works would pass with their names to the latest posterity? And could they suffer the thought that their reputation would be tarnished in the eyes of that posterity, by having it imagined they believed such idle tales as were broached by the priests of their times? Could Plato, Socrates, Seneca, and Cicero, be unconcerned for their fame among future generations, and future philosophers? And what should we at this day have said of those great men, had they been so political, or hypocritical, as to have entirely concealed their sentiments with regard to these matters?

The two 'positive religions' referred to were paganism and idolatry. Paganism was the established religion of all the nations except the Jews: a doctrine taught by priests and protected by sovereigns. Idolatry was the religion of the populace. The Encyclopaedists' typology survives hardily in the widespread assumption that true religion is a form of philosophy, and that deviations from this ideal are due to false civic pretensions and private superstitions. It has the merit of taking religion to be institutionalized before it generates an intellectual synthesis.

I take it here that religion is above all an organizational achievement. If the institutions come to be co-ordinated enough to make a coherent way of living, the religion acquires coherence along with the rest of the intellectual life of the community. Religions are usually sustained by fragmentary and conflicting institutions. Philosophers and theologians try to create new intellectual syntheses when changes in the institutions call for more inclusive doctrines, or for narrower, more exclusive boundaries. The intellectuals may succeed in creating the themes and slogans on which religious wars are fought, but these are not the same as the religion. The place where religious forms take shape is in the minds of individuals determined to co-operate, looking for compromise, or when that fails, trying to coerce one another into collective action by threatening divine sanctions. Arguing about the practical implications of belief and dogma, inventing tests for demonstrating loyalty, looking for signs of disloyalty that can be used as accusations, this is how religions are clarified.

3. *Images, Magic and Monotheism*

When the unique achievement of Judaism is recounted, the first religious innovation mentioned is usually monotheism. By straight comparison with the polytheistic religions of the region this may seem innovative but the word monotheism does not say enough. A religion may be counted monotheistic even if it recognizes many levels of divine beings. Monotheism only requires the supreme creator and lord to be uniquely identified in the pantheon. The monotheism of Israel is thoroughgoing in excluding a pantheon of lesser deities and spirits. After monotheism, the rejection of images is cited as Israel's special contribution to the history of human spirituality. Then the list goes on to include rejection of magic, divination and occultism. In effect, the central principle which embraces all of these is the rejection of images: from this the rest stem. So in approaching the Bible the question cannot be avoided: where does the anti-icon bias come from? Israel is an example of a religion that rejects all images whatever, and with images, all magic. An iconic religion pays great respect to images representing the dead, or angels, or saints, or the deity; they may be thought to be powerful, even magical. It is not just that they are a physical local manifestation of the revered one. Touching or holding them may in itself transmit a blessing, whether the contact is conscious or not; a prayer addressed to the picture may be more effective than a prayer said in its absence. Judaism is a religion that is settled in its rejection of images. This doctrine, so central to Judaism, is not accounted for in the current explanations of iconoclasm. The great Iconoclastic Controversy which racked Byzantium in the eighth and ninth centuries has been a rich field for historian's theories. On a simple historical view, iconoclasm is an expression of enmity, a straightforward revolutionary attack on the icons of a hated regime. But why do revolutionaries not replace the images of rejected rulers with their own respected images?

The first kind of explanation is a control theory. Peter Brown's survey of the Iconoclastic Controversy points out the threats to authority that would be presented by independent centres of holiness, the rise of cults of civic saints, and the danger of allowing uncertified images to become the focus of worship.[1] The second is a contagion theory. A nation at enmity with its neighbour would wish to destroy the latter's sacred images as part of delegitimating the rival religion. It accuses the enemy of idolatry, the accusation is felt keenly by some sections of the accused population, which uses it as a political weapon against its rulers, so iconoclasm spreads by contagion. This is basically the argument underlying Patricia Crone's defence of the old idea that Byzantine Iconoclasm was a response to the rise of Islam. The military success of Islam and its successful proselytizing gave rise to Christian heart-searchings and refinement of doctrine: no one wanted to be accused of bowing down to idols, so iconoclastic movements spread within Byzantine Christianity.[2] Islam got its anti-iconic attitude

1. P. Brown, 'A Dark-Age Crisis: Aspects of the Iconoclastic Controversy', *English Historical Review* 88 (1973), pp. 1-34.
2. P. Crone, 'Islam, Judeo-Christianity and Byzantine Iconoclasm', *Jerusalem Studies in Arabic and Islam* 2 (1980), pp. 59-95.

from Judaism. This line of argument is specially attractive to local combatants in so far as the charge of idolatry really hurts the priests of the religions which use images in the normal way. An accusation of idolatry is embarrassing in any religion. But the explanation is no help as to why a religion should ever have adopted an aniconic doctrine in the first place. The theory is historical: one people start to revolt against their neighbours or rulers, attack their sacred images, and so set off the complex chain reaction.

The control theory makes a double association with authority: on the one hand images emerge with civic authority, and on the other, iconoclasm arises with fear that the power attributed to images will get out of hand. The contagion theory tracks the oscillations set off in interdenominational politics. The combination of the control theory with the contagion theory is a complete, dynamic explanation of the rejection of images but it is a theory external to religion, which starts with politics and brings religious doctrines limping along second. The cultural theory of religion which I will develop in the next three chapters shows how in the internal development of a religion the concept of God may take an aniconic slant without reference to a dislike of foreign images or the desire to hold power. As the control theory leads us to expect, a community set against conspicuous leadership and wary of any authority would have an aniconic religion. Logically, if a people are determined not to allow any centres of power in their society, images will have little place in their religion. A famous example are the Nuer of the South Sudan whose political system dispersed all power and authority, and whose religion was without magic or images. For them the system of sacrifice was enough, though they said that of recent years a few emblems for curative magic had crept in from their neighbours, the Dinka.[1] It is theoretically convenient to distinguish three kinds of religion, one where civic authority is established, sustained and embellished with images, one in which private persons seek to use images to gain magical benefits for their own purposes, and one in which there is a fury against political control as such, a disgust with images and a contempt of idolatry.

There is no getting away from the fact that the use of icons is primarily for magical purposes. Magicality is not normally embarrassing for the adherents of iconic religions. Why should the faithful not be

1.   E. Evans-Pritchard, *Nuer Religion* (Oxford: Clarendon Press, 1956).

encouraged to pray for results? Why should they not seek to deflect sorrow and to secure their comfort? Why should they not want help? And what is helpful but some tangible good? In such religions material answers to prayer are not called 'magic' but 'miracles', and it is right and proper to ask for them.

Iconic religions teach the faithful to have recourse to miraculous images and amulets as an expression of their faith in divine intervention. Aniconic religions have a different theology of divine intervention. To pray for immediate, personal results is a debased form of spirituality. Worshipping God for his own sake requires resignation to his will, true worship is fundamentally opposed to a mercenary quest for the good things of life. Here we have a profound disagreement. On either side of the divide, for or against magic, the other religious conflicts line up. As its implications are worked out in the crises of life, a principled set against magic tends to entail an objection to a complex pantheon, devotion to the monotheist doctrine, antipathy to speculation about the fate of the dead, concern about defilement, and rejection of icons. Anti-magic, anti-ghosts, anti-icons, pro-purity, pro-monotheism, the tendencies go together as a bundle. The bundle is part of what we shall distinguish in the next chapter as the typical enclave religion.

In the Bible the Lord is credited with power which keeps the universe in good state. If the Lord's power is withdrawn it unleashes climatic disorders, drought, plague and famine; for humans it controls prosperity and victory or defeat at arms. Averting calamities by due performance of sacrifices and by honouring the Sabbath day is not magic. In the Bible there are also stories of the Lord being persuaded, as when Abraham interceded for Sodom, and when Moses pleaded for the people of Israel not to be destroyed. But the divine power could never be brought under human control, and never bought or sold. The very idea sounds extraordinary, yet there are religions in which the believer trucks with deities, expecting them to intervene privately in return for gifts. The essential point is that Judah's God cannot come under human control. He intervenes, but there is nothing automatic about his action. Only the Lord's accredited agents can perform miracles, and then only when they act formally as his instruments. It is very much disapproved of for individuals to claim private access to the source of sacred power.

When the Lord allows Elijah or Moses to perform miracles the miracles are not magic. In the Bible, magic is the secret lore of magicians, essentially working through spells and ritual formulae performed upon images: the demons and spirits of Canaan, and the false gods of Egypt and Assyria can be brought under human control by the use of images. The first three commandments of the Decalogue suggest that the prohibition of magic and icons is part of a programme against foreign religions, but this is to miss a deep incompatibility between the enclave culture and claims of individuals to exercise sacred power. First there is no other God but the Lord; secondly, no images are to be made and no one is to bow down to them; thirdly, the Lord's name is not to be taken in vain (Exod. 20.2-7). The three commands spell out the implications of the one command to worship one God only. The second commandment of the Decalogue says: 'You shall not make for yourselves a graven image or any likeness of anything. . . you shall not bow down to them or serve them' (Exod. 20.4-6). Images and magic are seen as a threat to monotheism: for Isaiah the three things are connected, as his accounts of false gods and their magic cults make clear (Isa. 8.13; 19.4; 44.9-20; 46).

The command not to take the Lord's name in vain (Exod. 20.1-7) would effectually forbid attempts to put God under human control by spells that are bound to work if his name is correctly invoked. Egyptian, Mesopotamian and Greek graven images were expected to be effective if the right instructions were followed about how to draw them, what to recite to them, what time of day or night or moment of the year to do the rite; knowing the name of the demon or spirit power is crucial, for invoking their names is the regular method of magic for bringing them under control.[1] Unequivocally, Israel's forbidden images are images of the proscribed other gods; taking a spirit's name in vain is a magical practice performed to force the spirits to do the behest of the magician. The first three commandments are one commandment, to worship the unique, pure God of Israel and abjure all others. The aniconic character of the religion cannot be separated from its strict monotheism, but the strict monotheism cannot be appreciated fully without its setting of a minority facing all the

---

1.   H.D. Betz *et al.*, *The Greek Magical Papyri in Translation* (Chicago: Chicago University Press, 1986); R.K. Rittner, 'Horus on the Crocodiles: A Juncture of Religion and Magic in Late Dynastic Egypt', in W.K. Simpson (ed.), *Religion and Philosophy in Ancient Egypt* (Yale Egyptological Studies, 3; 1989), pp. 103-15.

political external and internal difficulties of an enclave.

The antipathy against magic and magical images in enclave religion follows from the weakness of authority. Some communities have a strong resistance to allowing any member (or outsider) to claim religious power. An enclave's power to mobilize its population is weak compared with the effective mobilization available to hierarchies and to individualist regimes. The typical sectarian religion is part of the enclavists' effort to resist fragmentation and loss. Its desperately precarious authority, ambiguous and diffuse, is always vulnerable. Since this kind of community cannot allow any one to coerce the others, claims to magic powers are seen as very threatening. Magic generally involves using images and objects. Images of God tend to have power attributed to them and to imply magical advantages for their owners. It is the weakness of authority which underlies the rejection of images in enclave religions. And the theological claims about the unimaginability of God are part of the system of ideas which does not allow that God can be located in an object or submitted to the common uses of granting miraculous interventions at the request of common people.

Magic needs a word in its defence, since it is liable to be held in low esteem by the scientifically developed culture we live in today and since it is rejected as evil by the religion I am studying. However, magic is pervasive, and nearly irresistible. Even the community that officially disapproves of magic will find itself condoning magical images which depict the attributes of God or the letters of the alphabet which capture his name. Even persons with no particular religious affiliation carry amulets for luck, wear medals for protecting travellers, buy love potions and magic cures. Theologically speaking the difference between magic and miracle is a fine one. The distinction depends on the relation between reality and the transcendant godhead. The line is difficult to draw because it comes into question as an intellectual problem that arises at the constitutional level of thought: antimagic first comes into argument as part of a wish to constrain individual bids for influence. Miracles belong properly in cultures where competition for control is perfectly legitimate. Magic is acceptable among isolates together with all kinds of occultism, whereas hierarchies tend to be tolerant about the difference between magic and miracles. The task of placing Numbers in context will involve locating the different sectors of the population in Jerusalem at the time of redaction, and identifying their commitments.

4. *The History*

If it is true that an anthropologist cannot interpret a text without having a good sense of its origin and its destined readership, the need to know the community in which the text has issued is even more necessary for cultural theory. It is axiomatic that a sacred text is not recorded for archival purposes alone, there is always a current context in which the archive has present meaning. Numbers is about land promised by God to Abraham and his descendants, and the record of how under Moses' command they took it from the Canaanites. The eschatological sense of 'the promised land' could be an ultimate goal or a way of living; in a political sense it could be a particular national territory, or 'land' could refer to particular plots and particular rights. The word could have all these meanings at different levels, and indeed the boundary of the promised territory varies through the book. Furthermore, that context is bound to be political. So dating is a paramount need for an anthropological reading. But Bible scholars are not agreed. So rather than give up the project it has seemed best to take a date that seems to work well, and about which there is a large measure of support from scholars.

The Bible attributes a decisive transformation of the religion to the reigns of Hezekiah (716–687) and Josiah (640–609). By the end of the seventh century BCE the Northern Kingdom of Israel had been conquered, worship began to be centralized in the Jerusalem temple, the high priesthood emerged at the top of a hierarchy of religious orders, along with attempts to control the other sources of holiness. Some of the old agricultural festivals of sowing, and the two harvests, were incorporated into the story of Israel's foundation, but the rejection of other gods and other cults turned into a rage of denunciation against defilement. Sorcery, magic, divination, necromancy, which were evidently widely practised, became synonymous with false religion. Other gods were denounced either as useless wood and stone or as demon spirits. All the variety of Canaanite rites aimed at fertility and success were rolled into one abominable bundle, idolatry, associated with cult prostitution, homosexuality, demonism and death.

This study has followed those who consider that the editing of Numbers, along with the rest of the priestly work, was put in hand during the exile in the sixth century and completed in around the fifth century BCE, when Judah was a fief of Persia. At that time the people of Israel who had been exiled in Babylon had just returned to their own land and were settling down among those who had never gone away. Clearly the priestly work would have had as its central concern the reform and protection of the cult,[1] but to achieve it the priest's concern would extend to the political scene. Organized religion is always involved with politics. If the priests intended to stay in charge of the definitions of sin and purity, they could not avoid taking a political position.

It was a heady time of prophecy and messianic hope. At an early stage the return of the monarchy under Zerubbabel was enthusiastically expected, but he disappeared early from the record. External politics divided parties between those in favour of reunification with the remains of the Northern Kingdom, and the separatists who hated Samaria.[2] A major political issue could not but be also a major theological issue since Samaria and Judah were both inhabited by the descendants of Jacob, and therefore both had good claims to be heirs to the promises. In Numbers Benjamin and the sons of Joseph receive the same recognition as the other sons of Jacob descended from Rachel. But it cannot be accidental that the heroes of the years in the desert are a man from Ephraim and a man from Judah, and that Joshua, the Ephraimite, is commissioned as Moses' successor.

Apart from the foreign policy issue of how Samaria should be treated, as brother or alien, there was an internal policy problem about the immigrants, refugees and displaced persons who now inhabited Judah. Among them, it would seem from the book of Ezra, were genuine Jewish communities from Samaria who asked to be allowed to help with the rebuilding of the temple, claiming to worship the same God (Ezra 4.1-5). Their offers of help were rejected, and Nehemiah voiced grave suspicion of plots being hatched against Israel by the governor of Samaria and his friends.

The priests could not be indifferent to the question of whether intermarriage with the people whom Ezra called 'the people of the land' and 'adversaries of Judah' was permissible. Ezra decided to grapple himself with the problem of idolatry, and demanded that any

1.   F.M. Cross, *Canaanite Myth and Hebrew Epic: Essays in the History of the Religion of Israel* (Cambridge, MA: Harvard University Press, 1973).

2.   M. Stern, 'The Period of the Second Temple', in Ben-Sasson (ed.), *A History of the Jewish People* (London: Weidenfeld & Nicolson, 1976), pp. 185-306.

Jews who had intermarried with idolators should divorce them. Nehemiah made it clear that intermarriage with Samarians, even, or specially, with high ranking ones, was not acceptable to the government party.[1] The priests who were not in the government party were likely to resent the government arrogating to itself the decision as to who was an idolator, and who was defiling the priesthood, and who could or could not be married.

Ezra had a document from Artaxerxes, the Persian king, empowering him to appoint magistrates and judges, and giving him authority for life and death, banishment, imprisonment or confiscation of property, to be used against anyone who 'will not obey the law of your God' (Ezra 7.25-28). To carry out his responsibilities, Ezra gathered around him leading men from Israel, that is leading men who had come with him from Babylon (7.28; 8).

Shortly after they arrived in Jerusalem certain of the leading men complained to the governor that the people of Israel, lay and clerical, had not 'separated themselves from the people of those lands' and insisted that officials and leading men were foremost transgressors. H.G.M. Williamson remarks[2] that, though the Persian kings are presented as the political agents through whom God is at work in Jewish history, Ezra and Nehemiah present their local officials in a much poorer light:

> Whatever may have been their motivation at the time, these officials are presented as stopping at nothing in their resistance to the work of God in Jerusalem...By showing that the difficulties which the post-exilic community encountered were due to corrupt local officialdom rather than to the Persian court as such, these books reinforce their case for loyalty to the imperial power itself.

While the governor is praying and weeping over the news of his apostasizing officials, a great assembly gathers. He calls on the whole congregation to repent and to send back their spouses, formerly lawful but now declared unlawful (Ezra 9.10-15). With encouragement from the returnees he makes those present take an oath that they would put away their wives and children. But who has been doing this intermarrying with the adversaries? If, as is made out, it is the local

---

1. Neh. 13.6.

2. H.G.M. Williamson, *Ezra and Nehemiah* (Old Testament Guides; Sheffield: JSOT Press, 1987), pp. 88-89.

officials who never went away who are accused, the scene reads like a performance in which the returnees accuse themselves of sins which only those who are not returnees will have committed. The latter are probably not even present, for Ezra then proclaims that all the children of the captivity must assemble together in Jerusalem, and that any who refuse to come will forfeit all their possessions and be expelled from the congregation (Ezra 10.7-8). The coercion is unabashed. Not surprisingly in view of the threat, the assembled congregation weeps and promises to divorce the defiling wives and disown their own children.

Although the biblical precedent is hard to justify, the purity code of Judaism came in this way to be used to empower the priesthood, ensure the flow of wealth to their families, ensure their pre-eminence in public affairs, and justify their in-marriages.[1] The demand for the purity of women and the brutal punishment of women of the priestly caste accused of adultery, justified in the name of purity,[2] would have been a practical corollary of their demand for a pure genealogy. This reading supports the commonly held view expressed by Max Weber that the priesthood of the Second Temple community instituted the in-group/out-group mentality which, in his opinion, led eventually to the pariah status of the Jews in the West.[3] However, Numbers was not supporting a separatist policy, yet Numbers was a priestly document. There was not one but many different views on how the boundary of the congregation should be drawn, with the strongest separatists being the government party. The evidence of Numbers, as interpreted in this study, suggests that there were priests who would have opposed them strongly, and who edited Numbers to record their view.

Ezra/Nehemiah provides important information for the state of politics in Judah at the time at which the book of Numbers was undergoing its final redaction. It was a deeply divided community of

1. J. Jeremias, *Jerusalem in the Time of Jesus* (London: SCM Press, 1969), pp. 221-222, 216-18, 333. High priestly families tried to marry their daughters to priests, and pushed their sons-in-law forward to high office; several high priests were sons-in-law of officiating high priests (p. 218).

2. 'Under Agrippa (AD 41–44) when Jews could exercise criminal justice, the priests burnt publicly in Jerusalem a priest's daughter guilty of adultery' (Jeremias, *Jerusalem*, p. 221).

3. Weber, *Ancient Judaism*, pp. 336 ff.

self-differentiated sectarian parties.[1] Given the state of factional strife it is noteworthy that in Numbers the twelve tribes are all there, ranged around the tabernacle, all counted as heirs, all expected to take their part in winning the promised land regardless of any curses or blessings that Jacob spoke to his sons, each given their portion in the partitioning. It will be argued below that the reiterated catalogues of the twelve tribes in the book of Numbers held a friendly political message for the sons of Manasseh, dwelling in the province of Samaria.

The book certainly does plenty of inveighing against enemies, internal and external. Anyone who comes to Numbers with the prejudices of our culture finds that the interpretation offered here turns our own history on its head. Heirs of the Enlightenment, we are used to being taught that the priests take the narrow ritualistic view of religion, the priests are xenophobic, the priests' primary concern is for the survival of the cult and of their caste. But in this case, unprecedented it would seem, the concern of the priestly editor is to constrain a populist xenophobia. If there was what Max Weber called a 'negative attitude', if there was an increasingly rigid rejection of community beyond Judah, this reading of Numbers shows that it did not emanate from the priestly editors. So, far from hostility to Samaria, the priestly editors were still grieving for the separation of the two kingdoms of Israel. The book teaches that all the sons of Jacob should be included as heirs to the promise. This interpretation depends on examining the structure of the book. This is found to be a very symmetrical form of ring compositions with an internal structure of parallelisms. It is another surprise to find that the editors were masters of sophisticated literary skills exercised in the region at that period.

The structure of the book of Numbers stands up well to interrogation. It has used a number of literary devices based on parallelism to make one event become the lens for seeing another and for putting events of different periods into the same perspective. Its literary techniques implant the ancient prophecies in the text, annihilate time and deepen the theological reference. A literary masterpiece of this kind would only be possible for writers in a well-established grand tradition. The Babylonian conquerors of Jerusalem carried off the skilled and learned, the noble and rich families. Their life in exile was urban and literate. Before exile they would have already known

---

1. S. Talmon, *King, Cult and Calendar in Ancient Israel* (Jerusalem: Magnes Press, 1986), p. 176.

enough mathematics and astronomy to discuss the calendar with other exiled scholars and with the Babylonian specialists. In exile they would have had every facility for improving their skills in science, literature, music and the arts.

It is curious that the book of Numbers was read so differently five hundred years after it was given its final form. Perhaps it was unacceptable. Numbers carries the triumphant message of prophecy fulfilled, a message which might have seemed plausible before the second destruction of the temple, but afterwards a mockery. Jacob Neusner's explanation for a different mode of interpretation is compelling: the second destruction of the temple and total devastation of Jerusalem were too shocking for the old reading to be borne.[1] The rabbis looked in the scriptures for meanings less at variance with their experience, for simple moral lessons that could be focused on the present rather than on the painful past.[2]

Current biblical scholarship is relatively less active in interpreting the priestly work. If the histories and prophets engage more time and interest, this may be because of lurking anticlericalism which implicitly ranks the priests with the forces of reaction and the prophets with progress. In a typically Weberian view, if there was strife in the religious community, the lines of division would separate the priestly caste from the people, and therefore separate them from the prophets who inveighed against injustice and poverty—an idea which makes no sense in view of the writings in Numbers and Leviticus on both themes.

In his commentary on Numbers Philip Budd attributes the revolt of Korah in ch. 16 to priestly machinations. He sees it as a conflict between the priests and the government in which outspoken, egalitarian Korah is the victim, the priests are the villains and the democratic government party would have been the hero had not the hierarchical priests won the day:

1.   J. Neusner, 'Judaism in a Time of Crisis, Four Responses to the Destruction of the Second Temple', *A Quarterly Journal of Jewish Life and Thought* 21.3 (1972), pp. 313-27.

2.   J. Neusner, 'Form and Meaning in Mishnah', *JAAR* 45.1 (1977), pp. 27-54; 'Judaic Uses of History in Talmudic Times', in *Essays in Jewish Historiography* (ed. A. Rapoport-Albert; Middletown, CT: Wesleyan University Press, 1988); 'The Case of Leviticus Rabbah', in J.M. Lundquist and S. Ricks (eds.), *By Study and Also by Faith* (1990), pp. 332-88.

Korah represents Levitical opposition to the priestly hierarchy proposed by the settlers from Babylon...Thus the author's main concern in this section is to substantiate his vision of the priestly hierarchy.[1]

This interpretation assumes that the priests of the Second Temple community succeeded, against liberalizing pressures from government, in imposing separatism supported by doctrines of defilement. The priests on this assumption are expected to be interested primarily in maintaining their hierarchy and their own place in the community. Concern for larger issues of statesmanship and for sensitivity to the plight of the people, concern for the well-being of the whole community, highmindedness in general is implicitly credited to an anti-priestly faction among the Levites. This view makes the priests in Jerusalem responsible for Israel's isolation among the nations.

It is by no means clear that the priestly party responsible for the redaction of the first four books of the Pentateuch were the winners in the political contest. The argument of the following chapters is that they were the losers, and the winners were the extreme separatist parties. The separatists won, held power and controlled the interpretations. Numbers written from a diametrically opposed standpoint would naturally be difficult to interpret in later times. The biggest surprise in the anthropological reading is to realize the magnanimity of Numbers' political message. The surprisingly open political vision is supported by the cosmopolitan literary style, and above all by the benign doctrine of defilement which cannot be left without explanation.

1. P. Budd, *Numbers* (WBC; Waco, TX: Word Books, 1984), pp. 188-90.

Chapter 2

THE POLITICS OF ENCLAVES

1. *A Cultural Typology*

Judaism rejects images and magic, this is one of its central features. Any useful typology of religions has to offer an account of icons, their presence or absence. According to Max Weber and some of his followers the important condition that favours images is illiteracy.[1] Does the ability to read and write make such a fundamental difference to the typology of a religion? The rejection of graven images in Judaism is not seriously to be written off as an adventitious by-product of literacy. This chapter will characterize the bias of a certain type of culture, which I call here the sectarian or enclave community. In the typology of cultures, this is the community which has good reasons for preferring an aniconic religion.

In the introduction I showed that the community of the Second Temple period was far from homogeneous. There was the government party, supported by Persia, and, counting the returned exiles among its most committed members, there were the various rural communities, including representatives of many peoples, among those native to Judah some established immigrants, some recent newcomers of different regions, some from Samaria. Among the priests, those who had stayed behind and those who had come back from Babylon would probably have been divided, some allied with the returned remnant and others more pastorally involved with the people who had

---

1. Following Weber, E. Gellner finds this syndrome of religious tendencies well-assorted with urban life: he believes that towns make literacy possible and valuable, literacy makes possible the worshipper's direct access to revelation and makes intermediaries dispensable. At the same time it facilitates the disciplined observance of rules, disfavours excessive emotionalism and favours egalitarianism, monotheism, absence of graven images, and a religious bias generally called 'puritanism' (*Saints of the Atlas* [London: Weidenfeld & Nicolson, 1969], pp. 7-8).

stayed. The theological divisions which became prominent in later times may have well been present between those who saw Judaism as a nationalist religion and those who saw its message as universal. Only historical evidence or, in default, surmise can suggest how that alignment would have distinguished the pro-Persian party and the others, but there is a suggestion that the government party, who got their power and authority from Persian backing, would have felt it was in their political interest to emphasize the uniqueness of the Jewish religion and its distinctiveness in the surrounding region.

In this complex scene we have recourse to cultural theory, which gives four kinds of religious bias, one suited to the entrepreneurial, politically minded individualists, one to the hierarchical traditionalists, one for sectarians, the vast majority of the population, and one for those who refuse to be aligned or involved in the major debates of their day. It will help in the interpretation of the book of Numbers to realize that the priestly editors as a hereditary priestly caste would have been imbued with hierarchical tendencies which would put them at variance with the generally sectarian environment of their congregations. We will need to reflect on what is involved in being committed to a hierarchical culture, the nostalgia, the hopefulness, the sense of long tradition. None of this will be necessarily shared by political opportunists operating the government system as pragmatically as they are able in difficult circumstances.

The word 'culture' has many meanings; here it will be used in a specialized sense for a distinctive pattern of claims. Think of a community as a field of relationships: when seen too close no pattern appears. Relationships seem to be fluid over most of the range, but here and there steady forms emerge, hold their shape, expand and stabilize a large part of the scene. At the same time other patterns of relations disintegrate. In the competition a system of claims emerges victorious enough to oust incompatible claims. So for example the claims of the house of David to restore the monarchy became unrealistic and lost credibility. To some extent claims that are compatible support one another, but the dominant pattern is always precarious.

Every moment that a settled system of claims survives is owed to the work of committed persons. Nothing guarantees that their commitment will be sustained. Temptations to subvert the cultural bias abound and it can easily be subverted: anyone in a sect can move out. Natural disasters change allegiances, as do political changes. Ancient origin is no guarantee that tradition will be observed. As our questions probe into the conditions of stability, we find that a community stays the same only by grace of willing, working and persuading. The people's resolve to uphold certain principles and reject others, their vision of what is a good society: this is what makes the culture what it is, as shown by their actions. The theory is not a form of social determinism, or cultural, or economic, or materialist, or even historical determinism. The constraints on what one person wants to do are made by other persons at the same time and place, other persons who decide to uphold some constraints and dispense themselves from accepting others. To give a contemporary example, the Catholic church in our day is upholding an anti-birth-control and anti-abortion doctrine which is not necessarily received by the faithful.

Paradoxically the greatest source of strength for entrenching a particular cultural bias is the mutual hostility between cultures.[1] Each type of culture involves a specific pattern for the use of space and time and makes specific demands on personal availability. As the bearers of an individualist culture move into a new zone, they see space that from their perspective is unused, time that is frittered, persons doing nothing. If they succeed in taking over that space, they disrupt the local culture that was disposing of these assets in its own distinctive way. This is illustrated very clearly in conflicts over urban planning, where the same space cannot be used for a major motorway and still be home for a local community of artisans. Each exponent of a cultural bias is acutely aware of threats to the chosen way of life, and so endemic cultural conflict sustains the definition of each culture.

The principal distinctive types of culture can be defined along two dimensions, one based on the concern with the outside boundary, the other on the articulation of the social structure.[2] The two dimensions enclose a social field of possible stable environments, of which four are usually identified. One may take first the commitment to hierarchy as a potentially stable cultural type. It produces a strong boundary round its population, and a strongly articulated, self-repeating structure, with distinctive sub-divisions. The sect is quite different:

1. In their well-named book, *Divided We Stand*, M. Thompson and M. Schwartz compare the conflict between cultural types with the conflict between species competing for resources in an ecological zone (Hemel Hempstead: Harvester Wheatsheaf Press, 1989).

2. M. Douglas, *Natural Symbols* (Harmondsworth: Penguin Books, 1970).

sometimes called faction, commune, egalitarian group, enclave is the term that will here be used. An enclave is usually formed by a dissenting minority, it becomes a social unit which maintains a strong boundary but unlike the hierarchy it tends to be egalitarian, and so to have a weakly articulated social structure. Thirdly, there is a distinctive culture of competitive individualism. In this environment group membership is not important, the individual is expected to negotiate his own status unconstrained by group allegiance or prescriptive rules.

CULTURAL BIAS

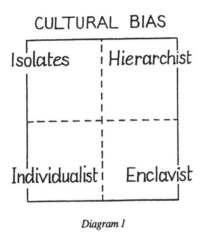

Diagram 1

These cultural regimes are patterns of accountability, ways in which individuals can organize themselves into a community. Not everyone wants to belong to a community, to hold or be held accountable. So in the scheme of cultural bias we have to allow for the possibility of isolated individuals, not belonging to a group, and exerting no power or influence. The culture of the isolate is the most interesting of all. Some persons are so constrained by the structure made by others that they have little space in which they can choose to do as they like: in the midst of a bustling, busy community they do not belong, no one needs their advice or offers them any. Some are isolates by choice, and use various ploys not to be drawn into other people's worries or recruited to their politics. In modern industrial society there are probably more opportunities to live as an isolate than ever. The girl at the cashier's checkpoint in some supermarkets has been cited as an example, because as far as her work goes she has no options or occasion to use her judgment; for all the human relations she enjoys at work she might as well be on a desert island.[1] A constitutional monarch is so hedged with rules, the timetable so filled by official requirements, scope for friendship and marriage so restricted, that, compared with the officials whose suzerain she is, such as parliamentarians, ministers, and bishops, the Queen is relatively speaking an isolate. Another example of a well-salaried role with the same conditions which prevent the incumbent from exerting influence is the champion weightlifter: his profession demands nothing from him in the way of judgment or skill, still less opinion; all he has to do is to lift the weight. But to earn his big income he has to observe such a strict regime of food and exercise that he is so completely under the control of his trainer, he might as well be a champion race horse. These examples are worth mentioning, even though they will not directly illustrate the arguments to come, because they do illustrate the mixture of free choice and external constraint that aligns persons to a cultural bias. The isolates, however diverse their lives may be, tend to take the generally benign view of the universe that one would expect from those who are not trying to persuade or coerce others and who stand aside from arenas of conflict. The other cultural types arise in distinctive conditions which I will describe.

Each of the three cultures practises its own distinctive power of exclusion, and what each does is abhorrent to the alternative cultures. Our civilization is convinced of the virtues of individualism and of the evils of hierarchy and sect, while the latter are equally convinced of the opposite. The processes of individualism downgrade the economically unsuccessful, and cannot but create derelicts and beggars. Members of an individualist culture are not aware of their own exclusionary behaviour. The condition of the unintentionally excluded, for example beggars sleeping on the streets, shocks visitors from other cultures. Neither hierarchy nor enclave excludes in this unconscious, unintentional way. Hierarchy is essentially based on grading, so it must tolerate the idea of a recognized bottom level and make provision for it. The very explicitness of hierarchical grading shocks the sensibilities of enclavist and individualist alike. Enclavists have reasons to avoid grading their members altogether: their habit is

1. G. Mars, *Cheats at Work, an Anthropology of Workplace Crime* (London: Allen & Unwin, 1982), pp. 75ff.

outcasting rather than downgrading: their exclusions all work on the outer boundary, the difference between belonging and not belonging. Their virulent hatred of the outsider is shocking to the other cultures.

As a method cultural theory implies nothing about theology, it says nothing about how God is, or about transcendentalism. As to religion it simply studies the claims that persons make against each other in the name of God and other spiritual beings. Different kinds of claims cancel one another, compatible claims coalesce as cultural patterns. The method is to work out what claims would be made in a particular cultural type, including specially religious claims. The terms hierarchical, sectarian and individualist are chosen in the hope that they are not so distracting and inappropriate for a typology as Protestant and Catholic, Buddhist and Hindu. At least they do not carry the heraldry of denominational conflict, but they still suggest the wrong meanings. Hierarchy suggests a multinational industrial corporation. 'Sect' sounds a pejorative note, recalling the bitterness of denominational feuding. 'Individualism' comes straight out of the rationalist philosophy of Utilitarianism. But the clumsy nomenclature at least has the merit of emphasizing the dependence of the form of religion on the form of organization. Hierarchy is a system of positions, its members will be making claims on God to safeguard their positions, and to safeguard the whole pattern without which they would not have any positions to protect. Individualist culture is an environment of expanding personal networks in which persons will be invoking God in their own name: we could call it a personal religion. The religion of an enclave tends to be that of a dissident minority, so sectarian. The question will be whether the religion of the book of Numbers should be classed as a hierarchical, an individualist or an enclavist religion. Part of the answer depends on how defilement is used.

We will go round the diagram and work out what kinds of claims we would expect to be supported by the religion in extreme examples of each type. All the priests in a community will not turn up in the same corner of the diagram; priests and their congregations will not take a unified view. For example, take a Catholic country such as Ireland: it has one official religion, organized by a hierarchical priesthood. But the hierarchy of the religion, with its ultramontane allegiance to Rome, does not mean that the congregations are organized as hierarchies: parish by parish their community life will probably be based on families competing and collaborating opportunistically, with

a large dose of factionalism between communities, and at least a few
isolates.

The diagram is a model of social mobilization. The whole right-
hand side of the diagram represents the collectivist cultures in which
community claims have priority over those of individual members.
We should get used to thinking of defilement as a cost-effective way of
diffusing the costs of mobilization. It is self-operating: every one
understands that defilement is dangerous, that it should be avoided,
that, if it occurs, it has to be penalized and precautions taken against
the spread of contamination. So long as they are cherished in the
hearts of the people, boundaries become self-maintaining, thanks to
spontaneous accusations of defilement. When commitment weakens,
defilement loses its force. Defilement is a popular concept, it arises
easily and follows demarcations which the congregation are interested
in preserving. It would be extremely difficult to impose a new concept
of defilement on a community which did not agree to the distinctions
it would create.

Up and down the left-hand side of the diagram the claims of community take second place. A community that has located itself on the
bottom left is not able to demand directly from its members altruistic
contributions to the collective good. Its typical form of mobilization
has to be to appeal to individual self-interest. Such an appeal can be
very effective in producing wealth, political concentration, and
armies. We should not expect that defilement is used as a coercive
weapon in this kind of culture in which other more dependable forms
of coercion are available.

Defilement in a hierarchy is elaborately differentiated between persons and places. The people have put themselves in a state of potential
mobilization at all levels. Making their collective claims on one
another they actively keep each other aware of the need for defending
the collectivity. Through the whole system they have structured their
personal claims into symbolic forms that remind them of the demands
of the whole. Danger of defilement keeps them aware of the collective
loss if the system were to crumble. We have observed how very
remarkable it is that the purity laws of Numbers and Leviticus do not
make distinctions between persons. The inference from this would be
that the community for which the purity laws were written was not a
hierarchy, because purity is not being used to shore up social distinctions. Religiously, Judaism is egalitarian, but the editors of Numbers

cannot be assigned to the slot for enclave cultures. In the enclave the main source of pollution is the evil of the outside world. Preoccupied with its frail consensus and without formal authority or effective power, the enclave tends to use defilement to accuse and reject unruly members and to mobilize loyalty.

Defilement in the Bible would follow the typical pattern of the enclave community if its attention were turned to separating the pure faithful from the impure outsiders, but it does not do that either. Contact with the foreigner is not defiling, only idolatry. Here is the puzzle. Since the hereditary priestly hierarchy was surrounded by a lay enclave, the province of Judah, we should first examine the conditions of enclave culture.

2. The Enclave Repeater Mechanism

Military defeat and colonial dependency always put a damper on regimes of individualist competition. A culture well-suited to expanding empires and trading routes would have been impossible under Babylonian or Persian foreign rule. So formative Judaism developed in an enclave. In its history it suffered the typical humiliations and rejoiced in the typical pride of an enclave, and like all enclave cultures it generated its own repeated destruction, resentment and renewal. An enclave community can be recognized and described. It is not mysterious nor unique. It starts in a characteristic situation and faces characteristic problems. These invite specific solutions, the institutions in which the solutions are tried call forth a specific type of spirituality. The religion offers a reasonable response to dilemmas facing individuals. In one set of conditions, the culture of individual competition works best, in another hierarchy is viable.

Religious difference appears in the form of doctrines and ideas, but it is rooted in preferences for distinctive ways of life. Consequently ideology describes but does not explain religious difference. Max Weber, in substituting ideology for historical materialism, reinforced the intellectualist bias inherited from the Enlightenment. He expected that what he called 'the spirit of the age' could carry the same kind of explanatory weight as control over the forces of production in Marxist theory. Are we to suppose that the believers are passively under the sway of ideology? If so, how may one account for change? To attribute independent power to ideas is to use a magic wand for explanation. At worst, it is a licence for prejudice. How can the spirit of Judaism explain anything at all about Judaism?[1] Correlation between the spirit and the institutions of a period are easy to find, but so are strife and disharmony. Sometimes the spirit of the age is not strong enough, sometimes another spirit is able to overcome it. The idea of religion as an independent variable is a formidable obstacle to the spirit of enquiry. It leaves a blank on the very topic it pretends to explain. Jacob Neusner having located resentment as the key emotional attitude for the continued relevance of the Torah then looks for a repeater mechanism that maintains the resentment. To ask the question is a profound insight. In a Weberian mode, he builds his answer upon a discrepancy between the fantasy world of the Torah and the grim reality of the Jewish existence: the shock of every now and again realizing the disparity generates the resentment upon which the system renews itself. For an anthropologist the role of fantasy in this explanation is uncongenial. The peoples whom anthropologists study can never be assumed to be more given to escapism than anyone else. Or if fantasy has an unusual power over their minds, that is another thing to be explained. To say that a religion grips the minds of its adherents just because it does not fit the reality around them raises more problems about religion in general than it answers about a particular one.

It is certainly possible for a community imbued with resentment to regard the nations outside as steeped in sin and death, and to turn in on itself and its exclusive traditions. With this attitude it may regularly behave so as to bring catastrophe on itself, and regularly interpret the ensuing disasters in the same way. If it does all of this, it runs on some kind of repeater mechanism, but it is not plausible that the mechanism is in its sacred books. The follower of Weber is supplied with no theory of generative systems, and consequently no theory of change, nor any theory of stability. The Weberian approach to religion is as much a hindrance to understanding religion as the Marxist because, like Marxism, it starts by separating the ideal from the action. Idealism, either right way up or inverted, is facile. A description of a religion needs to bring the ideal and the actual into some coherent relation. For a reasonably uncontroversial discussion of religious change, the main assumption has to be that the ideas are in

1. J. Neusner, *Self-fulfilling Prophecy, Exile and Return in the History of Judaism* (Boston: Beacon Press, 1987), p. 60.

some way part of the institutions. They work inextricably together in the process of making and resisting claims.

The theory is that the extreme types of culture are viable, stable cultures. There are conditions conducive to each, and conditions unfavourable to each. When the conditions change, the people may seize the opportunity to live together differently, or they may try to reject the new opportunity. This is not a determinist theory. The Jews, when the Hasmonean kings gave them a chance of spectacular military success, took the opportunity to modify their closed, enclavist sectarianism, and started to become an imperial power again. Most communities develop a mixed regime to solve their problems of organization. Of any two peoples living as neighbours one may give more scope to the hierarchical principle, or more or less to the sectarian or the individualist, but the other cultural principles need not be completely excluded. Contradictory principles can survive quite well in the same community so long as they are relatively segregated in the community's total space. An enclavist political scene with concealed and fragile authority can tolerate hierarchical families in its midst, so long as the family does not enforce its mode of organizing on politics.

3. *The Fears of the Enclave*

The characteristic preoccupation of an enclave is leakage of members. No coercion can be exerted to hold or punish deserters, for they will only go away all the faster; the only control that can be exerted is moral persuasion. This is the overwhelming problem facing sects. But dissident religious communities are not the only example. Sectarian behaviour belongs to a much wider class than the minority religions to which the word is commonly applied. The experience of Central African communities under colonial rule is quite typical. In the villages of the Lele of the Kasai in the days of Belgian control the middle-aged and older people used to make quite explicit their concern to keep the younger ones as permanent members of the village, but the younger ones would continually threaten to move off if they were reprimanded or abused. The result was the vacuum of authority and mutual accusations between neighbours which characterized their culture at that time.[1]

1. This has been analysed in numerous publications, including M. Douglas, 'Techniques of Sorcery Control', in J. Middleton and E.H. Winter (eds.),

This mutual mistrust and absence of authority are the basis of sectarian behaviour. In the same sense it must be acknowledged that the culture of the postexilic community was sectarian.[1] The word sect has a pejorative sense in the politics of European and American denominations. Faction will not quite do as an alternative, for it has pre-eminently political associations. The word enclave covers both sect and faction, meaning any kind of community whose main problem is defecting membership and which tries to solve that problem in the sectarian way.[2] In biblical studies the word sect has a well-established usage. The Essenes are called a sect on account of their separateness from the main community of Judaism. In this context it is not an appropriate term for the hierarchical priesthood, though it can well apply to the groups within the Second Temple community.

If ever there were anywhere in the world a dissident minority group, this is what the exiled leaders would have been in Babylon, and after the return they would have been a minority among other enclaves of Jews who had remained.[3] The whole region had become a colonial dependency of Persia. There was an external Persian authority and its local representatives would have suffered from the politically crippling weaknesses well described for African chiefs under colonial rule.[4]

Witchcraft and Sorcery in East Africa (London: Routledge & Kegan Paul, 1963); *The Lele of the Kasai* (IAI; Oxford: Oxford University Press, 1963); *How Institutions Think* (Syracuse: Syracuse University Press, 1987).

1.   M. Smith, *Palestinian Parties and Politics that Shaped the Old Testament* (London: SCM Press, 1987).

2.   Colleagues in cultural theory use other terms, depending on what aspect of the cultural bias they wish to emphasize. Aaron Wildavsky refers to the enclave as an 'egalitarian group', or simply 'egalitarians'; Steve Rayner calls them 'egalitarian collectives'. Their bias towards egalitarian distributive mechanisms is a response to their situation as dissident minorities, and to the resulting weakness of authority endemic in their organization. In the case of postexilic Judaism the decisive factor is subjection to colonial rule, so enclave is an appropriate term.

3.   Smith, *Palestinian Parties*; S. Talmon, 'Addendum to Max Weber', in *King and Cult* (1979).

4.   Although by a system of indirect rule the Zulu chiefs were allowed to govern themselves by their own laws, specially in religious matters, they were not allowed to apply the supreme punishment. If they encouraged their subjects to express their discontents, they would be ousted from office by the colonial power, but if they backed the demands of the colonial power for tax or labour, they would lose the backing of their people. So native authority under colonial rule would be inherently

The initial difficulty for an enclave is that it has not got normal access to the resources of the main community. For example, if it is a minority religious community its members very probably do not like public education because of their dissident principles. But they cannot get national funds for their own schools, or refuse to pay taxes or keep their children out of the school system. And for the very reason that they are an objecting minority, they cannot use the coercive powers of government for obliging their members to conform to their minority rules. More usually their dissidence puts them at a legal disadvantage. They may refuse, as in historic cases, military service, or voting, or standing for office. Whatever it is that puts them apart, the more apart they are, the more the main community looks at them askance. They are suspected of subversion, they are persecuted and defamed, all of which reinforces their apartness.

As a result of these disadvantages, the leaders of an enclave have to work to keep their members. The main community outside, rich, powerful and alluring, tempts members away from their enclave loyalty. Figures that may show that the actual secession from a particular community are relatively low would not imperil the argument. Anxiety about loss of members becomes obsessional. Population may actually be increasing, but each mixed marriage is a cause of distress in an enclave. When internal conflict surfaces it is only too easy for the member who is censured simply to cut loose, to abscond. Leaders of a dissident group cannot engage the arm of the law to stop defectors. In confrontation with their own disloyal subjects, they have no authority. If they act repressively, members will move out more quickly. The central preoccupation of enclave leaders is how to stop defection. At the start, while they still have their original founder, they have not had to face typical organizational problems. If such a community has survived for a generation after the death of its founder, it will have met its problems of organization and found strategies for dealing with them. The range of strategies is limited, and their adoption inaugurates the typical enclave culture which entraps its members in a self-repeating system.[1]

---

weak. Living in such a regime it would always be tempting to secede and join the exciting life of the great empire. (M. Gluckman, 'The Kingdom of the Zulu of South Africa', in *African Political Systems* [ed. M. Fortes and E.E. Evans-Pritchard; Oxford: Clarendon Press, 1940], pp. 25-56).

1. See E. Sivan on the marginalization of religion in modern industrial

4. *Standard Solutions*

The first standard solution to the threat of defection is paradoxically to emphasize the voluntary character of membership. In religious terms the leaders will be saying how voluntarily god has chosen the community and how much their own voluntary response matters. Choosing will be an important element of doctrine. The religion of an enclave typically emphasizes the personal relation of the individual worshipper to god. In a hierarchy the outward form is highly valued, but in an enclave the pure heart and the pious inner intention are more important. Harsh though he is in punishing deliberate defiance, the God of Numbers is forgiving to unintended sins committed by his followers. Numbers seems to be expressing this normal enclave attitude when it expounds the action to be taken by the unwitting sinner to be forgiven (15.22-26). But it is out of line when it adds that the stranger who lives among them can get forgiveness too. This openness is atypical for the normal enclave religion which keeps its benefits for insiders.

The image of god tends to be kindly in an enclave, nearer, more emotional and more easily hurt by rejection than the distant god of a hierarchy. A hierarchical religion often divides up the various roles of the deity between different spiritual beings, so that severity and justice will be located in a supreme spirit, and loving-kindness in another member of the pantheon. An enclave generally worships one god, and so the same god is at times cajoling and tender, and at other times vengeful and angry, posing problems about how to please him and evoking doctrines of his inscrutability.

The second strategy of the enclave struggling to survive is to emphasize the unique value of each individual member and to reject discrimination. If the individuals threaten to move out, they are warned that they will be oppressed by the outsider institutions. Inside, they are equal and free, so why should they want to move? Equality is a strategy to avoid the accusations of free-riding and private profiteering on the sacrifices of members which beset the internal politics of enclaves.

Numbers tries sedulously not to discriminate between persons. Exodus has ordained for the ransoming of each person numbered in

society (essay for the Chicago Fundamentalism Project, awaiting publication).

the census, that each shall give half a shekel to the Lord: 'The rich shall not give more and the poor shall not give less, than the half shekel, when you give the Lord's offering to make atonement for yourselves' (Exod. 30.15). Numbers goes further: when the leaders of the tribes present their gifts for the tabernacle, the principle of equality between persons is extended to the tribes: each gives exactly the same gift.

Turning the lack of authority to advantage, the enclave claims to be governed by consensus. In practice, it is always difficult for it to take unpopular decisions. Its councils are typically plagued by indecision and blocked by vetoes. Leaders have to be devious in getting agreement, and try passing responsibility back to the community. For lack of authority and to avoid friction, distribution problems tend, predictably, to be settled by lottery. For allotting territories to each tribe Numbers prescribes casting lots (Num. 26.52-56). There is no arguing with a lottery's results. The man who gathered sticks on the Sabbath was stoned to death (Num. 15.32-36). Although the form of punishment was not the main point of the story, stoning is a form of execution that makes the whole group bear invidious responsibility.

The fear of defection makes authority weak: the leadership of the enclave have no backing against continual, merciless attack from their members. The charge will be that the leaders are idlers, or even profiteers. Trying to deflect attack the leaders disclaim distinctive prestige or personal profit. Whereas the culture of hierarchy celebrates its leaders and expects to reward them for taking on responsibility, the enclave is not in a position to give anyone more responsibility than anyone else. For any signs of exceptional prosperity the wealthy will be accused of exploiting their fellows. Any distinction is liable to backlash. Any initiative in taking responsibility on behalf of the community is liable to be repudiated. Typically, the enclave cannot delegate because it cannot guarantee to its envoy that on his return it will stand by the original instructions. To the extent that it has to reject differences between persons, declaring them to be all the same, without distinction of role or office, the enclave is forced also to live with ambiguity.

A hierarchical institution can give plenty of reasons for treating persons differently according to their service to the whole. Its fund of strategies for justifying these solutions holds down the incipient jealousy which racks the enclavist heart. In a hierarchy the centre holds, it accumulates resources and power, it provides incentives so that the population is not sucked away by rival states. If outsiders want to come in, they can because the hierarchy has means of incorporating them in separate compartments. Its major worries are not about its border with the outside but how to prevent disaffection in its lower ranks. In the enclave culture where these strengths are absent, its dominant problem of defection is exacerbated by jealousy and factions. Animosity runs high and life, though frustrating, is never dull.

In a hierarchy the regular strategy for bringing jealousy under control is to institute buffers between rivals, to cut down rivalry by prescribing eligibility in advance of conflict, to reduce ambiguity by formal titles and tasks, and by dividing up spaces so that potential rivals need not encounter one another. As such distinctions between persons are against the spirit of the enclave, and impossible anyway to apply to potential defectors, the enclave solution to jealousy is to institute community of goods, or common holding of certain goods, such as land, or regular recall of goods that have been distributed to members. Variants on the idea of a Jubilee in which debts and slavery are remitted is an instrument of these policies. In the enclave there is no room for conspicuous consumption, any more than any other kind of conspicuousness. Conspicuous consumption goes with the culture of individual competition. An enclave responds to internal criticism by adopting ever deeper-dyed egalitarianism. Faced with this, there is nothing that the organizers can do to reinforce their already weak authority. For these reasons, all stemming from easy defection, the enclave's normal state is to be rent by factions. Each faction attacks the others with moral obloquy. Paradoxically, though they define themselves as a community of the elect, the unfurling of their political agenda causes them to hurl vilifying accusations against their own members. The conflict between ideal and actual is explained by theories of conspiracy and infiltration from outside. The organizers (we can hardly call them leaders since there is so little scope to lead) can do nothing to soothe the anger in the enclave. Hence the characteristic sectarian rhetoric is blame and admonishment. But the preaching is in vain, for sermons do not stop the enclave from tearing itself apart.

It is characteristic of enclave culture to split. Replicas of the parent group separate as brother enclaves, adhering to some shared basic principles of protest against oppression by the larger world outside. Brothers in religion are not notable for fraternal love. After parting from each other with recrimination, enclaves tend to have more anger against their separated brethren than against the outside enemy. For mustering such fragile solidarity as they can against potential absconders, one resort is left, but it is an ineffectual resort: the members can vilify the larger community outside, describing it as utterly corrupt. To vilify the outsider is a way of justifying what they are trying to achieve. In the enclave the general explanation of any one's misfortune is conspiracy.

So-called sectarian behaviour has little to do with personal psychology. It would take heroic virtue to resist the pressures; anyone who tries to think and speak against the trend will be punished for their pains. The causes of the cultural bias are the difficulties that regularly crop up whenever a minority group defines itself as separate from mainstream power and authority. The typical culture of the enclave is a regular response to those regularly recurring conditions. In this way resentment is fuelled. In this way, the enclave system renews itself, setting itself ever more distinctly apart from the nations. The system unleashes generative energies to refuel resentment. As its history unfolds, it reinforces the initial response to its disadvantages, and produces the secession it was designed to stop. The organization of the enclave is the very repeater mechanism to which Jacob Neusner has pointed, the routine of which is hardest to break.

Another important sign that an enclave political environment surrounds the redactors of Numbers is the absence of reference to any system of checks and balances. In Numbers and Leviticus the risks of violent conflict are certainly foreseen, but they are apparently to be controlled quite simply by rules against defilement. There is no sign of any routinely honoured opposition to the leadership, no dual principle by which at least two sides of any point of view can be aired, no one commissioned to represent the majority, the followers, against the leadership. There is nothing like the deliberate entrenchment of alternative political expression which is necessary and possible in a hierarchy. This is understandable since leaders of an enclave never feel secure enough to organize their own opposition. Although Numbers makes much ceremony about transferring sacrificial priestly authority to Aaron and his line, there is no matching installation of any executive authority. Aaron has an elaborate inauguration but Joshua, Moses' adjutant and successor, receives only the briefest commissioning and is made subordinate to the chief priest except in the conduct of war

(Num. 27.15-23). The narrative describes no consultations between
war leaders, only commands from on high. Typically when criticism
does surface it is seen as an attack on the leadership, to be vehemently
repressed.

5. *Moses as Leader of an Enclave*

If Numbers seems to be more preoccupied than Exodus with factionalism, this could be simply because it has another agenda. However, it is
remarkable how differently Numbers treats claims to leadership and
authority.[1] In Exodus Moses actually does a few things on his own
initiative. For example, he appoints judges on the advice of his father-
in-law (Exod. 18). In Numbers he reports every crisis back to God
and gets told precisely what to do about it. Rightly so, for in typical
enclave politics it would be fatal to promote any intentions that might
seem to be his own. The only initiative he takes is to ask Hobab to be
their guide in finding camping places, a very dubious request considering that it comes in the middle of a passage about the guidance of
the cloud in directing their movements (Num. 10.31). The Moses
described in the book of Numbers is the only kind of leader that a
sectarian enclave can tolerate: a charismatic leader who never speaks
in his own name, who is always the servant of God. Leaders are not
everywhere supposed to be humble. But the Moses of Numbers is said
to be 'very meek, more than all the men who were on the face of the
earth' (i.e. Num. 12.3). In an individualist culture no one would boast
that he is the meekest man on earth. It would be acceptable in a
hierarchy, and in an enclave meek is what the leader is supposed to be:
it is not a boast but a normal, necessary defence. In an individualist
culture the parallel would be for an epic hero to claim a passionate,
headstrong temperament; Homeric heroes go into black rages without
apology.

Great leader, strong leader? In Exodus, yes, some of the time, but
in Numbers, no. Moses is a great follower, the meekest man on earth,
the ultimate humble backroom person. He does nothing on his own,

1.   The concern here is not to identify the various political regimes which show
up in the Bible stories about Moses, but only to identify the political bias of the book
of Numbers. What follows is influenced by Aaron Wildavsky's work on political
regimes, and particularly on those analysed in *The Nursing Father, Moses as a
Political Leader* (Alabama: University of Alabama Press, 1984).

and in the big crises the book underlines his role as God's lieutenant. The people have never given him authority. He can never remind them that they invested him with power, for they would not, could not, and they did not. God alone authorized him. At one point he is inspired by God to choose seventy elders to help him in the lonely task of government (Num. 11.16). He chooses them and they are filled with the spirit. They are supposed to be a great source of comfort and strength to Moses. But we hear nothing about him ever consulting them. In the Icelandic Sagas and in Homer the leaders take part in many councils of war, they quarrel, walk out of the meeting, come together to praise as well as to blame. In Numbers there are many wars, but no councils of war, unless the one disastrous time is counted when Moses is told by popular leaders that they are about to go off on their own to fight the Canaanites against Moses's advice (Num.14.39-45). There is the argument with Korah, the leader of the murmurers: having mustered a big following, Korah, the descendant of Levi, launches against Moses and Aaron the standard sectarian charge couched in standard sectarian terms:

> Since all the congregation are holy, why do you exalt yourselves above the assembly of the Lord? (Num. 16.3)

Moses replies first by scheduling for the next day a public demonstration of God's will, and then by the stock sectarian retort to the Levite faction: in being privileged for the service of the tabernacle they already rank above the assembly. What other honours do they want? Do they want the privilege of priesthood as well? This standard sectarian response catches the Levites in contradiction. How can they, in the name of equality, claim leadership for themselves?

Then Moses turns to the secular faction, and tells the leaders to come to him. They refuse to budge. They might have reproached his tactics or his conduct of the journey, but no, what bothers them is his making himself a prince, the standard sectarian complaint against self-dealing. Moses reads their complaint against the leadership as it has to be read in an enclave, as an accusation of corruption and bullying. He gives the stock sectarian denial: 'I have not taken an ass from them neither have I harmed one of them' (Num. 16.15). Leaders of an enclave are expected to be abusing their role and are bound to play down claims to privilege or even to leadership. In enclave politics it makes perfect sense for the Levites to have no inheritance in the promised land; it is even necessary for them to make a show of their poverty and political weakness, for those who are chosen by God cannot afford to be accused of self-dealing. So over and over again we read that the Levites have no inheritance, God is their inheritance.

Claims on God are not the only resource available to muster solidarity in an enclave. There is also the boundary. The committed enclave members try to resolve the practical contradictions of their estate by erecting a wall of virtue between themselves and the outside world, a world they never cease to revile. This is the role played by references to foreign gods and the filthy perversions of foreign cults. 'Avenge the people of Israel on the Midianites', God said to Moses (Num. 31.1): the holy war is a welcome distraction from internal strife.

Whatever it was before, at the point at which the final version of Numbers was compiled the message of the Bible became attuned to an enclave congregation. The calling of the Jewish people became the call to live in a self-repeating enclave culture. This would give to Judaism a special source of resilience. Though we can generalize about hierarchy in abstract terms, hierarchy is always a specific pattern of claims. It means loyalty to a particular dynasty, adherence to a specific place in a particular pattern which is not sustainable after the kingdom has been destroyed. With enclave it is the other way round. As a local political form a particular enclave is more fragile than a hierarchy, and more liable to split; but the enclave mentality exports well. It is not over-burdened with complexly balanced structures of authority: its attitude is sturdy criticism of authority. Its conspiracy theory of history fits a large range of oppressive situations. Its sense of divine election is a personal strength for its members.

6. Conclusion

The antipathy against magic and magical images in enclave religion derives from the weakness of authority. We have seen why the enclave suffers in this way. The enclave's power to mobilize its population is weak compared with the effective mobilization available to hierarchies and to individualist regimes. The typical sectarian religion is part of the enclave effort to resist fragmentation and loss. Its precarious authority, ambiguous and diffuse, is always vulnerable. Since this kind of community cannot allow anyone to coerce the others, claims to magic powers are seen as very threatening. Magic generally involves using and images and objects, images of God tend to have power attributed to them and to imply magical advantages for their owners.

It is the weakness of authority which underlies the rejection of images in enclave religions. And the theological claims that God is not depictable are part of the system of ideas which does not allow that God can be located in an object or submitted to the common uses of granting miraculous interventions on request.

How well does this model of the enclave culture help us to interpret the book of Numbers? At first sight it seems to fit well. The book reads as if compiled for an enclave culture: we can recognize the celebratory styles that are so unlike those of hierarchy and individualism, such as the simplicity of the calendar, the celebration of the whole community. But knowing it was edited by a minority hierarchy within the enclave, we should be prepared to find that the priestly editors were saying something about God and his people that might not be entirely congenial to some more committed enclavists in Judah at the time. There are some aspects of that book which do not fit at all with the enclave religion. This is particularly true for interpreting the teaching on defilement and purification. An enclave culture uses defilement for reinforcing its antipathy to the outsiders, but this function is not at all fulfilled by the account of defilement given in Numbers, nor in Leviticus for that matter. The priestly work sends a strong message of reconciliation, not what we might expect from an enclavist compilation.

In laying out a cultural context for the book of Numbers I have suggested reasons why at certain times and places the people of Judah would have been inclined to the sectarian bias of the enclave. I have indicated the basis for their leanings towards aniconic, anti-magical, monotheistic religious forms and their tendencies to xenophobia. I have offered reasons for why an enclave culture, preoccupied with its fractioning consensus and without effective authority, tends to prefer an aniconic god. An enclave would always take a wary attitude to icons from the cultures of kings or heroes. A dissenting minority has no political reason to make and display its own images of kings or heroes. Absence of images is a sign of a distinctive kind of solidarity, the cohesion of dissent. In the next chapter we will see how different this religious bias is from hierarchy and individualism. We now need to set up in the same way the culture that would have inspirited a corps of priests responsible for the cult. The fact that they were a hereditary group is enough to suggest strongly that they would be imbued with a hierarchical culture, and for that reason in many ways at odds with their congregation. They would be a tradition-loving group, running their lives by tradition-sanctified rules, with a stereotypic bundle of attitudes to sin and forgiveness which we need to unravel before we can judge the mutual adaptation of priests and their flock that appears in the finished theological statement.

Chapter 3

A PRIESTLY HIERARCHY

1. Anti-Hierarchical Bias

A prophet generally cuts a more sympathetic figure with us than a priest. In our history 'clergy' and 'cleric' are decidedly unheroic, 'priest-ridden' is an undesirable state for the laity, and 'anti-clerical' is a congenial posture. As to hierarchy, our cultural bias transmits to us a deep suspicion. Writing of Confucius, Benjamin Schwartz charges this attitude with hindering our understanding of philosophies of past times:

> To many modern sensibilities, this frank acceptance of hierarchy and authority as a necessary and even a good aspect of a civilized and harmonious society creates an enormous barrier to any effort at 'understanding' (*verstehen*) Confucianism.[1]

Hierarchy now is inevitably seen in association with colonialism and with strategies of imperialist separation and downgrading of subject peoples. But of course many of these peoples would have been enjoying the benefits of their own hierarchical regime (presumably of a more benign kind) if they had not been colonized.[2] We can add that contempt makes for naivety: we tend to confuse any stratified structure with the culture of hierarchy or suppose the latter to be present wherever we see a crowned head, or a multinational corporation chief executive. However, even brigands can get themselves anointed as kings. Neither the ritual of coronation nor the laws of incorporation can stop leaders from behaving like mafiosi if they can get away with

---

1. B.I. Schwartz, *The World of Thought in Ancient China* (Harvard: Belknap Press, 1985), p. 68
2. D.A. Segal, 'The European, Allegories of Racial Purity', *Anthropology Today* 7.5 (1991), pp. 8-9.

it. So we are down to asking what is the essential difference that distinguishes the culture of hierarchy.

A well-entrenched habit regards hierarchy as the natural organizational solution to adopt when a community has grown beyond a certain size. This is a mistaken idea. Scale has many influences on organization but it does not necessarily affect cultural type.[1] There can as well be massive enclave cultures as small hierarchies. An analogy from earthquakes and clouds helps to make the point: they are forms of organization which persist despite differences in scale:

> A large earthquake is just a scaled-up version of a small earthquake. That distinguishes earthquakes from animals, for example—a ten-inch animal must be structured quite differently from a one-inch animal, and a hundred-inch animal needs a different architecture still if its bones are not to snap under the increased mass. Clouds, on the other hand, are scaling phenomena like earthquakes. Their characteristic irregularity—describable in terms of fractal dimensions—changes not at all as they are observed on different scales.[2]

Likewise, scale is important for many organizational questions, but not for indicating cultural bias. The heart of hierarchy is a distinctive pattern of accountability.

In the old Christian usage the word meant the order of holy things, for example the episcopate or the angelic host. Another traditional meaning refers to a body of persons or things ranked in grades, an inclusive system of orders or classes, one above another. In early Christian political philosophy the dominant idea was of an encompassing, rationally integrated whole. By extension, hierarchy means rational integration, say of numbers, or a reasonable arrangement of whatever it is. In mathematics it means an encompassing structure. A library may exhibit hierarchy to a greater or less degree, or an arrangement of kitchen shelves to suit an orderly progression of purposes. Any rational disposition of things anticipates their unfolding over time, a temporal programme. By the same token, hierarchy also requires anticipatory allocation of space. Every family that allocates one space for sleeping and one for waking is making a proto-hierarchical dispensation of space and time between day and night. The days,

1. M. Douglas, *How Institutions Think* (Syracuse: Syracuse University Press, 1986), ch. 2.
2. J. Gleick, *Chaos, Making a New Science* (London: Heinemann, 1988), p. 107.

the weeks, the months and years may be arrayed, backwards and forwards. A calendar is a hierarchical ordering. The hierarchical pattern pre-empts what can happen. Anyone who has difficulty in recognizing home-making as an effort to create a rational integration would gain by reading about the cooking and storing of food, eating it and cleansing after eating it in a Hindu household.[1] Hierarchy has its own recognizable and complex project of bringing space, time and all the materials of living within the same pattern that governs the relations between persons, and making that pattern conform to the laws of the cosmos. Inevitably then it has a different pattern of responsibility than prevails in enclave culture.

2. *Hierarchical Principles*

One may take the defining feature of hierarchy to be the idea of the encompassing whole. The question is how this idea gets institutionalized into a distinctive system of accountability. Both hierarchy and enclave accept heavy claims in the name of the community. Both have for their primary purpose the generalized aim of keeping the community in being. However, no one would claim that either enclave or hierarchy is efficient for achieving any one kind of purpose. Efficiency is the key word for the individualist culture, where persons are organized around specific goals. Time wasted in a hierarchy or resources spent in bickering in an enclave are the favourite daily jokes of individualists. However, when a prime objective is to maintain solidarity what seems to be wasteful to an outsider may be efficient. Endless tea and coffee breaks, regular partying, ceremonies and gossip may pay a handsome dividend if well directed to protecting and enriching the collective good. Eventually the organization develops goals of its own and subsidiary institutions which have to do with maintaining itself in being.[2]

1. R. Khare, *The Hindu Hearth and Home* (Durham, NC: Carolina Academic Press, 1976); M. Douglas, 'A Kind of Space', in *The Idea of a Home* (Social Research, 58.1; 1990), pp. 288-307.

2. R.K. Merton described this as the difference between the latent and the manifest goals of an organization, terminology which is hard to improve upon ('Manifest and Latent Functions', in *Social Theory and Social Structure* [New York: The Free Press, 1949], pp. 73-138). But see a recent list of publications on the dysfunctioning of bureaucracy: A. Dunsire, 'Holistic Governance', *Public Policy and Administration* 5.1 (1990), pp. 4-18.

Enclave is unitary, and organized around a principle which sets it apart from the main society: if the principle can only be saved by splitting, the enclave will split. For hierarchy it is different, an encompassing whole cannot get rid of its dissident members. To preserve both its segmented character and its wholeness, it shows more care to stop a sector splitting off (and probably less for a member's defection). Everyone who is there at the beginning will be there still, till they die. This is what makes the biggest difference to the culture. There will be pensions schemes, or the equivalent moral pressure on individuals to look after their infirm and elderly. The old will have more political weight; their respected presence forces attention to the long term, if only because everyone expects to be elderly in the long run. Aiming for stability, hierarchy institutes rewards for long service: no one can be fired, every one has tenure, there is no exit.

The idea of an encompassing whole sets the scene for what must happen. Membership, not merit, becomes the basis for allocations. Hierarchy penalizes the quarrelsome character. The smart Alec who makes it uncomfortable for slow colleagues or who mocks the old is unpopular; if he is heard to doubt the value of cherished traditions, his loyalty is suspect. Loyalty is the prize virtue which everyone is called to demonstrate by public gestures such as attendance at funerals and anniversaries. No one must question that it is in the interest of the hierarchy to expand its sphere of operations and to improve its good name, so rivalry with outside hierarchies is normal. But inside the hierarchical unit, rivalry between its sections and between individuals must be controlled. For this hierarchy has a resource which is not available to the enclave: the latter cannot make distinctions between persons, so it cannot buffer their contacts. But hierarchy has enough authority to multiply special spaces and devise other means for limiting the casual encounters of potential rivals: separate discourses, in separate coffee rooms, committee rooms, and dining rooms, separate washrooms for every grade, more small partitioned offices. Hierarchy tries to keep calm and dignified as a means for protecting stability. Enclave has to let rivals clash, because its members adhere to the principle of equality: it cannot tolerate 'common rooms' which only certain privileged categories may use, or indulge in separations which look as if members are ranked. As everyone goes everywhere and meets everyone else all the time, the atmosphere in enclaves is much more exciting and confrontational.

3. *Contrapuntal Institutions*

All of this is very familiar, but it is the tittle tattle of sociology, and none of it explains why enclave authority is brittle and hierarchy is strong. Why should its authority be more secure? The argument runs in a circle if it claims that hierarchy can exert authority because it has power. How it makes its power legitimate is precisely what we are asking. It does not help to say that a hierarchy has power because it can accumulate control over resources. Both types of group would like to be able to count on revenues, for half of their worries about exercising control would thereby be dissolved. Its normal authority being weak, an enclave keeps its overheads low, and periodically raises extra funds by imposing levies for particular causes that move the public's heart, but it is hard to administer a community chest if each stream of income is earmarked for a particular expenditure. If it could fill its public coffers with unallocated income, its discretionary power would be greater, and some authority would accrue, but lacking authority to tax it cannot fill its coffers—a vicious spiral. How does the hierarchy escape this spiral? Most hierarchies manage to centralize funds for public purposes. How do they break out of the vicious spiral to attract enough authority to impose taxes?

The answer is in a set of ingenious adminstrative devices which institutionalize the commitment to keep all segments together. The effect of these devices is to blur sectional loyalties by giving dual memberships and balancing one source of power against another. One such is contrapuntal organization of complementary authorities. There are also techniques for enrolling individual members into potentially rivalrous slots to dampen sectoral loyalties that might conflict with loyalty to the whole. Both of these would be difficult to enact in an enclave, because of the value it sets on undivided loyalty and the uncomplicated sense of betrayal which it nourishes as part of its standard solution to its difficulties.

Louis Dumont would consider that complementary hierarchy is the only true form. Starting from a study of hierarchy in Hinduism, most of his recent work has been on Western political thought over the last 300 years, in which he shows hierarchical ideas to have been initially present in Christendom, and steadily eroded.[1] His typical hierarchy is

1. L. Dumont, *Essays on Individualism, Modern Ideology in Anthropological*

a community organized by two mutually opposed principles, one of which theoretically encompasses the other.[1] Louis Dumont's most detailed examples come from the balance of influence and the contests between church and state in the early history of Europe.[2] There are many modern and secular examples. Consider the bicameral structure

Perspective (Chicago: University of Chicago Press, 1986), pp. 60-149.

1. The principles which Dumont uses for identifying 'true' hierarchy may be summarized (perhaps too boldly) as follows:

   a.   First, 'hierarchy' is a system. Like a mathematical system, it is a relation between parts and whole. From this initial condition flow the others. The different sectors are primarily differentiated and ranked as elements of the whole.

   b.   Second, the true hierarchical system has a dual principle of organization: two authorities, one spiritual, pointing to the whole, one secular, pointing to the part. In Dumont's thought bi-polar authority is the essence of hierarchy. The polarizing is repeated at every level, so that each subordinate unit is constructed as a microcosm of the whole, with its complementary spiritual and secular principles.

   c.   Third, the principle that represents the interest of the whole encompasses the other principle. In his analysis the Hindu purity code is polarized against and at the same time encompasses the political system of kings, warriors, merchants and farmers.

   d.   Incommensurability: in hierarchy no direct comparison of ranking between the polarized principles can be attempted.

   e.   Capacity for 'self-transcendence': the principle that refers to the value of the whole is predominant. It creates the sphere in which credible claims can be made on behalf of the whole system over and above the claims of sectoral interests. For example, when the Christian king wields his power against dissident barons, since his power is held to be ultimately subject to God's authority, the same barons can invoke God in a claim to scrutinize the king's actions, but then they must engage the support of the Church.

   f.   The microcosm: the hierarchical social structure is projected on to the order of nature, so that claims to precedence or respect are reinforced by the fit between the two models. The social hierarchy is justified by its correspondence with the hierarchical order of the universe. In the philosophy of hierarchy the order of nature matches the order of society at every level as microcosm to macrocosm.

In practice hierarchy is messy, but in consequence of being composed of polarized, unequal yet incommensurable, structural elements, it incorporates internal checks against its own transformation into another kind of regime.

2. Dumont, *Individualism*, pp. 44ff.

of political representation in most modern democracies: the House of Lords and the House of Commons, Senate and Congress. The British hospital was a hierarchy in which, until recently, the authority of the hospital administration was balanced against the authority of the matron in charge of the nursing staff: she had to be consulted and could exercise a right of veto for the sake of the good of the whole. Or think of the authority of the army medical officer whose technically defined area of authority in a military unit might lead him into conflict with the commanding officer, but who could not be overruled if he declared a soldier unfit for duty. Or again, the mess officer in a battleship is supreme in the matter of hospitality: even if the commander asks for a particular politician to be invited to dine on board, he cannot overrule the officers' mess or its representative if the officers have a strong objection. A hierarchical home would be another example, where the wife, 'She who must be obeyed', has a defined sphere of responsibility and authority.

For Dumont the one powerful condition which prevents hierarchy from dissolving into a unitary command system run by individuals is complementary opposition: church and state need each to have enough independence of each other for a complementary dual system to ensure the rest of the hierarchical pattern. If either one is absorbed by the other, then hierarchy (as he defines it) has given way to a unitary state. Complementary hierarchy provides many of the constitutional controls on arbitrary rule which are known in later jurisprudence as checks and balances. Neither pope nor king can afford to lose the competition for support, for if either acts out of order, he will be called to account by his instituted rival seeking support from the victims.

A large ethnographic bibliography for West and Central Africa testifies to the use of cross-cutting institutions to control and punish bloodshed where authority is weak. Kinship ties are balanced against territorial ties, queen mother against king, matrilateral kin against patrilineal groups. In each case the system of authority has two peaks, a priest or priestess confronts a king or warrior, speaking for the whole community against arbitrary violence. But this is carried down to every lower level. The Cameroonian district and even village has its male officials balanced by the association of women who protect the community as a whole from misbehaviour and exploitation by the men.[1] Family structure, too, is organized by definitions of incest and laws of prohibited degrees which arrange marriage on a cross-cutting basis. Choice of spouse is controlled by the requirement to set up in each household two distinct lines of influence, maternal and paternal, which confront and complement one another.

Polarization multiplied into different contexts makes a system of complementary positions. Without every member having as good standing as every other, and without the absurdity of pretending that all have the same claim for a place at the pinnacle, every member can achieve a place where he or she belongs. In defence of of an instituted place the rest of the system can be activated. Ideally, polarized peaks of authority recruit support for claims in the name of the whole. Women can legitimately complain against the men, officials in conflict can appeal to a higher court. No complainer can be easily brushed under the carpet since the authority at the complementary pole will welcome a cause to take up against its polar opposite. Dumont implies that in the absence of some such checks from competing institutions, order in the community will depend on the use of force. He starts from the religious authority of Brahmin over and against the secular authority of ruler, and goes on to analyse medieval history in the same terms. I have added contemporary African examples. Lest the reader dismiss the analysis as pertaining to ancient times and distant peoples, consider some more recent parallels.

The principles of complementary opposition and encompassment are still worked out within the Catholic Church. Cardinal Ratzinger sees the orders, Benedictine and Dominican for example, playing the role of complementary spiritual 'Other' in their relation to the Regulars, that is the priests who come under the authority of the diocesan bishops. The claims and loyalties of one set of clergy, based on the local unit of the arch-episcopal diocese, criss-cross the claims and loyalties of the orders obedient to their abbots. It is like building a house of cards from a base of two, one leaning against the other. Take one away and the other collapses. In the external relations of the Roman Catholic Church, the hierarchical principle depended on conceiving the pope as counterpart to the king:

> The papacy is not one of the popular themes of the post-conciliar age. To a certain extent it was something that could be taken for granted as long as

1.　S. Ardener (ed.), *Perceiving Women* (New York: John Wiley, 1975).

it was counterbalanced by monarchy in the political field. But once the idea of monarchy was extinguished in practice and superseded by that of democracy, the doctrine of primacy lost its field of reference in the general pre-suppositions of our thought.[1]

Forgetting that this is how hierarchy works, our position in a later individualist culture may obscure our appreciation of the complementary roles of priest and prophet in early Israel.

4. *Contrapuntal Thinking*

It goes without saying that refusal to compare values or reduce them to a common standard is extremely inefficient for economic organization. And there are political problems. How does a system of control that institutes inequality answer demands for fairness? Partly by universalizing its distributive principles: 'One day you will be old and you will enjoy your turn to sit in the sun and do nothing'. Partly by putting certain priorities such as birth, birth order, and gender beyond question by finding them embedded in the natural order. This is also familiar ground for political philsophy. Less appreciated is the principle of incommensurability. Demands for fairness need standard measures. You need to know the amount of other persons' salaries to be able to assess the value of your own compensation. Though money is a standard of value, monetary comparisons are never altogether easy because of special kickbacks and irregular handouts. But putting work on to a common standard is even more difficult. At the best of times fair comparison is elusive, but when members of the community deliberately do not wish to compare, it is well nigh impossible. In a hierarchy demands for fairness have to be made in the name of persons in positions and not in the name of equality. Ranks, services, and recompense are treated as incommensurable. Attempts to reduce them to a standard scale are deplored as vulgar and insensitive. Fairness takes on a different aspect when everyone has something to gain from a balance of honours accorded to representative positions.

According to the principle of incommensurability hierarchy makes that which was superior in one context become inferior at the other one. So Dumont cites the case of the pope and emperor in the fifth century: they were not equal, nor were they unequal: their ranks were

---

1. J. Ratzinger, *Church, Ecumenism and Politics: New Essays in Ecclesiology* (1988), p. 21.

strictly incommensurate, each operating in a different sphere. In spiritual matters the pope held superior authority, in secular matters the emperor. This corresponds to Pope Gelasius's doctrine at the beginning of the sixth century:

> The priest is subordinate to the king in mundane matters that regard the public order. What modern commentators fail to take fully into account is that the level of consideration has shifted from the height of salvation to the lowliness of worldly affairs. Priests are superior, for they are inferior only on an inferior level.[1]

The expression 'only inferior at an inferior level' is so ambiguous that one cannot but recognize in its structure the same message that wives have been given with the equivalent doctrine of the balance between the head and the heart: 'Yes, dear, of course the heart really rules the head in all important matters, but this is a minor matter, for the head, where you are inferior (though we know that it is only at an inferior level)'. Thus a doctrine that is a resource for the whole unit becomes an instrument of control over the parts. The unfairness cloaked in these terms is mitigated if the public celebration of asymmetry ensures collective power to riposte. Later we will see that hierarchies generally recognize the need to make the asymmetries visible and to justify them in public ceremonies.

Strong complementary institutions take the counterpoint into the inside of its members heads. In each person's mind loyalty to the whole is implanted in the form of claims that he can make effective. Eventually, as we tease out the clever devices for stabilizing a hierarchy, we see that the answer to the question about the origins of power must point to a whole system, and not to any one factor. Thinking is different, classification works differently. Even the categories in which the universe is conceived conform to the pattern of asymmetric complementary forces: sun and moon are paired in their separate spheres, day and night, corresponding to king and priest, man and wife. Words are differently attached to what they signify, not more loosely, not less precisely, but less exclusively; for example, 'female' has multiple referents, implicitly invoking polarity at each level. Every verb and noun is liable to reverberate through the mental corridors, echoing across the latticed meanings. Every word has a

---

1. Dumont, *Individualism*, p. 46.

precise meaning in one context, but multiple meanings in the complex totality of discourse.

Such deep channels have not been dug and redug in the minds of individualists and sectarians. The enclave members have to live with each other, ideally their converse is direct, not mediated by go-betweens or separated by intervening structures. Even more direct is the discourse of competing individualists: a spade is a spade, and accounting should be complete. It is not necessary for them to hold in mind a model of the universe that reflects a convoluted society. Consequently clever and learned scholars whose thinking is not elaborately cross-referenced to the central scheme of analogies give any text a very prosaic reading. This also will be relevant for the history of reading the book of Numbers and other writings which have come under the hand of priestly editors. It explains why the plain, immediate sense has often had priority over the cosmic analogies indicated in the text.

When a community has somehow unwound the meshes of hierarchy, perhaps by suffering invasion, or by dispersal and immigration, its speculations on cosmology are freed from a governing pattern that seeks to reconcile concrete claims of political units. A mind trained in a hierarchical bent cannot confound polar opposites, so when in the Christian Gospel or the Bible the word 'father' is used, it cannot include 'mother'. When it does not have to serve the demands of a particular community, linguistic concreteness can yield to more spiritual, gnostic theorizings. Irenaeus of Lyons likened the gnostic use of words to the disassembling and rearranging of a mosaic that was originally designed by a skilful artist. The hierarchist reading the word of God addressed to Israel interprets a particular nation, a political unit, and a land, so that the word 'earth' in Ps. 24.1, 'The earth is the Lord's and the fulness thereof', has all of these concrete meanings as well as the eschatological one. But for the gnostic the earth is not the Lord's in any of the specific senses: the language of gnosticism presents salvation as a mental and mystic redemption.[1]

Historians of ancient hierarchies have assumed that such a peculiar knot of ideas as those which constitute hierarchy would not have arisen in diverse areas of the globe except by diffusion from some exemplary centre, perhaps China, perhaps India, perhaps Persia, a

---

1. S. Laeuchli, *The Language of Faith: Introduction to the Semantic Dilemma of the Early Church* (New York: Abingdon Press, 1962), pp. 13, 32ff., 41ff., 83.

variant of the spread of infection model. But how are we to account for the spread of such a complex notion? Has it only been seen in its perfection in the great civilizations of antiquity? Where did the idea of a self-repeating, self-transcending system of self-similars, of multiple levels and polarized sectors, mirroring and mutually controlling each other, where did it originate? And what is it? Is hierarchy a rationalization produced by the ancient high civilizations to justify the costs of their achievements? Since Judaism was only lightly touched by the hierarchical principle, on this approach Judah's immunity would have been due to lack of historical contact between Judah and the great hierarchical monarchies of the Middle Orient. But contact was certainly there. Cultural theory would invite us to think of hierarchy as a principle that emerges pragmatically as a possible solution to organization problems.

5. *Hierarchy's Self-Celebration*

We are now ready to note some distinctive elements in a hierarchical religion. The style of celebration depends on what is to be celebrated. We will be forced to the view that hierarchy of the hereditary priesthood had very little influence on the Judaic style of celebration.

A hierarchy has a lot to celebrate, above all the triumph of keeping all its divisions and levels in alignment. It keeps celebrating all the time, but there are some things it celebrates more than others. It is sometimes said that all religions celebrate the renewal of the social fabric, but this is mainly true of hierarchy. In the individualist culture formal roles are not in themselves honoured, so there will be no interest in periodic rites of renewal and life cycle rituals will be organized on a personal basis. The enclave, in its egalitarian fervour, will have eradicated so much structure that there is not much social fabric left to renew. Hierarchy does need initiations to regulate the flow of generations through the framework of office; when dignitaries have retired or died, their successors must be consecrated and duly installed. For longer intervals structural changes need to be recognized. The Bible gives us little evidence of these hierarchical concerns.

It is predictable that hierarchy's celebrations should be formal and precise. The transpositions of analogy from one contextual level to another are systematic. Zealous eyes are watching hierarchy's public statements to check lest a precious distinction has been slurred. Timing is also careful since there is more detail to be recognized in a day of celebration. The more complexly packed the sub-systems of meaning, the more information can be carried by smaller gestures, encoding a richly cross-referenced multi-level information system into surface behaviour. Indeed, so rich is the load of meaning in the smallest sign when everything refers to everything else, that the contrast of surface and deeper meanings hardly applies at all. In hierarchical symbolic systems every meaning is deep.

The long term of expectations engendered in hierarchy affects its treatment of time. Self-defined by commitment to the whole, all its members belong to it indefinitely. We have noted that the community must carry a lot of passengers, it must tolerate a lot of mediocrity, put up with regular cheating[1], and make arrangements for its indigent, old and infirm. The rhetoric leads members to expect their claims to be honoured in perpetuity. An example from modern industrial society may help to bring the comparison home: some great corporations are more hierarchical in their culture and others more individualist and market-oriented. The former hold on to all their staff from training to the grave; the other types take in their staff when they have been trained and fire them when they are no longer competent. Hierarchy's budget priorities being committed far into the future, everyone has an interest in making sure that the long term engagements are honoured. From this we would expect a distinctive celebration of the passage of time. Hierarchical time is cyclic, it has no beginning and it does not end, but moves steadily round in a work of recapitulation.[2]

In a market culture it is good to know when a transaction starts and when it ends, in order to clear the accounts, but hierarchy avoids sharp beginnings and endings. Some flexible vagueness, both as to the precise value of transfers, and as to the time of settling accounts, is

1.   Gerald Mars's analysis of occupational crime (*Cheats at Work*) is largely concerned with ways of milking hierarchies.

2.   The cycle of intergenerational exchange is made explicit in Central African (Lele) villages by a variety of devices: naming the newest generation of age-sets after the most senior one that is just passing out, naming children after their grandparents, repeating the marriage alliances of the previous generation, and trying in any way they can to bestow on personal relationships links with the past that counteract the fissiparous tendencies which drive them to schism at the level of village politics. (Douglas, *Lele of the Kasai*).

more convenient. Complete settlement is too like ending a relationship, and its accounting is too comprehensive to be able to be neatly charted. Individualists transacting together must make efforts to clarify what is owed by whom to whom. But the spirit of hierarchy is better served by the principle of incommensurability, by which everyone is in debt to everyone else all the time, in a system of unchartable generalized exchange. Both enclave and hierarchy are in agreement about the cyclic nature of time. It is a feature of corporate life. But the calendar of a hierarchy is more complicated. As well as recapitulating the central foundation story, its variegated lists of feast days recall local events, varying from one locality to another, and often celebrated with competitive games between rival localities. With its vested interest in reconciliation and incorporation of dissenting units, hierarchy's preferred solution to discord is assimilatory rather than any drastic cutting off. In the long perspective, history takes many turns, wrongs get righted by ironic twists of time. So the calendar will be more filled with days of rejoicing than days of mourning and repentance. Catholic and Hindu calendars honour hundreds of local saints with special days, special statues and pictures dedicated to their names. Without having been studied from this point of view, the Jewish calendar seems relatively austere, as if to match the aniconic decoration of the place of worship.

Perhaps the most telling distinction of the religion of hierarchy is the capacity for self-mockery, which is absent in enclave and individualism. Hierarchy is the form of political organization that is strong enough to bear criticism. It can allow reflexivity on the relation of the up–down dimension. One of the signs of a working hierarchy is that members expect their common interests to be served by those in authority. Justice is one of these common interests. 'Chiefship is slavery', Central African village chiefs used to groan, besieged by crowds of litigants. An oxymoron anywhere, and a puzzling paradox in an individualist culture, it echoes the pope's title in the Catholic hierarchy, 'Servant of the servants of God'. The most destructive weakness for a hierarchy is forgetting that leaders depend upon the led. Whereas in an enclave, tension is explicitly on the relation of inside to outside, in a hierarchy it is on the up–down dimension of authority. As soon as communication from the lower levels is blocked, the hierarchical system is in jeopardy.

The members of a hierarchy know that they do well to be aware of this. In the typical enclave's system of claims authority is too precarious to be joked about, and leadership too inconspicuous for horse-play to be funny. If it goes in for carnival, the humour has to be directed against outsiders. In an individualist system jokes turn sour because the incumbent holds the top post by superior force, and, as he will eventually lose it to a more powerful rival, his position is no joke. Only in a well-established, well-running hierarchy can real carnival be acceptable. Hierarchy allows (and needs) a spectacular, scatologic turning upside down to remind those at the top that they depend on those below. But how do those below find licence for political lampooning? Why are they not afraid of being penalized for their ribaldry? Carnival satire draws its energy from the protection given by the dual-crested, mutually constraining balance of authority. I shall draw on this to interpret the story of Balaam as a political lampoon which would be possible for a priestly hierarchy to conceive, but very unlikely from anyone else in Judah.

These differences which make the celebration of hierarchy quite different from the celebrations of the other cultural types derive from the nature of its organization. Apart from celebration, there are important doctrinal biases. Gender complementarity is used to signified polarized points of organization, male and female, phallus and womb. The more complex the system for which the polarized symbols are being used, the more they are likely to be transposed flexibly from one context to another.[1] Microcosm points to macrocosm and back, over and over again, allowing hierarchy to justify its dynamic pattern of balance and incorporation. Ascending ranges of complementary peaks which mark the hierarchical social system tend to find a counterpart in some doctrine either of male and female deities, or of the marriage of heaven and earth. The great imperial regimes of Egypt and Mesopotamia had male and female deities in their pantheons. Such a doctrine was incompatible with Israel's monotheism, even if the people were attracted to the cult of a fertility goddess. However, monotheism does not conflict with the idea of God as the mystic bridegroom and his people as his betrothed. Israel as the bride, unfaithful, but still loved, is an old and revered theme of the prophets, down to Hosea and Ezekiel. I will show that it is present in

1. M. Sahlins, *Islands of History* (Chicago: University of Chicago Press, 1985).

Numbers, though it disappears from the interpretations of later sectarian readers.

6. *Kings and Leaders in the Bible*

The political message of the priestly work seems to have been to teach the people of Israel that there would be no more freelance political entrepreneurship. Henceforth the regime was to be controlled by the word of the Lord. Above all there was to be no defection from the faith and no challenge to the authority of the priests, neither from prophets nor from political leaders. The top-ranking sin in Numbers after idolatry is 'murmuring against Moses and Aaron'. There is every symptom in the Bible of a dynamic individualism in the political life described in Judges, Samuel and Kings. Although this vitality would have been dampened by military defeat and colonial control, the tradition of political independence would still have inspired any one who could take advantage of the situation to promote his own purposes. It was completely antipathetic to the behaviour required in an enclave under foreign rule.

By our standards early Israel and even the Israel of Kings was extremely violent and competitive, even at the level of family life. Robertson Smith, writing admittedly about the Bedouin and extending what he observed to Arab society in general, said,

> it is only in war, or on the march, which is conducted with all the precautions of war, that the sheik of a tribe exercises any active authority. In other words, the tribe is not organized except for offence and defence; except in war and in matters ultimately connected with war the licence of individual free will is absolutely uncontrolled. There cannot be any greater mistake than to suppose that Arab society is based on the patriarchal authority of the father over his sons; on the contrary, there is no part of the world where parental authority is weaker than in the desert.[1]

These old observations are supported by more recent work.[2] The account of Arab families without strong governance is very different from family systems of Central and West Africa where complementary poles of influence are instituted by balancing the kin of the wife

---

1. W.R. Smith, *Kinship and Marriage in Early Arabia* (Cambridge: Cambridge University Press, 1885), pp. 55-56.
2. R. Murphy and L. Kasdan, 'The Structure of Parallel Cousin Marriage', *The American Anthropologist* (1959), pp. 17-29.

with the kin of the father and where every child therefore has two loyalties. The disruptive effects of sibling rivalry are deflected with a variety of taboos. Defilement is at work, keeping brothers apart, ranking them by seniority, prescribing avoidance behaviour and respect between younger and older.

We see nothing like this forestalling of conflict in the account of the family in the Bible, where inheritance and choice of marriage partners are not codified and where children must compete like everyone else. The people who went into exile were individualists, except of course for the priests among them. To some extent this is signalled by their preferred marriage pattern between a man and his own father's brother's daughter. Marrying back into the same inheritance group permits a build up of reserves.[1] Wealth can be accumulated, and with it control over wives, cattle, pasturage and movable goods. Power can be accumulated which in turn fuels more emulation. The competitive system, as it generates incentives to work, fight and trade, promotes the growth of wealthy centres of civilization. Being more competitive than hierarchies, its power centres are inherently unstable. As some clever, fortunate ones rise to wealth and fame, others go down to oblivion. Such ups and downs of fortune characterize the conflict of empires at the time of the return from exile. The pattern of unbridled competition moves between the sibling-based family conflicts to spectacular political confrontations.

It is possible that this highly competitive scene grew out of calmer beginnings. The patriarchs may have been hierarchical monarchs in some respects: reigning like bucolic kings in the Mediterranean hinterlands, in quasi-domestic style, commanding authority as the husbands of their people, using feminine gender for referring to the kingdom,

---

1. In other marriage systems being obliged *not* to marry brother's daughter has redistributive effects. When cross-cousin marriage is combined with a rule of residence that disperses families, each generation sees a new set of sons-in-law come from families defined as 'other', to accept obligations of support in return for spouses. Being obliged *not* to marry brother's daughter prevents links of alliance from being accumulated in the hands of one family or dynasty: the rule has a regular dispersive effect by sending daughters and sisters to spouses outside the extended family. Along the network of these claims, back and forth across family units, flows the stream of goods and services in the gift economy. The redistributive effects are particularly striking in the case of matrilineal systems (M. Douglas, 'Is Matriliny Doomed in Africa?', in *Man in Africa* [ed. M. Douglas and P. Kaberry; London: Tavistock, 1969]).

relating to God directly. In his lifestyle Abraham has some similarities with King Evander, who lived in pastoral simplicity in his Arcadian kingdom, who could muster armies, and who defied Aeneas to despise his dwelling which had not been too humble for the visitation of a god.[1] But there is no sign in Genesis of any separation of secular and spiritual office. Abraham made sacrifice himself. There is no sign of microcosm–macrocosm reflections, no sign of dual organization or gender complementarity. And Abraham's marriage to Sarah was an extreme version of the father's brother's daughter's type. The evidence suggests that there never was a tradition of complementary hierarchy in the Bible, although plenty of tradition of individualist command structures.

At first sight the roles of Aaron and Moses in Exodus and Numbers might seem to be formally choreographed for the hierarchical balance of ritual and secular authority. But the classic type of complementary opposition does not work: Aaron is not convincing as pope to Moses' emperor, since there is no competition for power between them. Nor can he stand as Hindu Brahman to Rajah, or African priest to king. Aaron once defied Moses in a weak and impulsive way (Num. 12) and was roundly defeated. On all other occasions he was in Moses' pocket and they seemed to work together as one. Neither provided criticism for the other, and the criticism that came against them from unofficial quarters was not accepted. There was no established principle of opposition.

In some respects the book of Numbers shows signs of incipient complementarity. When it provides for cities of refuge to protect unintentional homicides from vengeance, disputed cases come under the jurisdiction of the high priest. This is a step towards a balance of church and state. A hierarchical principle had also inhered in the sacred right of sanctuary, but the check it provided on the king's power was ineffectual. Remember that Solomon over-rode it to carry out his father's demand for vengeance (1 Kgs 2.31). Some religious control over the ruler is implicitly available in the high priest's ritual monopoly of sacrifice and purification, but Solomon was not bound by these restrictions. In pre-exilic times the principle of complementary kingship and priesthood was weak.

1. *Aeneid*, Book VIII.

There was a popular opposition to be reckoned with, emerging from time to time, which was not part of an instituted complementary opposition of king and priest. Whether David harkened more to the advice of priests than to the applause of 'all the people' or 'all Israel' would need a deeper study. Solomon seemed to have felt rather free to disregard advice and to despoil the northern tribes for forced labour. The signs are that the early monarchy had strong leanings towards an individualist regime. The priests did not constitute an independent, powerful body of opinion. There were elders who gave the king counsel, but the Bible says that Solomon's successor did not listen to them (1 Kgs 12.8). The fact that in the time of Kings the most consistent political critics were prophets only confirms that the dual system of king/priest did not apply. The kings could not quite do whatever they wanted but the main check on them was not the priesthood but lack of popular support. If there had been an instituted separation of powers there would surely be more evidence of it in the Bible.

There were discriminations of rank in the times of the late and early kings, but the most significant high-ranking persons seem to have been battle commanders, and were not hereditary. We do not read of rituals to celebrate hereditary social differences as part of a unified system. David is said in Chronicles to have organized the service of the temple by allotting to twenty-four priestly families half a month of responsibility each, thus covering the twelve months of the year's worship (1 Chron. 24). When each family takes turns to do the same as the other families it is not a very hierarchical way of proceeding. Israel's priests depended for their livelihood on tithes, not on assured income from hereditary estates. David assigned specialized tasks to the Levites,[1] which suggests an old basis for the hereditary ranking proposed for them in the book of Numbers. This is consistent with a hereditary priesthood and temple service, but not for a tradition of ritual power to gainsay the king.

It is true that Saul was replaced, and true that King Uzziah was struck with leprosy for not defending the faith, and forced to step down from the throne in favour of his son (2 Kgs 15.5). This says something for the emergence of separate spheres, ritual and secular. But much as they deplored what Israel's kings did in the matter of false gods, the priests were never powerful enough, even if they had

---

1. 1 Chron. 19.8-11; 23.4; 25; 26.1-29.

wanted, to enter into foreign negotiations like the priests of Babylon did and invite a new ruler to replace the king. The decorative trappings of monarchy do not signify that the kings of Judah and Israel even knew what it would be like to establish their command structure within a hierarchical regime. From Bible evidence, the political system would have been highly individualistic at every level and the monarchy itself would have been run on individualist principles.

So we have a hierarchical hereditary priesthood editing the ancient texts of an individualist culture. There is no sign that they are imagining that they could introduce a hierarchical community. We would expect the priests to be traditionalist in every one of the senses we have described: they would work for reconciliation of the divided kingdom; they would work for the inheritance promised to all the sons of Jacob. They would write as if differences can be obliterated by encapsulating history in eternity. Their calendar would deploy grand cycles, their book would point out the ironies of time, curious cosmic effects and witty coincidences devised by God. They do all this, but at the same time, their book is utterly republican in tone, there is no hint of looking to a messianic solution to the problems of Israel. It bears marks of a politically realistic project, edited in a hierarchy surrounded by opposed cultures. We shall find that it carries the kind of message that a responsible hierarchical elite might have considered necessary to deliver, whether it would be acceptable or not. This is going to be important for the whole argument, and especially for the last two chapters.

Chapter 4

THE QUESTION OF LITERARY FORM

1. *Problems with the Unity of Numbers*

There is a general scholarly consensus that the book of Numbers received its final form during the exile in Babylon and shortly after the return. It is also well understood that the materials from which it was compiled are very ancient, some coming from oral traditions, some written, some laws, some stories. Some modern commentators attribute to the editors a minimal role in assembling diverse items, and regard the priestly work more as an anthologizing task than compositional. On this view it is only to be expected that the anthology jumps from topic to topic, and the underlying unity derives from the unity of the theological intentions in making the compilation.[1] This view is compatible with finding parts of the text disjointed. It comes very close to charging the editor with incompetence, or at least with carelessness. The opposite view will be proposed here: that the book has been very carefully constructed and that the many repetitions and jumps of context are not accidental.

It is true that the narrative is continually interrrupted by ritual laws prefaced by saying: 'The Lord said to Moses, Say to the people of Israel...', followed by more of the statutes that the people of Israel should observe. Even the story, with the best will in the world, fails as a coherent narrative. Exodus clearly is a coherent story, and when there is repetition the story explains why, such as for instance why God had to give the tablets of the law twice over. Leviticus is mostly in the form of laws, but when it breaks into story (as about Aaron and his sons in chs. 8–10) the narrative relates to the rituals and so does not read as an interruption. However Numbers reads as a story

---

1. B.S. Childs, *Introduction to the Old Testament as Scripture* (London: CMS, 1979), pp. 190-200.

crudely interrupted by bits of laws, and laws interrupted by story. The severest critic of the redactor's editorial skills is the esteemed biblical scholar, Martin Noth, who wrote in the 1960s:

> From the point of view of its contents, the book lacks unity, and it is difficult to see any pattern in its construction. Seen as a whole, it is a piece of narrative, but this narrative is interrupted again and again by the communication of more or less comprehensive regulations and lists which are only loosely linked to the narrative thread... there are long stretches where the thread fades into the background so that it is almost lost to view.[1]

Noth found the same lack of coherence in the ordinances. Of ch. 15 he said:

> It is not quite clear why this rather unsystematically arranged collection of various cultic-ritual ordinances should have found a place at all at this particular point in the Pentateuch narrative; presumably, in view of the mention of the wilderness at the beginning of vv. 32-36, it has been added to ch. 13-14, at the end of which Israel is condemned to a further sojourn in the wilderness. The individual parts of this collection have no connection with each other. Some of them tie up with older laws and provide expansions of these.[2]

His commentary is sprinkled throughout with similarly deprecatory remarks such as:

> Verses 6ff. produce a disjointed effect and might be regarded as a later addition, were it not for the fact that the whole of vv. 1-7 is so disordered and lacking in unity that one can scarcely expect any consistency of thought.[3]

Though few modern commentators seem to agree with him about the alleged disunity, they have not disposed of all his objections. This being so, it would be improper for a visitor to Bible studies to make light of the discrepancies and interruptions in the Hebrew text. Yet it would also be improper to retain from the text only that which makes sense to a reader some two thousand years later and to discard the rest. It is equally dubious to select the narrative rather than select the regulations or to select the regulations as the real text and play down the narrative. If the book has been revered by the Jewish people and

---

1. M. Noth, *Numbers: A Commentary* (London: SCM Press, 1968).
2. Noth, *Numbers*, p. 114. See also p. 57 on Num. 6.21, and see p. 77 on Num. 10.29-36 as 'far from being a unified whole'.
3. Noth, *Numbers*, p. 135 on ch.17.

admitted in this form to their canon of sacred writings, it has to be taken as a whole. Any selection or addition has to be justified. Yet Bible scholars tend to have each their own version of where it stops, and what has been added later. So little sense does it make as it stands that some resort has been used to fictive chronologies of the editorial process to explain enigmas.

The pattern is admittedly as Noth says: a few chapters of narrative followed by a few ordinances and then the narrative resumed exactly where it had been left in Exodus. But the connection between the two books is not haphazard. If we take the narrative by itself it follows on the story of Exodus, but with some overlap. And note that Exodus itself is not unalloyed narrative; like Numbers it is also interrupted by long instructions for making the tabernacle and the ark of the covenant, the garments of the high priest, and regulations about the feasts and Sabbaths (Exod. 34.18-26). Perhaps in Exodus these regulations seem more skilfully woven into the story than the stark interruptions which jut into the story of Numbers.[1] It is widely held that the completeness of Numbers is found within the Pentateuch as a whole. On this view, Numbers really is incomplete and should not be subjected to a search for inner unity since its coherence lies within a larger frame. But we should not disregard the incoherences and loss of continuity indicated by the quotations from Martin Noth above, and to which references abound in every subsequent commentary on Numbers, whether they are called 'difficulties', 'contradictions', 'enigmas', or 'problems' with the text.

In spite of the complaints of modern commentators the story parts of Numbers have some overall unity. They narrate God's dealing with his people in clear sequence with the preceding books. The Exodus story ends with the glory of the Lord, in the form of a cloud filling the tabernacle. There is a brief episode of the Moses story in Leviticus, which covers the consecration of Aaron (Lev. 8-10), and another briefer story about the punishment of the Egyptian

---

1. A parallel problem about unity has been treated in exemplary fashion by Jacob Neusner. He asks whether the Mishnaic Law of Purities concludes when it does because its inner structure has been fulfilled. Unfortunately the important criteria he develops for completing the logical possibilities of a commentary on laws do not help with determining completeness when the genre has not been identified (J. Neusner, 'History and Structure: The Case of Mishnah', *JAAR* 45.2 [1977], pp. 161-92).

blasphemer (Lev. 24.14). Numbers goes back to Exodus to fix the dates of its own tale.[1] It starts with God telling Moses to number the men able to bear arms and to count the Levites separately. The story follows the people of Israel through the forty years in the wilderness and finally their arrival at the borders of the promised land, when they are numbered again. This slice of history gives the book some large scale continuity. It is framed by closure around a narrative time and space.

However, if this is the artistic structure of the book, it should stop at ch. 26, with the second numbering. On that view the book would be enclosed within the two censuses, but the decision would allow ten more chapters to hang loose and unaccounted. Perhaps the book need not end so soon; perhaps the real conclusion comes in ch. 27 after Joshua has been commissioned as successor to Moses. Chapter 27 would round off the story, but at the expense of ch. 31, where successful fighting against the enemies of Israel is explicitly a revenge for the story in ch. 25 in which the same enemies have seduced Israel away from their true God. To the visiting anthropologist there is something arbitrary about deciding that the book stopped before the completion of the two explicitly paired narrative episodes. So what about stopping it at ch. 33 which gives a summary of all that has gone before? Some scholars would be content to let it end there. That still leaves the last three chapters unincluded.

The most glaring instance of weak emplotment would be the last chapter which, instead of a rousing finale, lets the whole drama tail off into a rule about the marriage of heiresses. This detail of inheritance must surely have been overlooked and stuck into ch. 36 as into a rag bag of disconnected rules. Either it was added later, or at the very

---

1.   Numbers co-ordinates the time frame by celebrating Passover fourteen days after the day Moses set up the tabernacle: 'The Lord spoke to Moses in the wilderness of Sinai in the first month of the second year after they had come out of the land of Egypt' (Num. 9.1). Compare: 'On the first day of the first month in the second year the tabernacle was erected' (Exod. 40.17).

Numbers assumes that the date of the setting up of the tabernacle in Exodus is known and picks up the story directly from that point: 'On the day that the tabernacle was set up, the cloud covered the tabernacle, the tent of the testimony; and at evening it was over the tabernacle like the appearance of fire until morning...' (Num. 9.15). Compare: 'For throughout all their journeys the cloud of the Lord was upon the tabernacle by day and fire was in it by night, in the sight of all the house of Israel' (Exod. 40.38).

least it can be supposed that the idea of rounding off an artistic composition would have been far from the mind of the editors when they allowed their book to end with the banality of ch. 36. This is the problem: an unfitting conclusion.

We have to be wary of the very idea that the structure of a book is provided by narrative. Even for our own literary genres it does not always apply: poetry is not necessarily narrative, nor is prayer, nor songs or sermons, though they all can be. Though this text seems to have some but not all the signs of a complete and edifying story, the interpretive effort is gravely subverted by supposing in advance that narrative is the genre. Even if we were to consider Numbers as a narrative, and ignore the rest, it still would not conform to our ideas of narrative unity. Take for example the story of the prophet Balaam who was engaged by the king of Moab and the allied princes to curse the Israelites (22–24), but who is inspired by God to bless them instead. Though the story is beloved in Jewish traditions, many commentators find it hard to explain why it is in the book at all, still less why it comes where it does. This will be discussed in Chapter 12, below. The same complaint holds for the items of law; those which would seem to belong together are cut up and put into different parts. For example, the laws concerning the work of the priests are scattered through the story. And the rights of the daughters of Zelophehad get treated twice, once when they themselves draw near to Moses quite appropriately in connection with the distribution of lands in Numbers (27.1-11) and then again, making an apparently irrelevant and distracting intrusion at the very end. There are many other elements of surprise and contradiction that understandably dismay commentators looking for narrative coherence.

A few inconsistencies are only to be expected, but the interpretation of a sacred text cannot go forward comfortably on the assumption that the editors put it together carelessly. The problem then is to take the pattern we are given and try to understand it. We know that this is an authoritative book of the Jewish religion. It must be the wrong interpretive strategy to scratch for inconsistencies when some larger, antique structure might be holding the book together so firmly that the incomprehension of modern Christian editors becomes unimportant. At least we are certain that the book is built upon sequences of narrative interrupted by sequences of ordinance. Instead of being unwarranted intrusions, the interruptions could be a deliberate rhetorical device, intending that each narrative sequence be trimmed, as it were, 'with a cord of blue', as God enjoined the people of Israel to put tassels on the corner of their garments (Num. 15.37-41). Each piece of story would then be read as bordered by a section on the law, reminding the people of their separation to God. This does not take us very far, for though the story sequence is resumed after each set of ordinances, the laws on their own would not make a coherent development of legal and ritual themes. Nor is each set of ordinances justified by its piece of adjoining narrative. If the book fails to show any compositional unity, the scrutiny that an anthropologist would apply to a sacred book would have to be abandoned. We therefore have several reasons for extending the scope of our interest. The literary traditions of the place and period have to be taken into account.

2. *Antique Learning*

If indeed the book of Numbers was compiled in the postexilic period the learned editors would themselves have been the heirs of a scholarly discourse that had been going for at least two millennia before their return to Jerusalem. The Mediterranean and the Aegean were established centres of an ancient world system of trade, used to sailing over long distances out of sight of land, using navigational techniques that required astronomy, and mathematics that developed the necessary calendrical information for their journeys. How much that world was knit into one inter-communicating system of ideas, and how the connections have been concealed is now being appreciated.[1] There is a

---

1. F. Swetz and T.I. Kao explain that

> of course the historical figure of mathematical fame known as Pythagoras and born on the island of Samos in the sixth century BCE was Greek, not Chinese. But there is another 'Pythagoras' equally famous. He is the man who first proved the proposition that 'the sum of the squares of the legs of a right angle is equal to the square of the hypotenuse'. For hundreds of years this theorem has borne the name of Pythagoras of Samos, but was he really the first person to demonstrate the universal validity of this theorem?

The issue is sufficiently open to be controversial. The study goes on to expound a translation of an ancient text of Chinese mathematics with proofs and diagrams, some going back to 1100 BCE and much of it dating from the time of Confucius in the sixth century (*Was Pythagoras Chinese? An Examination of Right Triangle Theory in Ancient China* [University Studies No. 40; Pennsylvania State University Press, 1977], pp. 1-75). See also M. Caveing's account of a Babylonian mathematician's

tradition that Pythagoras of Samos himself learnt the theory of numbers from Babylon where he had been taken after the Persian conquest of Egypt. There, as an initiate of the mysteries, he would have learnt the 'golden proportionality', the formula which lies at the base of many important mathematical proofs.[1] The amount of divergence on where a basic mathematical theorem came from shows that it may well be rooted in much earlier times. Joseph Needham, reflecting on whether the widespread philosophical idea of the microcosm in the ancient world came from Pythagoras or from the Chinese, was 'tempted to seek a common origin, going back before Pythagoras and before the Chinese Naturalists to some source that gave the germ of the idea to both Eastern and Western civilizations'.[2] Wherever there were elaborate buildings for construction, land to be distributed, tunnels to be built, there would have been need for precise measurements of volume and space.[3] The learned men of Judah who had been in Babylon had access to Babylonian mathematical learning, and the priests of the Second Temple would have used it subsequently to be able to project the Babylonian calendar every year.

A humanist bias in our day separates and privileges literature above the sciences. The mythical stories associated with the constellations are assumed to be projections of Greek legends. But the reverse is more plausible: neither legends nor art were projected into the sky for their own sake or for the sake of religion, but the practical knowledge came first and the legends were pegged upon the constellations to prod the memory of sailors to search for faint guiding stars. Michael

dealing with a problem of dividing a trapezium into six parts, which shows that he knew Pythagoras's theorem well in the 16–12 centuries BCE. ('La tablette babylonienne AO 17264 du Musee du Louvre et le probleme des six frères', *Historia Mathematicae* 12 [1985], pp. 6-24).

The earliest records of geometry in Babylon go back to 3000 BCE and Babylonians were familiar with Pythagoras's theorem for finding the hypotenuse of a right triangle with known legs in 2000 BCE (J.L. Coolidge, *A History of Geometrical Methods* [Oxford: Clarendon Press, 1940], p. 5).

1. B.L. Van der Waerden, *Science Awakening* (trans. A. Dresden; Holland: P. Noordhoff, 1954), pp.93-94.

2. J. Needham, 'Fundamental Ideas of Chinese Science', in C.A. Ronan (ed.), *The Shorter Science and Civilisation in China: An Abridgement of Joseph Needham's Original Text*, I (Cambridge: Cambridge University Press, 1980), pp. 169-70.

3. Swetz and Kao, *Was Pythagoras Chinese?*, p. 11.

Ovenden's researches on antique astronomy takes the unobviousness of the constellations as indicating that the star patterns identified by astronomy were obscure to the eye, and had to be memorized by uneducated sailors by using the legends as pictorial mnemonics.[1] Ovenden concludes from his research in antique astronomy that the constellations were designed in the middle of the third millennium BCE, as a primitive form of celestial co-ordinates for sea-faring purposes.

As the area of the great volcanic eruption on the island of Thera 3500 years ago is being laboriously excavated the greatness of the Minoan civilizations emerges. From its ceramics we have evidence of the highly developed technical skills of the early Bronze Age; from its paintings, evidence of its artistic achievements; from pictures of harbours, evidence of its voyages; from storage jars and from lead weights, evidence of long-distance trade.[2] It now appears that learning, whose origins have been credited exclusively to the fifth-century Greeks, had been available and used in more or less explicit forms in all the civilizations with whom the people of Judah would have been in contact. A widespread infrastructure of knowledge would have connected Solomon's Jerusalem with the rest of the civilized world. Early Israel would also have shared common traditions in literature as well as on astronomy, mathematics, the alphabet, and music: how much more the Jerusalem of the fifth century BCE after the experience of Babylon and the then current connection with Persia. When the compilers are recognized as heirs to such traditions, it is plausible that the book of Numbers should be presented in the most elegant literary form of the day.

A primitivist religion which traces its origins to the earliest times tends to cast its record in a rustic idiom. This makes deceptive reading for those who would reconstruct its history from the text. The interpreter must allow for the enclave's love of littleness, and its

---

1.   From astronomical analysis of writings he finds that the constellation makers would have been great sailors, voyaging in a latitude north of the Persian Gulf and Indian Ocean where the Babylonian sailors were in the habit of going. Among Mediterranean voyagers he considers the claims of the Egyptians and the Phoenicians, but comes down in favour of the Minoans based on Crete as the original constellation designers (M. Ovenden, 'The Origin of the Constellations', *The Philosophical Journal* 3 (1966), pp. 1-18.

2.   C.G. Doumas, *Thera, Pompeii of the Ancient Aegean* (London: Farringdon, 1983).

abhorrence of grand pretensions. Deliberately set upon rejecting the trappings of the great foreign tradition, and suppressing its own monarchical past, the record of the religion must exalt simplicity. However, a pastoral scene of shepherds and shepherdesses does not encourage later readers to expect that the origins of the text were rooted in a civilization renowned for science and learning. The expectation of rusticity favoured in eighteenth- and nineteenth-century biblical criticism has to be dispelled before the book of Numbers can be read.

Unfamiliar genres of literature are only too apt to be dismissed as clumsy, primitive, or wanting in coherence. It is a paradox that the more highly structured a text is, the more it is likely to be condemned by latecoming outsiders as defective. Martin Noth's charges of incoherence are widely echoed by scholars trying to read other ancient sources. His bewildered comments on Numbers suggest a common difficulty. It is said, for example, that the motifs in the celebratory odes of Pindar (522–443 BCE) are so repetitive and so intricately interlaced that the organizing structure is liable to be overlooked.[1] This recalls the complaints listed above against Numbers. The Theban poet achieved his great reputation at about the same period that the exiles were returning from Babylon, and indeed Pindar's poetry marked one of the high points of an ancient literary tradition spread through Asia Minor. The constraints imposed by this antique genre may be relevant to reading Numbers if only to show the difficulties of later readers.[2] The ode's formal structure has three sections, each with its beginning, its quasi-ceremonial names and praises, then a three-part narrative also carrying standard catalogues of names, ending with praises of the victor.[3] The catalogues are a necessary part of some public celebration, and far from meaningless. In other parts of the

1. In Pindaric composition, 'intricate displays of poetic technique in their own right do not bear a clearly discernible relationship to the topical arrangement of the ode... examples of recurrence and repetition are so profuse and operate on so many levels simultaneously in any given ode that they seem to obfuscate rather than clarify the delineation of any over-riding pattern that could be described as a coherent poetic structure' (C. Greengard, *The Structure of Pindar's Epinician Odes* [Amsterdam: Hakkert, 1980], pp. 13-15).

2. R. Hamilton, *General Form in the Odes of Pindar* (Hague: Mouton, 1974), p. 73.

3. Hamilton, *Odes of Pindar*, pp. 58-59.

world where similar recitals are performed,[1] the representatives of
several shrines come together to perform a ceremony, and their right
to perform it will be part of their relative standing in the community.
The list of goddesses or nymphs or the catalogue of victories is a standard way of signalling relative political weight, likewise the catalogues of victims, or of fathers or mothers. This suggests we ought to
be looking carefully at the long and repeated lists of names in
Numbers, and that we should expect a different kind of unity from
that envisaged by Noth. Describing Pindaric odes as celebrated for
their obscurity, Elroy Bundy writes,

> If unity means 'oneness', the ode is a unity. There is never loss of con-
> trol, and apparent irrelevancy... is only comparative and as foil for a point
> of commanding interest. In the determination of sense and effect as they
> subserve the harmony of the whole, convention rules.[2]

Looking assiduously for a continuous narrative thread is guaranteed to
make an already obscure archaic text even more inaccessible to a later
generation. The controlling point of reference is more likely to be the
general structure than the story.

Perhaps more relevant than Pindar, an example of the principles of
a sacred text being dismissed by a later commentator is provided by
the sanskritist, Paul Deussen, concerning the Vedantas. He noticed
what he called an external structure that interrupted the sequence of
the exposition and decided to remove its traces from his translation.

> We cannot adhere to the order maintained in the Sutras, since they bring
> together the most heterogeneous material in the strangest manner, and, on
> the other hand, widely separate passages naturally belonging to each

---

1. D. Lewis, 'Why did Sina Dance?', in *Creating Indonesian Cultures* (ed.
P. Alexander; Sydney: Oceania Publications, 1989), pp. 175-98; 'A Quest for the
Source: The Ontogenesis of a Creation Myth of the Ata Tana Ai', in *To Speak in
Pairs, Essays on the Ritual Languages of Eastern Indonesia* (Cambridge: Cambridge
University Press, 1988).

2. E. Bundy, *Studia Pindarica* (University of California Press, 1986), p. 91.
Bundy goes on to say,

> The study of Pindar must become the study of a genre. No longer can we view the odes
> as the product of an errant genius whose personal interests cause him to violate the
> ordinary canons of relevance... I shall apply the principles established in this and the
> previous essay to the examination of odes celebrated for their obscurity or wilful irrele-
> vance, in the hope of arriving at a more satsifying conception of the technique of oral
> song (p. 92).

other... As this survey shows, the order of the passages, as they occur in the different Upanishads, is rigidly preserved. But apart from this, the passages are interwoven in a way for which we only here and there seem to recognize a reason... this much is clear, that this principle of arrangement is in fact an external one. Therefore in our statement of the doctrine, we ignore it altogether... [1]

This frankness from someone who has noticed a poetic structure and decided to take no notice of it helps to answer another question about Numbers. If it is governed by an elaborate formal patterning, why has it not always been known and used for interpretation?

Part of the explanation is that an unfashionable style seems to obscure the meaning. In this case a current theory of the role of imagination may be responsible. The imagination is somehow, and against all the evidence, supposed to be freer without the constraints of structure. It may be some comfort to Westerners who have missed the principles on which their own ancient sources were composed to know that the Chinese classical novel suffered the same fate at the hands of later Chinese readers. In the seventeenth century a Chinese writer, Jin Shengtan,[2] rehabilitated the Chinese classical novel of an earlier period from exactly similar charges as those levelled by Noth against Numbers. A novel ostensibly about highwaymen killing and plundering gives the impression of one story being told over and over again, so that,

many modern readers are disappointed and even annoyed by such repetitions and apparent clumsiness and until very recently the prevalent opinion was that *The Water Margin* and novels like it are episodic and lacking a coherent construction.

Jin Shengtan showed that the Chinese novel has a 'tight and finely wrought construction' wherein every word, every section, every sentence has an inherent compositional function or governing principle

1.   I am grateful to John Clayton for this example. P. Deussen, *The System of the Vedanta: According to Badarayana's Brahma-Sutras and Cankara's Commentary Thereon Set Forth as a Compendium of the Dogmatics of Brahmanism from the Standpoint of Cankara* (trans. C. Johnston; New York: Dover Publications, 1973 [1883]), pp. 120-22.

2.   H.L. Wu, 'The Concept of Parallelism: Jin Shengtan's Critical Discourse on "The Water Margin"', in *Poetics East and West* (ed. M. Dolezelova-Velingerova; Toronto Semiotic Circle, Monograph Series of Toronto Semiotics, 4; 1988-89), pp. 169-79.

which goes towards making up the text as a whole, all the principles of composition summed under the category of parallelism.[1] The rules of poetry had not been expected to apply to a mundane genre such as the novel, but it is now recognized that a Chinese classical novel is

> a multi-story hierarchy of parts and wholes. This hierarchy consists of textual units of varying size, such as words, sentences, chapters, and the whole text. At a lower level, each part is a whole in itself that functions as a constituent part at a higher level to form a whole... parallelism [which] organizes and promotes the sequence of the novel as a whole.

The Chinese tradition of writing seems episodic and disconnected because the connections are linking up the whole instead of the particular sequence. The structuralist teaching of Claude Lévi-Strauss has taught anthropologists since the 1950s to identify wholes instead of short sequences. What is attempted here is not an essay in structural analysis in the free style practised by anthropologists, but first an analysis of the rhetorical structure.

The standard complaint against structural analysis is that it is too free, too easily mustered, artificial and unconvincingly remote from what were the concerns of the people hearing and reciting the myth. Lévi-Strauss himself insists that with the best will in the world it is not possible to exhaust all the structures in a great literary work. This means that there is always scope for subjective bias to govern the analysis. There are two kinds of protection for the myth analyst. One is to be working on material whose meanings are so well entrenched in the local culture that a community of fellow scholars can be counted on to scrutinize and correct wild readings. An anthropologist coming in to Bible studies from the outside may propose an outrageous interpretation, at the price of staying on the outside. Within the strict control of academe, idiocy is denounced for what it is; fortunately, for the anthropologist does not want to be outrageous.

There is another method of controlling subjective bias in interpretation. If the analyst can manage not to take responsibility either for selecting the units of structure, or for the principles of relationship between the units of the text, the analysis of the structure will be more secure. The safeguard is to have some principle of selection that makes the interpretation a work of discovery, not of creation. One of these independent principles is given in the spatial references in the

---

1.   Wu, 'Concept of Parallelism', pp. 169-70.

text. Luc de Heusch's exegesis of the Luba myths of kingship[1] demonstrates this safeguard: instead of studying all and every myth, he chose only those that had to do with the enthronement of the king. In itself the connection to the royal family and to politics gave him a strong lead.

3. *Myth's Spatial Framework*

A myth locates its story in space; it locates itself in time, in history and prehistory; it salutes the seasons and enumerates the work of the calendar year. With this frame of spatio-temporal reference it makes the steady structure for unfolding the story. Or quite often the story is an excuse to unfold the framework. The Luba were once a great empire, inhabiting the southeastern region of Zaire. By focusing on the royal myths de Heusch tied his analysis to their rituals, these were already tied to their laws, and their laws to their marriage customs and inheritance, and these to the cycle of their work in tune itself with the succession of the seasons. The result was to reach a long arm into their most profound cosmological ideas and religious doctrines. Scanning the construction of the stories themselves for repetitive patterns he found that the dominant regulative principles were their ideas of east and west. Civilization was brought to them out of the east. No enclave culture this, their origins were not in some past golden age: the autochthonous first kings were clumsy, ill-mannered creatures; their subjects, the original inhabitants of the land, had always lived in the west, where they would have remained uncivilized but for the foreign prince who came out of the east. From him they learnt how to organize eating and drinking, sex and marriage, and it was he who established the kingdom. In biblical terms it would be as if the Bible were written by Canaanites about how they received their religion from the east.

Reading the Bible with this model as a guide, the first way to subdue subjective bias is to look for regular spatial patterns and the cardinal points. In Genesis the spatial orientation is clearly marked. The patriarchs circled between two rivers, the story is contained between the Nile and the Euphrates. The line of heroes is first found in the east,

---

1. L. de Heusch, *Le roi ivre, ou l'origine de l'etat* (Paris: Gallimard, 1972); ET, *The Drunken King, or, The Origin of the State* (Bloomington: Indiana University Press, 1982).

near the Euphrates, then they move westward. Terah, Abraham's father leading the movement from Chaldea to Haran in northwest Mesopotamia. Haran goes on being referred to as the place of the Eastern people.

a. From the east, Abraham moves south at the Lord's bidding (Gen. 12.1) to the land of Canaan, and then from Bethel to the Negeb. A famine sends him to the far western boundary, Egypt. Back from Egypt he returns to the Negeb (Gen. 13.1), and goes north to Hebron. The Negeb, Bethel and Hebron are in a straight line running north and south in the middle of the area between the eastern and western rivers.

b. After the destruction of Sodom and Gomorrah Abraham goes west again, as far as Philistinia, at Gerar (Gen. 20), whence he returns to Beersheba in the Negeb (Gen. 22.15).

c. Abraham sends his servant east to his brother to find a wife for Isaac, whom he forbids to go east (Gen. 24.6, 8).

d. Isaac goes to Gerar, in Philistinia; this is as far west as he is allowed to go: the Lord forbids him to go to Egypt (Gen. 26.2).

e. Isaac sends his son Jacob east to get a wife, where Jacob undergoes servitude for twenty years (Gen. 31.38). Jacob goes to Bethel in the heart of Canaan (35.6), and on to Ephrath (Gen. 35.16).

f. Joseph is taken from near Shechem (Gen. 37.12) to Egypt (Gen. 37.28), and raised to a position of influence. Famine brings Jacob and his other sons to Egypt (Gen. 46), where Jacob dies and where the people endure servitude.

g. His sons bury Jacob in Canaan, at Mamre in Ephron, where Abraham had buried Sarah (Gen. 23.17), in the middle of the area between Jerusalem and Beer-Sheba.

h. They return to Egypt (Gen. 49.13-14) and Joseph dies there.

The rest of the story begun in Genesis is told in Exodus and Numbers, the long journey eastwards back to Canaan, the promised land. On either side flow the great rivers, the Nile and the Euphrates, on either side great cities stand, places of high civilization, wealth and power, and predatory foreign empires, Egypt and Babylon. For the readers of the Pentateuch in the sixth to fifth centuries, Egypt, where the people of Israel endured their first bondage, would be matched by

Babylon, where they endured the second. In the deployment of mythic space Abraham forbids Isaac to go east, the Lord forbids him to go west, so the paths of Abraham, Isaac and Jacob cycle around the centre of the world.

The geography of the Bible is no imaginary space, like Trollope's Barsetshire, or King Arthur's Broceliande. Current political experience is funnelled through a mythic space that covers the real space of everyday. Each moment of historical conflict and separation is marked in the story by a notorious act of defilement. As past infamy colours the news of present depredations and treachery, current place names and the directions of the roads and rivers carry the myth's story. In the mythical framework of Genesis, east and west are real places. The geographic framework pegs the story to the sites of real empires and their real enmities.

The book of Numbers is entered squarely into the space-time structure prepared by the first two books of the Pentateuch. But it immediately establishes an internal set of space co-ordinates of its own. For Numbers east does not always indicate a place but an orientation; east is the direction in which the sun rises (Num. 3.38). East and west are relative: anyone may stand in a more easterly position than someone else. The book uses the cardinal points to structure the relations of the children of Israel to one another. This is stated in the first four chapters, and they are told to keep their relative positions, camping in due spatial order, and setting forth again in the same order. The repetitions warn us to look out for deeper meanings in the order of the host. We will find that the ordering presents an elaborate pun in space. The tabernacle is in the middle of the tribes, around it is a cordon of Levites, on the outer edges of the square stand in parallel lines the families of the other sons of Jacob. The two kingdoms, the northern kingdom of Israel and the southern kingdom of Judah, now become two Persian provinces, Judah and Samaria, are brought together by the ground plan into one grand council.

The spatial references of Genesis and Numbers structure the whole Pentateuch, just as the cardinal points of east and west structure the royal myths of the Luba. The book of Numbers stands before this background of circuits between the east and west river boundaries, with the short journey between Hebron and the Negeb as the steady centre. The geographical pattern reveals the message of Numbers as hope and trust in God. The congregation in the Second Temple community will have recognized the pattern: after the Egyptian bondage the Lord led them home and after the Babylonian captivity, he led them home again. The movement of their history, so disordered without the religious perspective, now appears as regular as the procession of the seasons. The tragic burden is lifted by showing the periods of exile in the east and west as parallel orbits through God's plan.

4. *Numbers' Commentary on Genesis*

Numbers' special role in the Pentateuch is to draw out the theme of prophecy fulfilled. It complements the other books by presenting a coherent mythic background for Judah's political situation after the return from exile. The story of the people of Israel is marked in Genesis by Noah's prophecy of conflict between the descendants of Shem and the descendants of Canaan. The founders of the great empires, Egypt, Ethiopia, Babylon and Assyria would issue from his son Ham; but he curses one of Ham's sons, Canaan (Gen. 9.25). Noah's second son, Shem, is the antecedent of Terah; Noah's third son, Japheth, is patriarch of the Gentile nations.[1] Terah begets Abraham and his brothers; one of them begets Abraham's weak and ambiguous nephew, Lot, who fathers his two sons on his own daughters. This defamation brings us nearer to the political history of Judah, for its geographically nearest neighbours and most hated enemies are those two ill-begotten sons, Ammon and Moab. The blessing on Abraham is confirmed (Gen. 12.1-3; 13.14-17; 15.5-6; 15.12-16; 22.15-18), and the land of Canaan specifically allotted to him and his progeny (Gen. 17.8). The promises are renewed for Isaac (Gen. 26.24) and for Jacob (28.13-15), and proved to have been triumphantly fulfilled in the story of Numbers.

The theme of fraternal rivalry drums a regular beat throughout Genesis. When Jacob has displaced his elder brother by a ruse, Esau goes to found his own kingdom, another close neighbour and enemy of Judah. Jacob's story records the rivalry of his wives, Leah and

---

1. Loren Fisher identifies in the structure of Genesis five histories modelled on the ancient form of patriarchal cycles which are based on a common structure ('The Patriarchal Cycles', in *Orient and Occident, Essays Presented to Cyrus H. Gordon on the Occasion of his 65th Birthday* [ed. H.A. Hoffner; Verlag Butzon and Bercker Kevelaer, 1973], pp. 59-63).

Rachel. When the book of Numbers is going through its final editing, Ephraim, descendant of Rachel, and Judah, descendant of Leah, will be the only two sons of Jacob whose descendants have survived with their own political territories. The crux of the whole book will be the burning contemporary issue of how these descendants of Jacob should treat one another. The regular parading of Jacob's sons through its chapters repeat the initial and ever-present confrontation of the sons of Joseph, represented by Ephraim and Manasseh, with the sons of Judah. We shall see that Numbers does not evade the political issue. Its consistent teaching is that all of the sons of Jacob are heirs to the promises, except Levi, to whom a separate destiny is reserved.

If ever a serial had a cliff-hanging end, pointing onward to the rest of the series, the end of Genesis does: Jacob is dead and his twelve sons locked into servitude in Egypt. Next, in the book of Exodus Moses leads the people of Israel out of Egypt. The story of their journey from Ramses to Sinai is interspersed with laws given by the Lord to Moses. The ten commandments are revealed; keeping the law is the condition of the sons of Jacob enjoying their promised inheritance in Canaan. Two strands of revelation, law and supporting story, have emerged by now as the governing principle of the genre. The third book, Leviticus, translates into daily minutiae the implications of the laws. We have had one book of story and promises, one book of mixed story and law, one book of laws. The part of the fourth book is evidently to sum and affirm the first three. Numbers combines interwoven stories and laws; it takes up the story part of Exodus by tracing the journey of the people of Israel from Mount Sinai to the borders of the promised land. Its own story documents the fulfilment of the Lord's promises to Abraham, Isaac and Jacob and the curse of Noah against Canaan. As Numbers works forwards from its beginning at Sinai to its ending in the Plains of Moab, it unfurls in reverse order the scroll of God's promises in Genesis. The beginning of Numbers starts with the end of Genesis and the ending of Numbers arrives by an inverted parallel at the beginning of Genesis:

a. Genesis 50.24: The dying Joseph's last words were an oath saying that God will visit the sons of Israel and bring them to the land which he has sworn to give to Abraham, Isaac and Jacob.
    Numbers 1: At the very beginning Moses is told to make a census of those who will bear arms, that is those who will

fight to win the land, separating them from the Levites who will not inherit any territory. In Genesis the people of Israel were serfs in Egypt, in Numbers they are about to become free-holders in the promised land.[1]

b. Genesis 49: On his deathbed Jacob blesses nine of his sons and curses Reuben, Simeon and Levi.

Numbers 2, 3: Immediately after the census Numbers deals with these curses and blessings and definitively settles the rivalry between Rachel and Leah. Their descendants are given their place around the tabernacle: the children of Leah stand on the east, while Joseph's sons and Benjamin have a place on the west.

c. Genesis 32, 33: Esau and Jacob, having earlier quarrelled, treat each other generously, with honour and gifts.

Numbers 20.14-21: The king of Edom, Esau's descendant, refuses safe passage to the people of Israel on their march to the promised land, but Moses conspicuously refrains from attacking him.

d. Genesis 25.23: The oracle of Rebecca about her two children: 'Two nations are in your womb, and two peoples born of you shall be divided; and one shall be stronger than the other, the elder shall serve the younger'.

Numbers 24.18: Balaam prophesies Edom's downfall which we know by hindsight of history will take place at the hands of David.

e. Genesis 19.30-38: The daughters of Lot seduce their father, and so conceive Ammon and Moab.

Numbers 25.1-6: The daughters of Moab seduce the men of Israel into apostasy.

f. Genesis 9.25: Noah curses Canaan.

Numbers 31.1-19: The armies of Israel start their victorious campaigns which deliver the Canaanites into their hands.

By the time we have reached the end of the book of Numbers, the Lord has given the tribes of Israel instructions on how to partition among themselves the promised land which they have now reached.

---

1. A. Wildavsky, *Assimilation versus Separation, Joseph the Administrator and the Politics of Religion in Biblical Israel* (New Brunswick: Transaction Publishers, 1993).

By walking backwards through Genesis from end to beginning, and forwards through Numbers step by step from beginning to end, we have come full circle to the opening theme of Numbers, the land of the promise. Numbers makes it clear that the sons of Joseph are included with the others in the promises.

The Plan of Numbers on the Plan of Genesis

Genesis

A The land promised to Abraham
  B Noah's curse on Canaan
    C Origins of Moab and Ammon by Lot seduced by his daughters
      D Esau, the founding of Edom's kingdom
        E Jacob's last words to his twelve sons
          F Joseph confirms the promises of land
            to Abraham, Isaac and Jacob

Numbers

          F Census of Jacob's inheritors
        E Jacob's twelve sons placed around the tabernacle
      D Moses's encounter with Edom
    C Israel seduced by women of Moab
  B Canaanites destroyed by Israel
A Promised land partitioned among the twelve tribes

This pattern of parallel promises and curses made and fulfilled is a consistent guide to the reading of the latter book. Referring back to the paired verses the references in Genesis to Judah's neighbours jump to the eye. The parallels between Numbers and Genesis, where the names of Moab and Edom are prominent, point to grave matters of foreign policy remembered by the Second Temple community. With this preliminary evidence of a coherent construction, we should not disregard the many repetitions and digressions, but consider them as playing a necessary part in an archaic literary form. It is rewarding to read Numbers in the ancient Chinese fashion, paying attention to the links connecting the parts to the whole structure, instead of going from point to point in the linear sequence required in Western prose readings. To call it half-jokingly the Chinese fashion is to defer to its antiquity as a style of writing, but we use the same synoptic eye when we read a sonnet. In the synoptic reading of the book of Numbers the meaning becomes coherent and very much more impressive, intellectually and theologically.

Chapter 5

TWELVE SECTIONS IN THE OVERALL PATTERN

1. *Identifying the Units of Structure*

I will first identify the building blocks of the structure. Instead of unwarranted interruption, the periodic switch back and forth between law and narrative is more like montage or cinema flash-backs (which indeed are often disruptive but intended by the film makers to enrich the chronological dimension). Rather than judge the book severely because the laws interrupt the narrative, we find that it is composed deliberately of two strands, one of law and one of narrative. By introducing the alternative mode each new section cuts off the previous section: the result is a pattern of alternating strands.

In Numbers the sections are marked off automatically by stylistic rules which anyone can check, without making reference to the themes developed within a section. The two modes, story and law, differ in their treatment of time. The law sections are not circumscribed by present chronology nor does the internal development of a law section have a temporal order. The laws are to be kept now, forever, and particularly in some time when the people arrive in the promised land. In the law sections there is no dialogue or interaction, and no plot. The Lord delivers his ordinances to Moses and sometimes to Moses and Aaron, but apart from these there are no other persons named in the legal sections. A typical law section never contains just one command, but several. Although law sections also start with the Lord speaking to Moses they report no dialogue except sometimes the obedient response of Moses. There is no other interaction. The first command is followed by another set of commands and often by yet another and another. Everything is impersonal and abstract, no names, no defiance, no changes of mind. The law section is a series of imperatives which conclude with a formal injunction that the law is eternal, or by a formal reminder of the Lord's authority: Do this, I am the Lord, your God.

The story sections always mark out their temporal and spatial structure. The storyteller locates the actors with precise dating, and the story proceeds to develop its internal chronology. The stories are distinguished by action and plot. When the Lord speaks, Moses then conveys the message or does something that he has been told to do. For example, a long story section runs from chapters 1 to 4, all in the story mode: the Lord tells Moses to number the people of Israel, tells him how to do it, in three stages, involving named leaders for each of the twelve tribes, and for the Levites. If events in the story are activated by divine commands, the commands are instructions for tasks to be carried out at once, not to be confused with ordinances to be observed for ever. Persons in the story mode are referred to by name, they respond to what is said; they gesture, run, throw themselves on the ground, or the Lord afflicts them with some penalty and they die.

When these criteria are applied systematically to the whole text, seven narrative sections emerge, alternating with six ordinance sections, making thirteen in all as follows:

Story	1–4	Counting the 12 tribes, heirs to the land, and danger of encroachment
Law	5, 6	Keeping faith and breaking faith
Story	7, 8, 9	Gifts to the Lord; cleansing the Levites, the Lord's gift to Aaron, the Passover, the cloud on setting out on the journey
Law	10.1-10	Blowing trumpets and appointed feasts
Story	10.11-14	The Wilderness of Paran
Law	15	Offerings for priests, guilt and innocence
Story	16, 17	Encroachment punished, twelve rods subject to Aaron's rod
Law	18–19	Offerings for priests, cleansing from blood
Story	20–27	The Wilderness of Zion
Law	28–30	The appointed feasts and women's vows
Story	31–33.49	Defeat of Midian kings, booty purified, offered to the tabernacle, summary of journeyings
Law	33.50–35	Destroy images, partition promised land, cities of refuge
Story	36	The sons of Joseph, and the land

These are the two strands of which the book is composed. The next question is how they have been arranged. I will demonstrate that they are an elaboration of the well-known poetic structure of parallelism which is typical of Hebrew poetry. Each section has its parallel, each law section matches another law section, each story section matches another story section. The match is loose, but the attempt to produce correspondences by repeating phrases that go across the book accounts for the repetitions which have given it a bad name for careless editing.

2. *Hebrew Poetic Structure*

The term 'parallelism' derives from Robert Lowth's 1753 lectures given as professor of Hebrew Poetry in Oxford, where he described a deliberate pairing of line, phrase and verse:

> so that in two lines (or members of the same period) things for the most part shall answer to things, and words, to words, as if fitted to each other by a kind of rule or measure.[1]

Thematic parallelism is sometimes called 'thought rhyme'[2] because the thought has two parts, the second pairing the first, running in parallel with it. Something asserted in the first part is repeated with affirmation or denial in the second part. The paired parts may be very complex: one complete pair being used as the first part of another, more comprehensive pair, and that, when completed, used as part of another. The pairs may run parallel, or one can be an introversion of the other. Such fracturing and reforming of the meanings by contraposition was very much the favoured style for the rabbis. A quotation from Jacob Neusner draws attention to its characteristic features:

> The dominant exegetical construction in Leviticus Rabbah was the base-verse/intersecting verse exegesis. In this construction, a verse of Leviticus was cited (hence base-verse), and then another verse from such books as Job, Proverbs, Qohelet, or Psalms was cited. The latter, not the former, was subjected to detailed and systematic exegesis. But the exegetical exercise ended up by leading the intersecting verse back to the base verse and reading the latter in terms of the former... a multiple-layered construction of analogy and parable. The intersecting verse's elements always turn out to stand for, to signify, and to speak of something other than that to which they openly refer. Nothing says what it means, everything important speaks elliptically, allegorically, and symbolically. All

---

1. R. Lowth, *Lectures on the Sacred Poetry of the Hebrews* (translation of *De Sacra Poesia Hebraeorum Praelectiones Academicae*; Boston, 1829), p. 157.

2. G.W. Anderson, 'Characteristics of Hebrew Poetry', in *The New Oxford Annotated Bible with the Apocrypha, An Ecumenical Study Bible* (RSV; Oxford: Oxford University Press, 1977), pp. 1523-28.

statements carry deeper meaning, which belongs to other statements altogether.[1]

This is a good summary of what Benjamin Harshov calls 'translogical discourse'.[2] The style, typical of Yiddish literature, uses three major principles which he identifies as associative digression, resort to a canonized textual store, and the assumption that all frames of reference in the universe of discourse may be analogous to each other. The effect for reading or listening, as Harshov says, is like that of a prism, shattering the world and presenting the shaken image through a kaleidoscope. A simple way of presenting parallelism is to say that a series of paired units make the rungs of a ladder.[3]

Semitic parallelism was originally treated as a genre of its own. But now the work of linguists and anthropologists of the last 50 years has produced a richly documented discussion of parallelism throughout the world. A magisterial review of the topic[4] places Roman Jakobson's analysis of Russian poetry at the beginning of modern understanding[5]. The techniques of parallelism are found in widely scattered regions of the world, including China, Vietnam, Burma and Thailand. The traditional poetry of Finland and North America influenced Longfellow's writing of *Hiawatha* in parallelisms. More intriguing than the widespread existence of this rhetorical form, which corresponds so closely to the basic demands of grammar and syntax, is the slowness of Western scholars to recognize it. Possibly it escaped recognition just because it is so pervasive.

Although G.B. Gray found parallelism in certain 'poems' of the Bible, in Psalms, the book of Job, Proverbs, Ecclesiastes, Lamentations, and Canticles, he declared it absent in the Pentateuch,

1. J. Neusner, *Self-fulfilling Prophecy: Exile and Return in the History of Judaism* (Boston Beacon Press, 1977), pp. 138-39.

2. B. Harshov, *The Meaning of Yiddish* (University of California Press, 1990), pp. 100-101.

3. Harshov uses this image for analysing Hebrew verse and Yiddish narrative style (*Meaning*, p. 106).

4. J.J. Fox, 'Roman Jakobson and the Comparative Study of Parallelism', in *Roman Jakobson: Echoes of his Scholarship* (Lisse: Peter de Ridder Press, 1977), pp. 59-90.

5. R. Jakobson, *Questions de Poetique* (Paris: Editions du Seuil, 1973).

Samuel, Kings, Chronicles, etc.[1] We owe to Jacob Milgrom the demonstration that the book of Numbers uses thematic parallelism:

> The main structural device, to judge by its attestation in nearly every chapter of Numbers, is chiasm and introversion. Chiasm is named after the Greek letter X and denotes a pair of items that reverses itself, yielding the structure ABB'A'. When there is a series—more than two members—for example ABXB'A' or ABCC'B'A', then the term introversion will be used. These two types must be distinguished, for whereas the chiasm is purely an aesthetic device, the introversion can have didactic implications. In the scheme ABXB'A', the central member frequently contains the main point of the author, climaxing what precedes and anticipating what follows...
>
> Smaller units
> 1. Simple chiasm
>   A If only we had died
>   B in the land of Egypt
>   B' or in this wilderness
>   A' if only we had died (Num. 14.2).
> 2. Complex chiasm
>   A If her husband offers no objection from that day to the next,
>   B he has upheld all the vows and obligations she has
>   assumed.
>   B' he has upheld them
>   A' by offering no objection on the day he found out (Num. 30.14).
> 3. Chiasm in subsequent repetition
>   A We will build here sheepfolds for our flocks
>   B and towns for our children (Num. 32.16)
>   B' Build towns for your children
>   A' and sheepfolds for your flocks (Num. 32.24).[2]

Milgrom gives many examples of whole chapters, laws as well as narrative, composed according to this pattern. It is a small step from these instances of poetic form in Numbers to finding two chapters entwined together in parallel, and the larger units made by these combinations worked again into even more comprehensive patterns. This is the grand illumination which opens a new perspective on the book.

---

1. G.B. Gray, *The Forms of Hebrew Poetry* (London: Hodder & Stoughton, 1915), p. 37.
2. Milgrom, *Numbers*, p. xxii.

The next chapter will be concerned with how to arrange these sections. First it is necessary to spend more time on how they are identified because this is always the slippery part of structural analysis. If, as is claimed, we have here an automatic, self-identifying set of units, analysing Numbers will be comparatively straightforward.

3. *Exceptions to the Rule*

Some exceptions to the smooth allocation of pieces of text to a narrative or an ordinance section are only to be expected. Rather, it is surprising that after all this time the simple criteria work as smoothly as they do. Astonishingly, there are very few problem pieces which do not slot easily into their appropriate section. Discussing them will give the reader an idea of how the identification of the alternating sections has been done.

a. *The lamp: chapter 8, section III.* Is this a law or a narrative? Now the Lord said to Moses, Say to Aaron, When you set up the lamps, the seven lamps shall give light in front of the lampstand (Num. 8.1-2). This command is an instruction for furnishing the tabernacle. It continues the narrative moment when Moses went into the tent of meeting to speak with the Lord and the voice from the mercy seat gave him this instruction. Supplying information as to where, and when and who, it belongs quite properly in the narrative section lying on either side of it, in the same way as the opening narrative section of the book starts with the command to number the people of Israel and to tell them where to stand. Aaron responds: 'And Aaron did so; he set up its lamps to give light in front of the lampstand, as the Lord commanded Moses' (Num. 8.3), and the narrative continues with another instruction: The Lord said to Moses, 'Take the Levites...' One command does not make a law section. There is no way in which Num. 8.1-4 should count as a legal section jutting up in the middle of the narrative.

b. *The woodgatherer: 15.32-36, in section VI.* Is this story a separate narrative section? Or is it a part of the law section? In the middle of a long section in the ordinance mode a man is reported for breaking the sabbath. Moses consults the Lord and is told to stone him. Immediately after the stoning the ordinance-giving is resumed. These four verses indubitably make an exception. If they were counted as narrative they would add a new section, changing the total number of sections and forcing a rearrangement of their pairing. As there are no names or dates, it is counted here as an exception, even treasured as the only real challenge to the consistency of the governing pattern.

c. *Moses' obedience (29.40), in section X.* Is this to count as a story? In the middle of an otherwise unbroken sequence of ordinances the narrative mode erupts, recording that Moses told the people everything, just as the Lord had commanded—that is all. Again, no one is named, there is no reaction to Moses' message. It is similar to the obedience of the people of Israel to the command to put lepers outside the camp in Num. 5.4. If these count as switching into the narrative mode, they are trivial exceptions because no narrative follows.

The ending, ch. 36, has caused head-scratching among the commentators, as we have seen. The problems of heiresses is definitely presented in the narrative mode and if it were counted as a new narrative section it would make an additional section and the sum of parts would be thirteen. It has been already noticed that ch. 36 makes an odd conclusion for a book such as this. However, the position of this narrative chapter at the very end is only a seeming anomaly. Once we start to analyse the structure of parallellisms internal to the sections, the marriages of heiresses turn out to be carefully placed in the structure of the book. They connect the end with the beginning and have to be treated as an addendum to the first section, making the total of sections for considering the structure as twelve in all. Although I need to consider it here as a separate section, in the last chapter it will show up as an integral part of the first. It is much too soon in our analysis to be looking at such fine brush strokes. At present we are concerned with the grand canvas and only need to ask the reader of this chapter to reserve judgment on whether ch. 36 is an anomaly in the general structure.

Another seeming anomaly, ch. 30 on women's vows, is attached to a legal section dealing with the annual festivals; it seems to be out of place by reason of its theme. But the strength of our method is that the divisions within the book of Numbers are not identified thematically. Any kind of themes may have been packed together inside the different story and legal sections which have been identified by other criteria. Recognizing why particular themes have been put together in one section is not our affair; for the moment the question is whether the sections can be clearly separated on criteria distinguishing narrative writing from law. Once that division has been made, and once the sections have been arranged with their pairs, we can use any scholarly insight at our command to understand why the chapter on women's vows should be placed just where it stands or the ending is what it is.

If the story of the woodgatherer and chs. 30 and 36 were counted as complete sections there would be fifteen pieces in all. Before we decide that they are to be counted as sections we need some other clues as to the structure of the book. These emerge as we shall show and point to an overall pattern of twelve matched pieces. For the present it is convenient to work with the thirteen clearly distinguishable sections. The first rule for identifying a section is the clear beginning and ending. Chapter 30 turns out to be the ending of a section, and ch. 36 has its own characteristic story beginning and ending. Only the woodgatherer story remains as an anomaly to the strict ordering of sections, but both the other cases fall into place when we have found the principles for organizing the main structure.

4. *Beginnings and Endings*[1]

Whether Numbers was compiled for oral recital or for reading, the editors would need to signal the shift from one mode to another. Warning of the approaching end of a section would be given in a strong peroration, and the next section would have an unmistakable opening formula. In looking for these opening and closing signals we are looking for automatic reinforcements devised by the editors to ensure recognition of the pattern.

Although we do find that the story sections use distinctive formulaic beginnings, conformably with the criteria for stories given above, their beginnings always identify a group of persons and/or locate the action in a time. Three of the six story sections begin with a date:

Section I, ch. 1.1	'On the first day after the second month of the second year after they had come out of Egypt'.
Section III, ch. 7.1	'Now it came about on the day that Moses had finished setting up the tabernacle' (the date is given in Exod. 40.17, the first day of the first month in the second year).
Section IV, ch. 10.11	'Now it came about in the second year, in the second month, on the twentieth day of the month.'

---

1. See David Goodman's *Note on Identifying Beginnings and Endings* appended to this chapter.

The other story sections begin with naming individuals and defining a population and sometimes with a date as well:

Section VII, ch. 16.2   'Now Korah, the son of Izhar, son of Kohath... and they rose up before Moses, together with some of the sons of Israel, two hundred and fifty leaders of the congregation.'

Section IX, ch. 20.1   'Then the sons of Israel, the whole congregation, came to the wilderness of Zin in the first month.' This both identifies the actors and locates them in space and time.

Section XI, ch. 31.4   This section starts with the Lord commanding Moses to send the people of Israel to war against the Midianites: 'You shall send a thousand from each of the tribes of Israel to the war.'

Section XIII, ch. 36.1   'And the principal fathers of the families of the children of Gilead... came near and spoke before Moses and before the princes, the principal fathers of the Children of Israel.'

Likewise, story sections have clear endings. They lead up to their conclusions with long perorations, replete with repetitions, inversions and plays upon names, often with a double peroration. Here are the story section endings.

Section I: The first peroration exhibits this double set of endings: the main peroration is the whole of ch. 4, which repeats much of what has gone before in chs. 2 and 3. The last three verses of 4.46-49 make an even more condensed ending as they summarize chs. 2, 3, and 4, the numbering and positioning of the Levites. The larger summary that contains a summary of itself is a sign to the reader that the section is carefully structured internally, as we shall see in the next chapter.

Section III: The next story section, 9.23 concludes with: 'At the command of the Lord they encamped, and at the command of the Lord they set out; they kept the charge of the Lord, at the command of the Lord by Moses.' But the real peroration starts earlier, from v. 15: 'On the day the tabernacle was set up, the cloud covered the tabernacle...' It goes on with a close-knit verse form, repeating and repeating over and over again the lead up to those last lines.

Section V: The fifth section is in the story mode and has a brilliant poetic signal for its ending. 14.39-45 is constructed upon a double axis, deliberate transgression and meet punishment, going up and going down. Up, transgression to the height of defiance, and down, the depths of humiliation: Moses told the people of Israel that they were cursed by God for forty years, they wept, they rose early, they went up to the heights of the hill country, they said they would go up, Moses said, 'Do not go up lest you will be struck down, and you shall fall'; they presumed to go up to the heights of the hill country, but the Amalekites and Canaanites came down, and defeated them.

Section VII: The seventh section is in the story mode, and it also ends with a vivid poetic structure which matches its paired section. The ending of section VII is the whole of ch. 17, the story of Aaron's rod which concludes the first half of the book. Of this there is much more to come below.

Section IX: The long ninth section is brought to its end by the whole of ch. 27. The stories of wandering close with the case of the daughters of Zelophehad whose father had died in the desert without male heirs. The chapter picks up all the main points of the preceding stories: Moses is allowed to see the promised land but reminded of why he may not enter it. The last verses of section IX fittingly conclude with the commissioning of Joshua as Moses' successor (27.22-23).

Section XI: The penultimate story section, section XI, has 33.1-49 as its peroration. The story has been about the partitioning of the promised land among the twelve tribes. Clearly the saga is drawing to its foreseen conclusion. The long peroration starts: 'These are the stages of the people of Israel when they went forth out of the land of Egypt by their hosts under the leadership of Moses and Aaron'. It goes on to count 42 stages of the journey.

Section XIII: Following the model for perorations, if the last chapter is a thirteenth story section, it has to be read as the peroration of the whole book. A whole chapter of this volume will be devoted to it, so we can leave it aside at this point, except to say that as well as referring back to its own opening theme, it repetitively carries the words back to the beginning of the book, where the tribes of Israel were numbered 'according to their father's houses' (36.7, 8, 9).

The law sections begin, without exception, with the Lord speaking to Moses or Aaron, and end with summary perorations.

Section II: 'The Lord said to Moses, Command the people of Israel that they put out of the camp every leper' etc. (5.1). That this is the opening gambit for a long law section is emphasized by the declaration 'that they may not defile their camp in the midst of which I dwell' (v. 3). It is followed by a long list of commandments. The ending is the Aaronic benediction and the words: 'So shall they put my name on the people of Israel and I will bless them' (6.27).

Section IV: 10.1-10 is the shortest of all the sections. If we did not have automatic criteria for telling when they start and end, we would be inclined to doubt that this is a whole section, but it conforms to all the principles of selection. It begins, 'The Lord said to Moses, make two silver trumpets...', goes on to detail the occasions when they shall be blown. Short as it is, the section still ends with the standard formula for concluding laws: 'They shall serve you for remembrance before your God: I am the Lord your God' (v. 10).

Section VI: Chapter 15 starts with the Lord telling Moses what offerings the people are to make when they come into the land which he will give them. These are the offerings to the priests of flour, wine and oil. Then there is a full disquisition on sins, intentional and unintentional, illustrated by the punishment of the sabbath-breaker who is stoned. The section concludes with an ending as clearly signalled as anyone could wish: the people are to put tassels and a cord of blue on the corner of their garments to remind them of all the commandments, an echo of the ending of section IV. And there is finally a further summarizing ending within the ending: 'So you shall remember and do all my commandments, and be holy to your God. I am the Lord your God, who brought you out of the land of Egypt, to be your God; I am the Lord your God' (15.40-41).

Section VIII: Starts with the duties of the Levites and goes on to say more about the offerings reserved for priests and Levites, first fruits, firstborn, tithes (ch. 18). The second part of this section is the rite of the ashes of the red cow, how to mix it with water and reserve it for sprinkling on persons defiled by contact with a corpse (ch. 19). The conclusion repeats the law of purification (19.20-21), mentioning that it shall be a perpetual statute for them. Note the parallelism holding between sections VI and VIII:

> A. Offerings ch. 15
> > B. Intentional sin ch. 15
> A2. Offerings ch. 18
> > B2. Purification ch. 19

Section X: This starts in the usual way, 'The Lord said to Moses, Command the people of Israel and say to them' (28.1), and goes on to prescribe the animals required for sacrifice through the year. Chapters 28 and 29 are the only statement in the book about the annual calendar of festivals ending with a summary, 29.39-40. The conclusion of this section is the whole of ch. 30.

Section XII: An untypical start, as it specifies the place at which the Lord gave his laws to Moses: 33.50, 'And the Lord said to Moses in the plains of Moab by the Jordan at Jericho', indicating that they are now on the very verge of arrival in the land promised. The Lord says: 'Say to the people of Israel, When you pass over the Jordan into the land of Canaan, drive out all the inhabitants of the land and destroy all their figured stones and molten images...for I have given the land to you to possess'. The rest of the section is about the boundaries of the land, how it shall be partitioned between the tribes, the 48 cities of the Levites, the six cities of refuge for the unintended homicide (with vivid attention to possibilities of unintentional killing).

The section has five verses of conclusion: starting in v. 29 with the injunction that this shall be for a statute and an ordinance throughout their generations, summarizing the law of homicide. It finally ends with the ending within the ending which we have noticed before, a repetitive pattern as follows:

> A. You shall not thus pollute the land
> > B. in which you live
> > > C. for blood pollutes the land
> > > 1. and no expiation can be made for the land
> > > 2. except by the blood of him who shed it
> A2. You shall not pollute the land
> > B2. in which you live
> > > D. in the midst of which I dwell
> > > D2. for I the Lord dwell in the midst of the people of
> > > ˛Israel (35.33-34).

5. *Matching the Paired Sections*

I now have advanced my rebuttal of the notion that Numbers lacks structure by finding thirteen well-demarcated units which run in alternation through the book. The laws are even numbers and the stories odd numbers. The next question is how the sections are to be grouped. The right place to look for guidance about the structure of the book is within the book itself. Given all that we have said about the rule of parallelism in Hebrew writing, and the depths of allegory and cross-referencing that the style makes possible, we would expect that the book itself will discuss the basis of its own pattern. The first section lays out the positions of the twelve tribes on the four cardinal points. If this design is going to be the structure of the book, we would look for twelve sections in all, arranged in a strong quartering pattern. Pursuing that idea, we note that the Jewish lunar calendar has twelve regular units and an optional thirteenth month, not brought in to use every year. We turn therefore to how Numbers arranges the calendar.

Chapters 28 and 29 which announce the law for celebrating sabbaths, new moons and fixed festivals, closely follow the calendar of Leviticus, which in turn elaborates that of Exodus. Leviticus adds to the week of seven days a week of seven years. One could also say of that series that Leviticus has an intermediate week of seven months, since it makes the seventh month (Lev. 23.23) into a kind of sabbath of the months. On the first day of the seventh month a solemn rest is to be proclaimed by trumpets, the 10th is the Day of Atonement, another sabbath of solemn rest, the 15th day is the feast of Booths or Tabernacles, to be celebrated for a week. The two mid-month festivals seem to have more or less equivalent importance.

> Appointed feasts of the year in Leviticus:
> First month
>   14th day, Passover (Lev. 23.4-8)
>   15th day, Unleavened bread, celebrate for 7 days, 7th day a holy day.
>   16th day, First fruits, offer 1 lamb
>
> Seven full weeks from First Fruits, Pentecost (Lev. 23.15-21); 7 lambs, 1 bull, 2 rams, 1 goat
> Seventh month (Lev. 23.23-44)
>   1st day, solemn rest, trumpets
>   10th day, Atonement,
>   15th day, celebrate for 7 days the feast of booths, a solemn assembly.

Numbers makes a long contribution to the subject of the ritual calendar. It supplements the Leviticus law by using the animals to be sacrificed as a scale for ranking solemn feast days. Measured by the numbers of animals to be sacrificed on each festival, a much larger quantity for the 15th day of the seventh month implies this festival's importance. The sheer scale of the slaughter announces a major calendrical point. The sacrificial requirement for mid point of the seventh month is increased from 2 bulls, 1 ram and 7 lambs required for the 15th day of the first month to 13 bulls, 2 rams, 14 lambs, and 1 male goat, and no work. Then Numbers gradually scales down the ritual time to ordinary time by seven days of special offerings in declining value.

Sacrificial requirements for the seventh month:

Day 1	1 bull, 1 ram, 7 lambs, 1 goat
Day 10	Atonement, 1 bull, 7 lambs, 1 goat
Day 15	13 bulls, 2 rams, 14 lambs, 1 goat
Day 16	12 bulls, 2 rams, 14 lambs, 1 goat
Day 17	11 bulls, 2 rams, 14 lambs, 1 goat
Day 18	10 bulls, 2 rams, 14 lambs, 1 goat
Day 19	9 bulls, 2 rams, 14 lambs, 1 goat
Day 21	8 bulls, 2 rams, 14 lambs, 1 goat
Day 22	7 bulls, 2 rams, 14 lambs, 1 goat
Day 23	1 bull, 1 ram, 7 lambs, 1 goat.

In this language of animals Numbers is using the scale of sacrifices to say that the joyful feast of Booths in the middle of the seventh month is more important than the corresponding feast of Unleavened Bread in the middle of the first month, a point not made in Leviticus. The Mishnah somewhat enigmatically treats the first and the seventh month of the year as each the beginning of a new year.[1] Whereas Leviticus makes them equal, Numbers ascribes the main honour to the old Jewish New Year in the autumn equinox, while also recognizing the Babylonian New Year in the spring equinox. Numbers is drawing our attention to a scheme for the calendar year which divides in half and starts again at the seventh section.[2]

Like the Jewish religious year the book is divided into two halves at section VII. The mid-year is marked at the mid-point of the two

1.   There are four New Years mentioned in the Mishnah: the first day of Nisan is New Year for Kings and Festivals. The first day of Elul is New Year for tithing cattle. The first day of Tishre is New Year for reckoning of years and for Jubilees. The first day of Shebat is New Year for trees. (J. Neusner [trans.], *The Mishnah, A New Translation* [1988].)

2.   Diagram from D. Meijers,

```
                 Beginning = End
                       1
           2                    12
           3                    11
           4                    10
           5                     9
           6                     8
                       7
                 End = Beginning
```

('The Structural Analysis of the Jewish Calendar and its Political Implications', *Anthropos* 82 [1987], pp. 604-10).

months, the 15th day of the first and the seventh months, leaving five months on each side of the divide. Like the climax of animal sacrifices, the mid-book is likewise marked by a powerful dramatic climax. If the book is deliberately composed on the model of the two halves of the calendrical cycle, the book's own structure would be a metonym of what it is celebrating; then what it describes in chs. 28 and 29 on the ranking of festivals has to be understood as referring also to itself. It may be that the Numbers Poet, for this is an appropriate name for the redactor, was using the composition to reinforce his views in some priestly controversy about the celebration of the year. It is plausible. But the parallelism which makes the structure of the book match the structure of the year may have had a more profound philosophical purpose. The poet may have been striving for an underlying consonance between logic and existence exemplified by both the organization of the book and of the cosmos.[1] It would be fitting that a theological book should itself conform to the structure of creation.

The speculative ideas that I have aired about rhetoric at the time of the sixth and fifth century, and the thought that the writer selected to be the Numbers editor would have had sophisticated literary skills, suggest that he would have been fully aware of how to manipulate the multi-layered meanings carried in any word, phrase, or verse, and competent in the current conventions of poetry. He would have used the most respected literary form for the task in hand. His book would be arranged in a circle, like the circle of the seasons, the circle of the years, and like the other great poems which are known as ring compositions. Arranged in a ring, with section VII as the mid-point, the

---

1.   The influence of Pythagoreanism on artistic form in fifth-century Babylon and Judah cannot be ruled out of court. It would be in the spirit of Vergil, who devoted to each book of the *Aeneid* careful mathematical attention and constructed each on 'the basis of the same Divine Proportion which appears in the Eclogues and the Georgics' (G.E. Duckworth, *Structural Patterns and Proportions in Vergil's Aeneid: A Study in Mathematical Composition* [Ann Arbor: University of Michigan Press, 1962], p. 45).

For those who think that poetry is incompatible with mathematical calculation, recall that Milton saluted the unity of knowledge and of creation by writing his masterpiece in exact numerical progression (J. Whaler, *Counterpoint and Symbol: An Inquiry into the Rhythm of Milton's Epic Style* [Anglistica, 6; Copenhagen: Rosenkilde & Bagger, 1956]).

following pattern pairs laws with laws, stories with stories in regular rungs across the book.

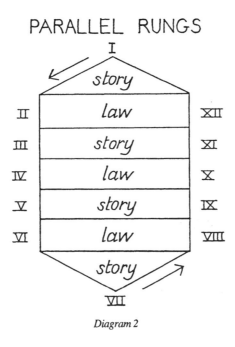

Diagram 2

Although Numbers' religious calendar needs to say nothing about a thirteenth month as there are no feasts for that purely pragmatic arrangement, its own construction has a thirteenth section, the last chapter about the daughters of Zelophehad and their inheritance. It counts as a separate story section by the several criteria we have applied above, named persons, interaction, plot, resolution, beginning and ending. The convention of ring composition allows for the last section to overlap and interlock with the first. In what follows, since the general pattern works so well, we shall assume that this is the correct way to place ch. 36 in the overall framework of the book. In this literary convention, for the end to come round to the beginning, there has to be a mid-point, the tropic, the turn, like the mid-point of a quatrain arranged in ABC × CBA form. The turn matches the beginning, and so does the very end.

THE BOOK IN A RING

SECTION I 1-4

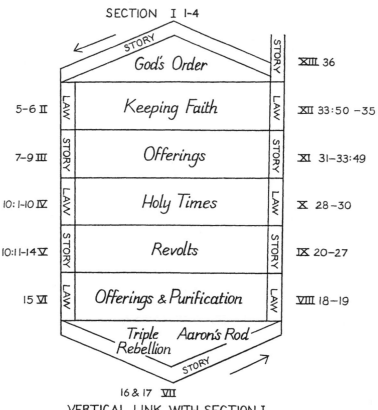

	STORY	
	God's Order	XIII 36
5-6 II	*Keeping Faith*	XII 33:50 −35
7-9 III	*Offerings*	XI 31−33:49
10: 1-10 IV	*Holy Times*	X 28−30
10:11-14 V	*Revolts*	IX 20−27
15 VI	*Offerings & Purification*	VIII 18−19

Triple Aaron's Rod
Rebellion
STORY

16 & 17 VII

VERTICAL LINK WITH SECTION I

Diagram 3

6. *Numbers in a Ring*

This is the pattern to be used throughout this volume as a frame for reading and interpreting the text, each item always to be placed in its relation to the paired sections making up rungs, and the rungs only to be read in their relation to one another and to the whole. The strong and flexible framework supports the claim that Numbers is a piece of extraordinarily skilful writing. But this is only the start. The headings which I have chosen to indicate approximately a community of ideas across a rung may seem to force the argument. In the following chapters when we shall have given each rung a close reading, rung by rung, we will see that apart from the elements held in common that have been named in the headings, many other shared references connect each side of a rung either in a formal parallel or in a chiastic pattern.

The first merit of the scheme that is here adopted is that it is an admirable device for including extraneous items. So it is well adapted to the editorial problems of an anthologist collecting very ancient pieces and putting them into a bundle with modern ones. Another of its merits is to account for the many repetitions as well as for the interruptions which have dismayed some commentators. Maintaining the parallels in each rung would have to be a prime concern of the editor. Sometimes a theme has to be interrupted in order to be spread across to the other half of the book, sometimes the signal is given simply by repetition. We shall come across many examples of both techniques. The result is not a crazy patchwork but a formal pattern divided down the middle, in which one half folds across the other. The two corresponding halves of the book match each other, but each has its own mood and message.

The chart below is drawn up to show how the famous repetitions in the book of Numbers are not in the least haphazard, but do the work of indicating the match between the two sides, upholding the rung structure.

Chart of Repetitions
Organized by Rungs and Correspondences

Section I   a) Counting
             b) Encroachment

Chapters 1–4

Israel numbered and ordered, tribe by tribe, tabernacle separated from profane persons and Levites, 'Lest they die'; tribes counted according to their fathers.

Chapter 36

Tribe by tribe, the people of Israel to cleave to the inheritance of their fathers (36.9).

FIRST RUNG: KEEPING FAITH

Section II: chs. 5–6
Taboo-breaking and breaking faith (5.5-10)

Keep pure 'the camp in the midst of which I dwell' (5.1-4)

The woman who may have broken faith (5)

The Nazirite's vow, cancelled by corpse contact (6.1-21)

Aaron's blessing on Israel (6.22-27)

Section XII: chs. 33.50–35.34
Destroy figured stones and molten images and high places (33.53)

Protect from blood defilement *'for I the Lord dwell in the midst of the people of Israel'* (35.34)

For the man who may have shed blood unintentionally, cities of refuge (35)

God's vows; the land he promised partitioned among the tribes: boundaries of their inheritance (34)

God's curse if they do not keep his commandments: 'And I will do to you as I thought to do to them' (33.56)

SECOND RUNG: OFFERINGS TO THE LORD

Section III: chs. 7–8
Tabernacle consecrated (7.1)

Purifying the Levites (8.5-26)

Section XI: chs. 31–33
War of vengeance against Midianites for leading Israel into apostasy (31.1)

Purifying the soldiers and prisoners (31.19-20)

Purifying the booty (31.22-24)

Levites offered to the Lord (8.13); Gifts of the tribal leaders to the tabernacle, gold and silver, waggons and oxen (7)

Gifts for the Lord from the victorious captains (31.50), gold for the tabernacle (31.51-54) and persons and cattle (31.32-47)

THIRD RUNG: FEASTS AND TRUMPETS

Section IV: chs. 10.1-11
Sound trumpets for alarm, for assemblies, war, gladness, beginnings of months and Appointed Feasts.

Section X: chs. 28–30
Offerings, daily, beginnings of months, sabbaths, Appointed Feasts (28); blow trumpets (29.1).

FOURTH RUNG: IN THE WILDERNESS

Section V: chs. 10.12–14
Arriving in wilderness of Paran in 2nd year, 2nd month (10.1).

Section IX: chs. 20–27
Arriving in wilderness of Zin in 1st month (20.1).

Weeping for Egypt, fish, cucumbers, melons, leeks, onions, garlic, 'nothing but this mannah' (11.4-9).

Weeping for Egypt, grain, figs, vines, pomegranates, and water (20.5); 'We loathe this worthless food' (21.5).

Miriam's encroachment on sacred power, her leprosy (ch. 12).

Moabite women cause apostasy, killing of princess Cozbi (25).

Joshua's loyalty tested and proved (14.6-10).

Joshua commissioned to succeed Moses (27.23).

God's curse: 'Not one shall come into the land...except Caleb the son of Jephunneh and Joshua the son of Nun' (14.28-35).

New census, (26.1-51); 'There was not a man left of them, except Caleb the son of Jephunneh and Joshua the son of Nun' (26.64-65).

Amalekites and Canaanites chase fighters to Hormah (14.39-45)

Canaanites, defeated by Israel at Hormah (21.3).

FIFTH RUNG: PROVISIONING THE CULT/DEFILEMENT

Section VI: ch. 15
Cereal and drink offerings with sacrifice (15.1-21).

Section VIII: chs. 18–19
Cleansing from corpse pollution, ashes of the red cow (18).

Defilement by unwitting breach of the commandments (15.22-36).

Food for priests and Levites, tithe (19).

MID-POINT TURN

Section VII: chs. 16 and 17

Chapter 16: triple rebellion, Levites and captains led by Korah, the Kohathite, encroach on the Tabernacle, people angry against Moses. Rebels destroyed, God's order prevails; Kohath family survives (16.57).

Chapter 17: Aaron's rod blooms, to end murmurings, 'Lest they die' (17.10).

NOTE ON IDENTIFYING BEGINNINGS AND ENDINGS

David Goodman

If a book is constructed with alternating legal and narrative sections the shift from one mode to the other would have to be easily recognized by readers and listeners. Either clearly defined openings or clearly defined endings would be enough. The Hebrew text shows that the openings, which vary considerably, provide an unreliable basis for marking the distinctions. On the other hand, the endings are carefully worked out, both for story and law sections. There are also syntactical, verbal and structural signals. Thirteen sections can be distinguished, as follows:

	Narrative		*Law*
I	1.1–4.49	II	5.1–6.27
III	7.1–9.23	IV	10.1–10.10
V	10.11–14.45	VI	15.1–15.41
VII	16.1–17.13	VIII	18.1–19.22
IX	20.1–27.23	X	28.1–30.16
XI	31.1–33.49	XII	33.50–35.34
XIII	36.1–36.13		

Markers for the Story Sections
Each of the narrative openings locates the plot in a specified time, space and community. The opening lines identify some of the questions of when, where and who, but only section IX gives all three types of information in its opening lines.

When?	I	:	III	:	V	:	:	IX	:		:	
Where?	I	:		:	V	:	:	IX	:		:	
Who?		:	III	:	:	VII	:	IX	:	XI	:	XIII

However, time, space and community indicators are not used exclusively for marking the shift of style, as they also appear in the middle of certain of the main narrative sections, marking the internal divisions of a section and structuring its composition. For example in the middle of section III we find 'when?', 'where?' and 'who?' answered:

> And the Lord spoke to Moses in the wilderness of Sinai, in the first month of the second year after they had come out of the land of Egypt... (9.1).

Other examples:

> Then the people of Israel set out, and encamped in the plains of Moab beyond the Jordan at Jericho (22.1).

> After the plague the Lord said to Moses and to Eleazar the son of Aaron,
> the priest, 'Take a census of all the congregation of the people of Israel,
> from twenty years old and upward, by their father's houses, all in Israel
> who were able to go forth to war' (26.1-2).

By contrast, the endings are clearly marked. Sometimes a concluding
sentence applicable to a subsection also concludes the whole section.
For example, in section I, the expression, 'according to the commandment of the Lord by Moses (*'al pī YHWH bĕ-yod Mošeh*)'
occurs in the summation of the numberings of Kohath, Gershon and
Merari, and then again in the conclusion to the whole tribe of Levi. In
fact, 4.34-49 contains the final peroration to the whole section, repeating phrases from earlier passages.

In sections I, IX and XIII, the final peroration is a summation of the
narrative passage immediately preceding it, and is often in itself a
repetition or rephrasing of a formulaic passage (e.g. divine command,
Moses' response, conclusion/confirmation of action), so that in the
context of the whole section, it stands out clearly as a conclusion.

Sometimes the overall structure of the section points to its own
completion. For example, sensing that sections usually consist of four
parts arranged in a chiastic structure followed by a summary would
give strong clues about the approaching end of the section. This can be
found in the composition of section III:

> tribal offerings to the tabernacle, 7.1-88
> seven lamps in front of the lampstand, 7.89-8.4
> purification and offering of the Levites, 8.5-26
> observance of the passover at its appointed time, 9.1-14
> the movements of the tabernacle and the cloud, 9.15-23

Although the first four passages are each written in a very different
style, together they make up a coherent theme about the cult and the
tabernacle, to which the fifth provides the epilogue. Consequently,
before reaching the final passage (9.15-23), the reader has already
received an implicit signal from the structure that the section is
drawing to a close. Or else it is signalled by means of an embedded
message, such as a word or phrase repeated three (or more) times.
For example, section V has a short concluding piece (14.40-45), characterized structurally by four pairs of couplets, two of which are
arranged chiastically and are situated in between the other two to give
the sense of the passage's lexical keys, 'rising' and 'falling'. The first

half (14.40-42) contains the root *'lh* ('to go up') three times and begins with *way-yaškimū*, 'they loaded up...' In contrast, the second half has the similar threefold semantic associations from:

> ...and you shall fall...and they came down...and defeated them and pursue them (... *ū-něpaltem...way-yēred...way-yakkūs way-yakkětūm*) (14.43-45).

Likewise the conclusion of section XI (33.5-49) contains a long list of locations, with repeated 'setting out' (*ns'*) alternating 'encamping' (*ḥnh*). In general, the narrative sections make use of long, repetitive perorations, and do not rely on the last one or two lines to flag endings as do the law sections. However, notice that in section III, the concluding phrase *'al pī YHWH*, 'at the command of the Lord' is repeated three times:

> At the command of the Lord (*'al pī YHWH*) they encamped, and at the command of the Lord (*'al pī YHWH*) they set out; they kept the charge of the Lord, at the command of the Lord (*'al pī YHWH*) by Moses (9.23).

In section VII the verbs (*gw'*, *'bd* and *qrb*) are each mentioned twice:

> And the people of Israel said to Moses, 'Behold we perish (*gāwa'nū*), we are undone (*'ābadnū*), we are all undone (*'ābadnū*). Every one who comes near (*haq-qārēb*), who comes near (*haq-qārēb*) to the tabernacle of the Lord, shall die. Are we all to perish? (*li-gwōa'*)' (MT 17.27-28/LXX 17.12-13)

All the narrative sections follow one or more of these patterns in their endings.

Markers for the Law Sections

All the law sections start with the phrase, 'The Lord said to...' (*wa-yědabber YWHW 'el...*). However, the majority of the legal sub-sections also begin with this same formula, as do a number of the narrative sections (I, XI). Consequently, the main indication after the peroration of a narrative section that a new law section has begun comes from the subsequent use of characteristic legal phrasing.

Law endings are marked by individual words or groups of words repeated twice or thrice. In section II, the root *brk*, 'to bless' is used three times, in section VI *'elōhēkem*, 'your God' is repeated three times and the phrase 'I am the Lord your God' twice; in section VIII, the root *ṭm'*, 'to be unclean' is repeated three times. In section XII, the final law section of the book, the words *dām*, 'blood', and *ha-'ārēṣ*, 'the land' are mentioned three times, as are different words associated with 'unclean' (*ḥnp, ṭm'*) and 'dwell' (*yšb, škn*).

II The Lord said to Moses, 'Say to Aaron and his sons, Thus you shall bless (*těborăkū*) the people of Israel: you shall say to them, The Lord bless you (*yěborekěkā*) and keep you... 'So shall they put my name upon the people of Israel, and I will bless them (*'ăborăkēm*)' (6.22-27).

IV On the day of your gladness also, and at your appointed feasts, and at the beginnings of your months, you shall blow the trumpets over your burnt offerings and over the sacrifices of your peace offerings; they shall serve you for remembrance before your God: I am the Lord your God (10.10).

VI So you shall remember and do all commandments, and be holy to your God (*lē-'lōhēkem*). I am the Lord your God (*'elōhēkem*), who brought you out of the land of Egypt, to be your God: I am the Lord your God (*'elōhēkem*)' (Num. 15.40-41).

VIII And whatever the unclean person (*haṭ-ṭāmē'*) touches shall be unclean (*yiṭmā'*); and any one who touches it shall be unclean (*tiṭmā'*) until evening (19.22).

X These are the statutes which the Lord commanded Moses, as between a man and his wife, and between a father and his daughter, while in her youth, within her father's house (30.16).

XII You shall not thus pollute the land in which you live; for blood pollutes the land, and no expiation can be made for the land, for the blood that is shed in it, except by the blood of him who shed it. You shall not defile the land in which you live, in the midst of which I dwell; for I the Lord dwell in the midst of the people of Israel (35.33-34).

The two exceptions are sections IV and X, which are discussed in a separate note on trumpets in Chapter 6, and which have a very clear internal construction as well as important verbal repetitions.

Chapter 6

THE PEOPLE OF ISRAEL NUMBERED

1. *Prologue*

Now our introduction is done, and the rest of this volume will read Numbers through its own structure. Characteristically for the literary forms of the period, the book of Numbers has two prologues. We first learn (1.1-46) that the book's main theme will be about the count (and accountability) of the men of Israel who are able to go to war. The second theme is the place of the Levites, called to serve the tabernacle (1.47-54). A dangerous crisis is warned against but it is not going to happen until section VII. When they are read in sequence, the two paired story sections, I and VII, are continuous, and there are clear intimations that the second completes the story that has been opened in the first.

THE VERTICAL LINK

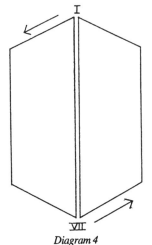

Diagram 4
Section I, Numbers 1–4 linked with section VII, Numbers 16–17

The first section describes in story form the numbering of the people of Israel. It divides into two parts. The first, chs. 1–2, is about the numbering of the twelve tribes who are to inherit the promised land, explicitly excluding the Levites. The second part, 3–4, also divides into two, both about the numbering of Levites, making three parts in all. In effect, the counting, which also means to hold to account and so controlling or governing, brings into focus three distinct categories of persons. The first focus is on the named tribal leaders, that is the fathers or the heads of houses, who do the actual counting of the arms-bearing men, chs. 1–2. The second, though it is a count of the Levites, is also a count of the firstborn of the whole congregation, who are redeemed by the exchange of Levites for firstborn, ch. 3.

The third focus is on the families of Levites, especially on the family of Kohath which is made prominent by being listed first (whereas in the previous count the order of birth was followed, with Gershon first and Kohath in the middle), ch. 4. These three categories, fingered as it were in the first section, will be the main categories of actors in section VII. There will be three rebellions, one by the Levite descendants of Kohath, one by the leaders of the inheriting tribes, and one by the whole congregation. And there will be three corresponding punishments, earthquake, fire and plague, one for each of those three categories.

The structure of the first section seems to be very simple. The three numberings are organized in strict parallel. Each begins with a count, each count is followed by a rule that separates the Levites. The separations are progressive: first the people are separated from the Levites who are to protect the tabernacle from encroachment, second Moses and Aaron are separated from the other Levites and told to stand apart, third, among the Levite families, Kohath is singled out for special warning about the sanctuary. Each of these verses that call for separation tells of danger that will otherwise befall: in the first, wrath to be averted, in the second, death to the encroacher. And in the third, danger of death is reiterated for Kohathites lest they even set eyes on the holy things that they have the privilege of carrying on their shoulders:

i)   'they must not touch the holy things, lest they die' (4.15).

ii)   'Let not the tribe of the families of the Kohathites be destroyed from among the Levites...' (4.18).

iii)   'that they may live and not die when they come near the holy things' (4.19).

iv)   'they shall not go in to look upon the holy things even for a moment, lest they die (4.20).

The mounting menace is not resolved in this first section. There is no turning point in the section that integrates the theme of danger with the opening verses. Instead, the opening is repeated for each of the three parts. The danger is not dealt with. A menace hangs in the air. There is no concluding section which takes the whole development back to the beginning so as to resolve what has been said in a new synthesis.

Outline of the Structure of Section I

Numbering the Tribes	Levites redeem first-born of Israel	The Kohathites
A. Number the arms-bearing men; twelve tribes numbered (1.1-46).	A. Number the Levites from one month; three families counted and given places and assigned charges (3.14-37).	A. Number the adult Levites, by their three families (4.1-3).
B. Separate the Levites to protect the tabernacle and avert God's wrath (1.47-54).	B. Moses, Aaron and Aaron's sons separated to keep charge of sanctuary; death to the stranger who approaches (3.38).	B. Separate the Kohathites' family (4.4-20) not to see the holy things, lest they die.
A2. Camps assigned and numbers repeated for twelve tribes (2.1-34).	A2. Summary of Levites numberings (3.39).	A2. Numbering of Gershon and Merari families (4.21-33).
B2. Levites presented as first-born of Israel (3.1-13).	B2. Levites exchanged for first-born of Israel (3.40-51).	B2. Summary of Levites countings (4.34-49).

The completion of section I has been deferred until section VII, which makes a parallel in the book with the ending of the Jewish year and the beginning of the new year. The anticipated encroachment will take place in the seventh section, there will be dying, the threats of danger will be horribly fulfilled, God's might will be demonstrated, but the time is not ready. If we read straight on to section VII we find the transition is smooth, the rest of the intervening text can be dispensed, the tension leads straight from the wrath which threatens in the first to the defiance launched by Korah the Kohathite at the very beginning of the seventh section. The four times reiteration of danger will be repeated six times more in section VII when the transgression has been done. The family of Kohath is in danger (as the Lord warned above in 4.15, 18, 19): it is about to be led in a rebellion by one of its sons, Korah, and Korah will die, though the family of Kohath will survive (Num. 26.57). The repetition in close sequence of 'Lest they die!'/'Lest we die!' ties the dangling end of the first section to its completion in section VII.

2. *Three Rebellions*

As soon as section VII starts, the suspense breaks. Korah, the Kohathite, leads the rebellion of the Levites (16.1). The first to rebel belongs to the last population to have been counted (a favourite chiastic pattern). As Korah speaks for the Levites against Aaron's authority, he has roused the population of Israel who were the subject of the second census. He also collects to his banner other malcontents, led by sons of Reuben, and 250 of the leaders: that is a significant number of leading men from the first category identified by the census of the men bearing arms.[1] There follow two altercations, between Moses and the Levites (Num. 16.8-11), and then between Moses and the Reubenites (Num.16.12-14). Moses, outraged by their defiance, proposes the test of the censers, telling the Levites and the 250 captains to take their fire-pans and put incense on them and bring them to the tabernacle precinct. At this dramatic juncture Korah assembles all the congregation before the tent of meeting. The glory of the Lord appears, the earth opens, Korah and the Reubenites are swallowed up and go down to hell alive.[2] That first punishment disposes of the men

---

1.   Jacob Milgrom (*Numbers*, pp. 414-23) has unravelled the elements in the rebellion in this way, which makes the connection with the counting in the first section easier to trace. He has four separate rebellions woven into one, but it would be three if he did not count Moses' answer to the rebels, in which Moses assumes that their attack is against Aaron alone, as a fourth rebellion. Here I take the course of supposing that Moses' reply was strategic within the third event, not a separate item in a chronicle of separate events.

2.   According to old traditions studied by Milgrom it is not too clear who is killed in the earthquake, and who is killed in the next punishment, the fire, and it is not

of Korah, the Levites and the leading Reubenites. Divine fire then consumes the 250 leading men who have come to the sanctuary with their censers in their hands. That disposes of the leaders of the first census. But the congregation is still there, all the people of Israel whose first-born were exchanged against the Levites, and who are not contrite. They dare to be angry with Moses for all this carnage (Num. 16.41). But God's anger responds to theirs and he sends a great plague which starts to annihilate them. Moses tells Aaron to get holy fire from the altar and to make atonement in the midst of the people, because 'wrath has gone forth from the Lord' (another linking phrase; compare Num. 1.53 where the Levites are supposed to avert wrath). Aaron runs, waving his censer, the plague is stopped and he has saved the people (although the plague has killed fourteen thousand seven hundred).

The drama concludes with brilliant focus on Aaron as he stands histrionically 'between the dead and the living'. This is exactly the intermediate protective role envisaged for the Levites in the first section. Thus in the conclusion the population of the second census, the whole congregation, has been tested, has failed and been punished. Judgment has done its round. The ending has been securely fixed to the beginning: the three censuses have been followed in due order by three distinct rebellions, and respectively by three precisely targeted punishments. Furthermore, the first section has found its inescapable conclusion. God's threats were not vain, approaching the tabernacle proved to be really dangerous, Aaron was proven master and mediator.

We should pause to notice the craftsmanship that splices the first and the seventh section so cunningly together that we might miss the joins if we did not pay attention. I have drawn attention to the matching of the three populations distinguished in the census with the three rebellions and three punishments, and also to the verbal clues ('Lest they die/ Lest we die'), and to the pinpointing of Kohath as a future focus of danger. Before any of that we have been reminded that the offering of fire is fraught with danger. In the first section, as soon as the Lord tells Moses to number the Levites, the count is interrupted by an apparently digressive reference to the deaths of two of Aaron's sons who had died when they offered strange fire (3.4). But it is not a

even clear whether Korah himself goes down, as my reading suggests, in the earthquake (Milgrom, *Numbers*).

digression, it is a a trail that is laid to evoke something that will happen when in the seventh section the rebels will die offering fire. The sons of Aaron who died in Leviticus are providing another link between the beginning and the ending of this half of the book.

3. *The Rod of Aaron*

Now we at the very turning point. In the metaphor of the calendar this is where the old half year has run its course, but in a calendar every ending is a beginning. After this dramatic resolution we should be looking out for the second beginning. Since it will cleave the book in half, we should expect this second beginning to match the first beginning as its unmistakable pair. Still in the narrative mode the second part of the book of Numbers is opened by the story of Aaron's rod. After the triple rebellion has been quelled there follows immediately the test of the rods (Num. 17). Moses tells each of the heads of the tribes to put their name on their rods, twelve in all and to give them to Aaron. The rod of the Levites has Aaron's name. He will put thirteen rods in the tabernacle overnight and next day they will see the judgment. In the morning they find that Aaron's rod has miraculously burst into bloom.

The words for rod in the Bible have several connotations:[1] the staff, the rod of power and chastisement, the sceptre, the wand of office, the descendants or the tribe descended from a man. In popular parlance, when legs or feet are mentioned the staff between the legs also signifies the potency of procreation, even a colloquial circumlocution for the male organ. Dying Jacob blessed Judah in both senses:

> The sceptre shall not depart from Judah, nor the ruler's staff from between his feet (Gen. 49.10).

The book of Numbers has opened with counting the twelve tribes of Israel according to their fathers' houses. Counting has some of the meaning of holding accountable, standing up and being counted. At the new beginning, cowed after their terrible punishment, all the tribes obey the order to hand in their rods. To Aaron's charge they have symbolically given both their claims to rule and their hope of posterity, the two meanings of the word. In the first beginning, the twelve fathers' houses have been allotted their places around the

---

1. See David Goodman's note appended to this chapter.

tabernacle and submissively obeyed. In the second beginning, the rods representing the same twelve fathers' houses are taken into the tent of meeting and superseded by the rod of Aaron. The two beginnings are a pair.

When the people saw the burning of their leaders, they were enraged, when they saw the miracle of Aaron's rod, instead of rejoicing, they panicked. We hear the echoing response to the phrase 'Lest they die' that was so strikingly repeated in the first section. Moses is told to keep Aaron's rod as a 'sign for the rebels, that you may make an end of their murmurings against me, lest they die' (Num. 17.10). Three or four repetitions of a key idea signifies that the structure is being reinforced and made obvious. Here we have one warning from God (17.10) and five more repetitions. The people at last are overwhelmed by the reality of their danger, and cry out in terror:

> Behold we die, we perish, we all perish. Whosoever cometh anywhere near unto the tabernacle of the Lord shall die. Are we all to perish? (17.12-13).

Since coming near the tabernacle has never been mentioned in any of the dialogues or actions in the three rebellions the repetition is a cue to read this section as dealing with the menace that hangs over the first: it is the postponed conclusion of the first section. But the word 'encroachment' in this constrained context is very significant. No one has committed a physical transgression against the tabernacle or the sanctuary, or threatened to look at forbidden things. All the encroachment was against Moses' authority. This ties up the revolts and murmurings in the desert with the opening section, showing that the warning of danger was against all kinds of encroachment. Here is a tentative model of how the two sections fit together.

Section I: chs.1–4
    A. Numbering of twelve inheriting tribes
        B. First-born of Israel numbered and exchanged with Levites
            C. Levites numbered and warned, Lest they die!

Section VII: chs. 16, 17
            C2. Triple rebellion and triple punishment: they die!
    A2. Submission of 12 rods to Aaron, Behold we die!

The writing turns out to be more complex than it seems at first. The material is richer than this implies and there are other ways in which the matching of the two sections could be traced. At least organizing it to show the links suggests a deeper reading.

It is generally assumed that when Aaron's rod triumphs, Aaron has won a victory over the other priests and the Levites: then the great objective would seem to be only to settle priestly bickering for priority. But in a presentation that requires the two sections to be read together, the political stakes have become higher. In the first numberings the priests and Levites are separated; Jacob's blessing on Judah will be fulfilled, and Judah will keep the ruler's staff for its allocated position on the east affirming its hegemony over the other tribes. Aaron and Moses are given their place parallel to that of Judah: they are on the inner square, while Judah is on the outer. The placement does not necessarily mean anything more than that priests and rulers have separate spheres of authority. But when the two sections are put into a single pattern with the twelve tribes matched by the twelve rods, another meaning emerges. At the end of the paired sections all the rods, including Judah's, are given to Aaron's charge. The issue is not a matter of priestly families squabbling to be first, but the perennial question of church and state. Aaron's flowering rod asserts that God's authority prevails. Not Judah at all, but Moses and Aaron (and not they, but the Lord) is arbiter of who is sinning and whether the sin is intentional or unintentional. The theocratic political solutions of the enclave are here at the very beginning of the book.

We find that at every stage Numbers positions its themes in harmony with Genesis. This being so, we should surely ask how the Levites as a tribe have suddenly acquired their priestly privileges. In Genesis their ancestor was roundly cursed by Jacob. Why are they now doing so well, and apparently without explanation or comment? When we study the disposition of the sons of Jacob round the tabernacle we find the story of his deathbed looms over Numbers. In Deuteronomy Moses praises Levi because he denied his father and mother and his brethren (Deuteronomy 9). This is taken to be a reference to the day when Moses called the Levites to his aid in the matter of the golden calf, and the children of Levi slew three thousand men, 'every man his brother, every man his companion, and every man his neighbour' (Exod. 32.27). Numbers does not overlook discrepancies between the curses of Jacob and the survival of the other two cursed sons, but for Levi it has a different solution, without either summarily cancelling or ignoring the curse.

Instead, the words of the curse are fulfilled. In conformity with Jacob's saying that they 'shall be scattered in Israel' the Levites are explicitly not to be heirs to territory of their own in the promised land. In effect, it means they are not to be a political unit. This is made the basis of special legislation giving them cities in the lands of the other tribes. Second, they are taken out of the list of the twelve inheriting tribes and made over to be a new kind of tribe. The curious scene of the redemption of the first-born of Israel by the Levites and the establishment of the latter in this new rank of first-born of Israel is directed to this end. Third, the guilt of their ancestor Levi is transferred to Korah, the Kohathite; the Levites are purged when he and his followers are destroyed. In this way the Numbers poet is faithful to the record from Genesis and to his own project of showing that all the curses and blessings were marvellously fulfilled.

4. *Marking the Quarters*

The mid-point of the book has been superbly celebrated with high drama and a comprehensive cast. Numbers is also quartered, like the arrangement of the twelve tribes around the tabernacle, east, west, north, south. The halving is at section VII, and at the quarter point section IV points directly and obviously to its completion in section X and clearly divides the book into four parts.

Section IV, 10.1, is very short, only ten verses. It starts with the Lord telling Moses to tell Aaron to make two silver trumpets and then gives the rules for when they are to be sounded: when to sound once and when to sound twice, for assemblies, wars, days of gladness, beginnings of months and 'for the appointed feasts'. The subject of blowing trumpets would seem to be completely covered, except that we are not told when these feasts occur. Reading laterally, straight across the diagram, the parallel section picks up the theme directly. It consists of chs. 28 and 29, which we have just been studying for the analysis of the law of offerings, and also ch. 30 about vows. The first part, ch. 28, describes the offerings to be made to the tabernacle starting with the sabbaths and the new months; the second part, ch. 29, gives the sacrifices to be made for the seventh month. It says:

On the first day of the seventh month you shall have a holy convocation: you shall do no labour. It is a day for you to blow the trumpets.

It concludes in 29.39 with a summary, adding 'These are your appointed feasts'. The combined repetition on each side of the rung of 'blowing' trumpets and 'appointed feasts' signal the parallelism. The paired sections IV and X contain law chapters; the legal rung that they compose cuts across the main framework of the book. We have already seen how important this cross section is, the appointed feasts metonymically providing the model of the calendar favoured by the Numbers poet for structuring his own composition. The separation of ch. 10.1-11 from its development in chs. 28–29 is an example of how the topics are divided up so as to uphold the pattern of the rungs.

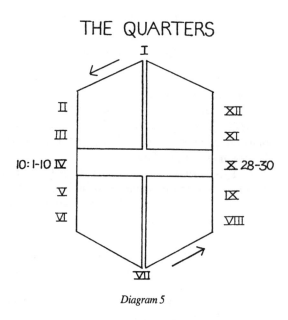

Diagram 5

The model of four quarters is used in Numbers for the division of the tribes of Israel on four sides of the tabernacle. The 'four quarters of Israel' are specifically mentioned in the story of Balaam (23.10), and it is not likely that this quartering of the people of Israel is accidental since Balaam is quoting part of the Lord's covenantal blessing on Abraham in Gen. 28.14, where the four cardinal points are named.

In addition to reflecting the structure of the universe and the promises to Abraham the quartering of the book also produces a verse structure. Numbers has become a quatrain, submitted to the laws of poetry, the first element announcing the theme, the second expanding it, the turning point at the third, and the concluding elements winding the whole into a synthesis that incorporates the beginning. Numbers itself plays this fourth element in the Pentateuch, signalled by its own internal construction.

Arranged as five rungs of a ladder, each section merges with its pair to produce thematic parallelisms that hold the book together in the lateral dimension: six law sections to make three rungs, and four story sections to make two rungs. The law sections (all even numbers) should be read laterally, likewise the story sections (in odd numbered pairs). Reading any one of them out of the context of the pattern leaves interpretation open to the wildest vagaries; reading any one of them in the context of the pattern is the discipline that refers the meanings to the whole structure as we were advised to do by our reflections on antique styles, whether Chinese, Greek, or by recent examinations of structure of the Hebrew texts of the Bible.[1] We therefore should take the quartering seriously too.

As we trace how the book's contents are deployed over the four parts we will observe a different tone in the stories of each quarter. In the first quarter, the stories in chs. 1–4, 7–9, are calm, the people are law-abiding, the prophecies are recalled; in the second quarter, the stories in 10.11 to ch. 14, there are the murmurings and trying of the patience of the Lord which lead up to the debacle at the end of the first half; in the third quarter the people of Canaan and the Moabites make their appearance, Balaam foretells their defeat and recalls again the prophecies; the last quarter is the triumphal march of the people through enemy land, and their arrival at the borders of the land that they are to inhabit, on which all the laws have been focused.

The editor has all the time in the world, he takes the long view, he is not writing in a hurry. He is a member of a hierarchical priestly elite in which polarity, balance and counterpoint are as important as the content. It would be destructive of the work's beauty to put all the

1. W. Roth, *Hebrew Gospel: Cracking the Code of Mark* (Oak Park: Meyer Stone, 1988).

references to trumpet blowing and the calendar in one place for easy
reference for readers in a rush. Notice how the line that divides the
book in half on the model of the year is crossed by the rung that gives
the annual festivals. The plan is bold, but well considered: the vertical
pair gives the whole story, the cross-bar gives the whole cult.

5. *Political Implications*

We are not told the full meaning of the Levites being counted separately until 18.20-21, where the Lord tells Aaron that the people of
Levi are to have no part in the inheritance of land, but are to live by
the tithes given by the congregation. The first section simply distinguishes the Levites from the warriors, those who are able to bear
arms. Nothing is said about the inheritance. But the connection is
made clear in 26.62, where the counting of the arms-bearing tribesmen is repeated after they have come out of the forty years in the
desert: the sons of Levi were not numbered among the children of
Israel because there was no inheritance of land for them. This means
that the first numbering was a numbering of heirs, and the fact that
the Levites were not included makes it all the more significant that all
the other twelve tribes were counted. This is one more instance of the
full meaning being delayed for a later revelation.

The separation of the Levites from the warrior tribes is heavy with
other political reference. In the days of kings the Lord chose his
favourites, named them his son, or his beloved son, or his first-born
son. But the days of kings are over. Numbers is firmly republican in
loyalty. Evidently something has to be done about the now vacant
status of the first-born. In Exodus the Lord sends Moses trembling to
proud Pharoah to demand that Israel be released, naming Israel as his
first-born (Exod. 4.22). In Numbers the Lord declares that he has
taken the Levites instead of the first-born of Israel, recalling the day
that he smote all the first-born in the land of Egypt, when he hallowed
to himself all firstlings in Israel, man and beast (Num. 3.13). Because
they belong to him, he can present them to Aaron and his sons,
(Num. 8.19), to do the work of the tabernacle. In the elaborate
exchange between the tribes of Israel and the Levites, the latter
ransom the first-born of the former by their service of temple
dedication. The complex transaction cuts down the old circle of
equivalences between first-born of the flock presented by the owner

to the tabernacle, and the privileged position of the monarch as the first-born son of God himself, so uniquely dedicated to him. The circle truncated now comes to an end in the Levites, who do not stand for their own political stake, having none, but for the first-born of the people of Israel. By implication, the first-born son of God is Israel, but in Numbers the theme is not further developed. It is difficult to press that analogy while it competes with the old analogy of Israel as the betrothed bride of God.

Having demonstrated the link between the first and the seventh section, and shown how scrupulously it has been elaborated, we are ready to read the law sections through the same framing perspective.

NOTE ON RODS AND TRIBES

David Goodman

The reading offered above of this section pairs section I with section VII, placing the latter as the mid-point, the turning which divides the book of Numbers into half. The case is that the twelve tribes counted and ranged around the tabernacle in the first section are paralleled by the twelve rods placed in the hands of Aaron and by him in the sanctuary in the second. The Hebrew emphasizes the parallel between the stories, since the word used for rod in section VII is used in section I to mean tribe or line of descent.

In the Bible three different Hebrew words are used for rod. Of these, one, *mĕḥōqēq*, the *pōʿel* participle from *ḥqq*, 'to cut in, inscribe, decree', means legislator and so a commander's staff, but does not connote tribe or descent. It is rarely used in the Bible: once in Genesis (Gen. 49.10), twice in Psalms (Ps. 60.9; 108.8) and only once in Numbers in the song to the well, where the princes dug the ground with their sceptres and staves and water came out (Num. 21.17-18).

The other two words have this double connotation, and are frequent in Numbers:

i　*šēbeṭ*
    a.　　rod, staff, club, sceptre
    b.　　tribe
ii　*maṭṭeh*
    a.　　staff, rod, shaft
    b.　　branch
    c.　　tribe

Although *šēbeṭ* can be interpreted as tribe, Numbers generally prefers the word *maṭṭeh*, though not exclusively (e.g. Num. 4.18). The question raised here is whether the use of one word for both connotations was intended to draw our attention to the pairing of the sections.

Another question is whether Aaron's rod which blooms miraculously in Numbers is the same as the rod which turned into a serpent before Pharaoh in Exodus, and which brought water out of the rock at Meribah. All we can say here is that the same word for rod is used. The book of Numbers uses *maṭṭeh* for Aaron's blossoming rod (MT 17.16-28), and for the miracle at Meribah in which Moses is told by the Lord to 'Take the rod (*ham-maṭṭeh*), and assemble the congregation...' (20.7). Exodus uses the same word for rod for the miracle before Pharaoh (Exod. 7.9) and for its version of the Meribah story (Exod. 17.5).

NOTE ON BLOWING TRUMPETS

David Goodman

The English translation suggests that section X responds so closely to section IV that the former is a condensed prologue to the main discussion of the cult for the holy days of the religious year. However, as this impression depends on the frequent use of phrases about 'blowing trumpets', and as there is more than one word for trumpet in Hebrew, it needed to be checked. Examination of the Hebrew texts supports the idea of deliberate cross-referencing between these two sections, and particularly emphasizes the hallowed connection between the priestly office and trumpets.

In section IV and in other passages in Numbers the unusual word *ḥăṣōṣĕrōt* is used. The word is of unknown origin and is found principally in Chronicles, Ezra–Nehemiah as well as two passages in Numbers:

> The Lord said to Moses, 'Make two silver trumpets; of hammered work you shall make them; and you shall use them for summoning the congregation, and for breaking camp' (10.1).

> And Moses sent them to war, a 1000 from each tribe, together with Phineas the son of Eleazar the priest, with the vessels of the sanctuary and the trumpets for the alarm (*wa-ḥăṣōṣĕrōt hat-tĕrū'āh*) in his hand (31.6).

The most familiar word for 'trumpet' is *šōfār*, which is found mostly in earlier texts:

> Then you shall send abroad the loud trumpet (*šōfār tĕrū'āh*) on the tenth day of the seventh month; on the day of atonement you shall send abroad the trumpet (*šōfār*) throughout all your land (Lev. 25.9).

Another phrase in Leviticus bears a similarity to Num. 29.1:

> And the Lord said to Moses, 'Say to the people of Israel: in the seventh month, on the first day of the month, you shall observe a day of solemn rest, a memorial proclaimed with blast of trumpets (*tĕrū'āh*), a holy convocation' (Lev. 23.23-24).

On the first day of the seventh month you shall have a holy convocation; you shall do no laborious work. It is a day for you to blow the trumpets (*těrū'āh*), and you shall offer a burnt offering (Num. 29.1).

The third word that is used for trumpets is *yōbēl*, 'ram, ram's horn, cornet'. *yōbēl* is used literally, as in 'at the sounding of the horn of the ram' (*bi-mě šōk bě-keren hay-yōbēl*), as in Josh. 6.5; Exod. 19.13; and figuratively, as the designation of the fiftieth year, marked by blowing of cornets, as described in the two passages, Lev. 25.8-55 and 27.16-33. The only non-Levitical occurence of the word in this sense is in Numbers, in the second account of the daughters of Zelophehad:

And when the jubilee of the people of Israel comes, then their inheritance will be added to the inheritance of the tribe to which they belong; and their inheritance will be taken from the inheritance of the tribe of our fathers (Num. 36.4).

It is thought that the *hǎṣōṣěrōt* were long, straight, slender metal tubes, with a flaring end, thus distinguished from the *šōfār* which was originally a ram's horn, and probably always retained the horn shape. The *šōfār* is constantly mentioned in the earlier literature, and was used by watchmen and warriors, as well as priests. The two words are sometimes found in parallel:

Blow the horn (*tiq'ū šōfār*) in Gibeah
    the trumpet (*hasōṣěrāh*) in Ramah
Sound the alarm (*horī'ū*) at Beth-aven
    tremble Benjamin (Hos. 5.8).

With trumpets and the sound of the horn (*ba-hǎṣōṣérōt we-qōl šōfār*), make a joyful noise before the King, the Lord! (Ps. 98.6)

In Joshua and Judges the words *yōbēl* and *šōfār* are used for the war-like occasions rather than *hǎṣōṣěrōt* (Josh. 6.4-5; Josh. 6.8-9; Judg. 7.16-18). *hǎṣōṣěrōt* is found most commonly in the books of Chronicles. It is included in a list of other musical instruments:

And David and all Israel were making merry before God with all their might, with songs and lyres and harps and tambourines and cymbals and trumpets (*ha-hǎṣōṣěrōt*) (1 Chron. 13.8).

However, in the parallel passage in 2 Sam. 6.5 the phrase 'and cymbals and trumpets' is read in the Hebrew as 'and castanets and cymbals', possibly suggesting either that the word *hǎṣōṣěrōt* was not known at the time of writing of the earlier book; or simply that *ḥăṣōṣĕrōt*: were not associated with cultic practices as they were later. Throughout the later books of the Bible, the *ḥăṣōṣĕrōt*: are associated with the priests (*kōhănīm*): Shebaniah, Joshaphat, Nethanel, Amasai, Zechariah, Benaiah and Eliezer, the priests, should blow the trumpets (*maḥṣĕrīm ba-ḥăṣōṣĕrōt*) before the ark of God (1 Chron. 15.24). In this passage *ḥăṣōṣĕrōt* is also found in a verbal form. The differentiation with the *šōfār*, found in the poetry, is also found here:

> So all Israel brought up the ark of the covenant of the Lord with shouting, to the sound of the horn (*qōl šōfār*), trumpets (*u-ba-ḥăṣōṣĕrōt*) and cymbals, and made loud music on harps and lyres (1 Chron. 15.28).

In 1 Chronicles David appointed musicians for the ceremony of bringing the ark of the covenant to Jerusalem:

> Asaph was to sound the cymbals, and Benaiah and Jahaziel, the priests, were to blow trumpets continually (*ba-ḥăṣōṣĕrōt tāmīd*), before the ark of the covenant of God (1 Chron. 16.4-6).

> With 120 priests who were trumpeters (*maḥṣĕrīm ba-ḥăṣōṣĕrōt*); and it was the duty of the trumpeters (*la-mĕḥaṣṣĕrīm*) and singers to make themselves heard in unison in praise and thanksgiving to the Lord. And when the song was raised, with trumpets (*ba-ḥăṣōṣĕrōt*) and cymbals in praise to the Lord... he house of the Lord was filled with a cloud, so that the ministers could not stand to minister because of the cloud (2 Chron. 5.12-14).

In 2 Chronicles the *ḥăṣōṣĕrōt* are used to sound the battle-cry against Israel's enemies (2 Chron. 13.12, 14), and at times of rejoicing (2 Chron. 23.13).

Finally, the *ḥăṣōṣĕrōt* were used in association with the cult (Num. 10.10; 2 Chron. 29.26-28), and with the priests and the temple in Jerusalem:

> They came to Jerusalem with harps and lyres and trumpets (*u-ba-ḥăṣōṣĕrōt*) to the house of the Lord. (2 Chron. 20.28).

As this study of Numbers assumes that the final work of redaction took place in the postexilic period, it is relevant to note that the word *ḥăṣōṣĕrōt* had currency in the postexilic period, and particularly in the circles of Ezra and Nehemiah. The uses of the *ḥăṣōṣĕrōt* were remembered by both Ezra and Nehemiah at the time of the dedication of the Second Temple and the rebuilding of the walls of Jerusalem, and referred back to the connection with David (Ezra 3.10-11; Neh. 12.35, 41).

Chapter 7

THE LAWS

1. *The Law Sections*

The laws in Numbers deal with the two main topics: the first covers all kinds of sin and uncleanness, including the difference between intentional and unintentional transgression, and purification from contact with blood. The second includes offerings for the priests, the sacrifices to be made on appointed festivals through the calendar year, and vows. There is no way in which these diverse topics can be made to cover all the laws of a community. We should recognize at the outset that they are a selection. Even if the style of law sections is modelled on other ancient law codes, and even if Numbers is taken as sharing the account of law with Exodus and Leviticus, in so far as they are to be seen as parts of a single law book, the combined laws give a very incomplete coverage. Since Numbers is written in two intersecting strands of narrative and law, the so-called law or ordinance strands must be important. So it behoves us to find the principle of selection by which the editor chose the ordinance sections.

In many ways Numbers' laws extend and complete those defined in Leviticus. Leviticus gives the law of sacrificial offerings (chs. 1–7), Numbers amplifies the calendar of festivals (chs. 28–29), and specifies what numbers of beasts are to be sacrificed on each day; Leviticus gives the rule against eating blood (chs. 7, 17), and Numbers gives the rule against contact with blood, and the rite for purification: in these and other instances there seems to be complementarity between the laws, but the idea that the fourth book supplements systematically the laws that have been broached in the third just does not work. For example, Leviticus has legislated for debt, slavery and the right of the kin to buy back land that has been distrained by creditors (ch. 25). Numbers ends with a chapter on the rights of daughters to inherit the land when their father dies with no male heir. It can hardly be claimed that in this Numbers is putting a final touch to the topic of inheritance, since the topic still remains quite incomplete. Nothing in either book indicates the rights of a son to any given portion of his father's patrimony, or what a daughter receives on marriage from her father's property, or the rights of the children on divorce. We cannot explain the curious selection and incompleteness of the laws in each book as due to the rest of the topic having been covered in one of the others.

Not only is the selection of laws a problem but on a straight reading the laws given in Numbers seem not to fall into any obvious order. Gordon Wenham observes that many commentators have found the abrupt transition from the spy story to the strange collection of cultic laws in ch. 15 quite baffling.[1] While they are evidently not offered as a comprehensive body of law, those topics that are treated are dotted around the book. Why, for example, should the priest's functions come after instead of before the obviously subordinate function of the laity in contributing to the support of the Levites. Again, though he has his own explanation, Wenham remarks of the liturgical laws in chs. 28 and 29:

> But why should these laws about sacrifice come here? to the Western mind it would have seemed much more logical to have grouped them with other laws dealing with the festivals and sacrifices. Modern commentators have no answer to this problem, generally contenting themselves with the observation that Numbers does mix law and narrative in an incomprehensible way.[2]

The priests' duties are given in chs. 18, 28 and 29, while the duties of the laity in bringing them food offerings and tithes are divided between chs. 15 and 18, separated by the story section VII and some laws. Milgrom, commenting on ch. 15, which he calls 'A miscellany of laws', points out that the chapter clearly interrupts the narrative sequence of the spy story, chs. 13–14, and suggests several reasons based on similarity of themes for why this chapter should have been placed where it is.[3] But why is ch. 15 such a miscellany?

If we are beginning to suspect that Numbers is not at all an incoherent composition, we can start considering the law sections as justified

1. G. Wenham, *Numbers, an Introduction and Commentary* (TOTC; Leicester: Inter-Varsity Press, 1981), p. 126.
2. Wenham, *Numbers*, p. 196.
3. Milgrom, *Numbers*, p. 117.

by their role in developing the theme of the book. Numbers and Leviticus each has a dominant theme and each provides a foil for the other. At the most bare, Leviticus is an essay on atonement, Numbers is about the prophecies for Israel; Leviticus is concerned with the cult, Numbers more with the constitution of the nation. So we can regard the selection of laws in Numbers not as part of an autonomous process of legal writing, but as part of the development of the book's theme, the destiny of Israel (comprising both Judah and Israel), prophecies fulfilled, sorrow for the rift between the two kingdoms and for the fate of the Northern Kingdom, now Samaria.

LEGAL SECTIONS ALTERNATING WITH STORY

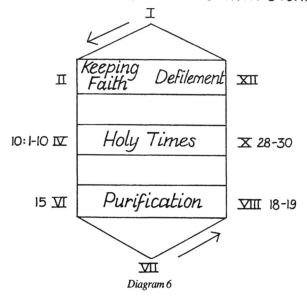

Diagram 6

When read in their rungs instead of in their linear sequence, the laws make a clear pattern. The first and third rungs present a systematic account of defilement and purification. The law of sacrifice for sabbaths, new months and holy days is given in the middle rung. This pattern suggests that the paired sections forming part of a single rung should be read synoptically. On the reading by rungs the expectation that the priests' functions should have priority, and be read before the laity's role in provisioning them, is satisfied. The rungs have to be read across, or rather, both sides of a rung have to be taken in simultaneously. As when reading a poem already known, the whole shape of the poem is in mind as a setting for each consecutive line; each rung is what it is by its place in the pattern of rungs. The reading goes round the inside of a rung, rather than down and along. The first legal rung, comprising section II (chs. 5 and 6) and section XII (33.50 to end of ch. 35), deals with defilement in its various kinds. The second legal rung, composed of sections IV (10.1-10) and X (chs. 28, 29, 30), expounds the formal celebrations of the cult. The third of the legal rungs (section VI, ch. 15, and section VIII, chs. 18 and 19) completes the set by summing the whole doctrine of defilement. Reading by rungs, the duties of the laity are only encountered in the third legal rung, and so follow on the duties of the priests in the second. The order of the legal rungs across the book provides a clear structure, and studying the order of the legal sections teaches us how to read the rest.

The Three Rungs of the Law

Blessing and defilement	First Law Rung
The cult	Second Law Rung
Purification Offerings	Third Law Rung

In the organization of the book the positive cult is located on the inside, layered between two parts of the negative cult, as the sanctuary on the inside of the tabernacle is protectively surrounded with spatially defined degrees of ritual contamination.[1] It should not surprise us to find that a visual effect from the writing parallels the matter, so that the pattern of the laws follows the pattern of degrees of sacredness that the laws declare. It may even have been more than a poetic conceit.[2] 'Concrete poetry' may have been the proper way to write of sacred matters for a culture which paid respect to the letters forming the name of the Lord.

The book of Numbers has already received its comprehensive introduction in section I. When we read sections II and XII together

---

1. W. Rehfeld, 'Deuteronomic Time', in *Proceedings of the Ninth World Congress of Jewish Studies*, I (Jerusalem: World Union of Jewish Studies, 1986), pp. 121-25.

2. H.D. Betz (ed.), *The Greek Magical Papyri in Translation, including the Demotic Spells*. I. *Texts* (Chicago: Chicago University Press, 1986).

we notice that they announce their place as the first legal rung with a new introduction, not to the whole book, but specifically an introduction to the laws. The internal construction of the law rungs is a dissertation on defilement which covers methodically, once on each side of a rung, what defilement comprises, and how to treat the two legal issues of uncertain guilt and inadvertent transgression. The first legal rung opens in section II with a promise of the divine presence:

> outside the camp shall you put them, that they defile not the camp in the midst of which I dwell (5.1-3).

Section XII concludes with a twofold repetition of the same theme:

> Defile not, therefore, the land which ye shall inhabit, wherein I dwell; for I, the Lord, dwell among the children of Israel (34.34).

The columns show the two sections in correspondence:

Section II begins:
A. Drive out the lepers and not defile within the camp wherein the Lord dwells (5.1-4)

Various kinds of breaking faith with the Lord (5.5-10)

B. Ordeal for the woman suspected of broken faith (5.11-31)

B1. Inadvertence: vows broken unintentionally: conflict of principle between consecration to the Lord and corpse contact: the consecrated Nazirite innocently contaminated by corpse (6.1-21)

Section XII begins:
A. God's threat if they do not drive out the idolators (33.50-56).

Naming the boundaries of the land (34)

B. Cities of refuge for the suspected manslayer (35.1-15)

B1. Killing with intent (35.16-21)

B2. Inadvertence: innocence depends on intention (35.22-28). The congregation judge and rescuer of innocent manslayer (35.24-25)

A1. Peroration (35.29-33);
Not to defile the land with blood, the Lord's promise to dwell in the land (35.34-35)

C. The Lord tells Moses to instruct Aaron how to bless Israel (6.22-27)

The end of ch. 35, though it is the end of the laws, is not quite the conclusion of the book, which ends with the much debated ch. 36 about the inheritance of heiressess, the reference to the jubilee and the duty of the people of Israel each to cleave to the land of their fathers. The last chapter has switched into the narrative mode, and is counted as belonging with the first section of all, the turning point which takes the end of one year straight into the beginning of the next.

If a commentator asks now what the woman in ch. 5, suspected by her husband of infidelity, is doing in this section, the answer is in the strong structure which holds the matched pair together, two kinds of suspicion, unproven. Section II switches abruptly from defilement to Aaron's blessing, but as the blessing marks the chiasm of the two sections, the moment of turning, it sheds a benediction on all the harsh threats against defilement. Section XII takes up both the opening and ending theme of section II. Whereas section II says at the beginning that the Lord dwells with his people in the midst of the camp, section XII says at the end that the Lord dwells in the midst of the land. Thus the missing completion of section II is provided by section XII which rounds off the opening passage and gives a deeper meaning to the command to exclude lepers by repeating the promise that God is to be there with his people. The assurance of the Lord's presence together with the requirement to have no defilement in the camp/land makes the double statement even more apocalyptic: God will live there, among his people, and the land will be free of defilement. The discomfort for the lepers, which for the modern reader eclipses the rest of the meanings, has to be read in the context of the millennial vision of a pure people living with their God in a pure land. The play between 'camp' in the first rung, and 'land' in the second is no accidental shift; it is there to remind us that the laws are about the land.

The same simple verse structure applies to both sections:

A	The camp/land undefiled	
	B	uncertain guilt
	B2.	intention
A2.	Blessing/promise/threat	

The middle sections also pair off into minor rungs: inadvertent corpse defilement matches inadvertent bloodshed; all the trespasses which are to be understood as breaches of God's taboo in section II are paired by the Lord's inexorable book-keeping in section XII where the promises he made long ago are redeemed by correct allocations of land to each tribe. The arrangement adopted here runs anti-clockwise, putting section II on the left side of the rung and section XII as the right. The driving out of lepers and the driving out of idolators make a parallel at the beginning of each section, and likewise the matching of the Aaronic benediction with the Lord's promise to live in the land at the end. By telling us that these chapters are a ring that brings the end to the beginning, the pairing tells us how to read the book, as a movement that ends where it starts.

2. *Purification*

The middle legal rung dealing with the calendar of festivals has already been discussed. This is the rung comprising sections IV and X, the first announcing the use of trumpets. This rung, which also quarters the book of Numbers, is at the centre of the whole book. The centring implies that the laws are the main message of the book, reversing the judgment of those commentators on Numbers who considered the laws as interruptions of the narrative.

Recalling, then, that the middle rung of the book has been prefaced by the rung of laws on defilement, and is followed by the rung of laws on purification, it will be wise to comment on the first and third legal rungs together, since their common topic, defilement and purification, are two sides of the same coin. Notice that the laws in section VI follow directly on the laws about sacrifice in the second rung. These two law rungs are members of a parallelism.

Section VI	Section VIII
A. Rules for meal, oil, and wine offerings to accompany sacrifice (15.1-13)	A. Holy things dedicated to priests and Levites (18.1-18)
the same for the stranger (15.14-17)	the tithe, because they have no inheritance in the land (18.19-24)
rules for a dough offering (15.24-29)	a tithe of the tithe to be offered to the priests by the Levites (18.25-32)
B. Unintentional sinner to bring beasts for a burnt offering (15.24-28)	B. Burning the red cow and gathering its ashes for purification (19.1-9)
B1. One law for him who sins unwittingly, for him who is native and for the stranger sojourning among them (15.29)	B1. The same statute for the stranger (19.10)
	Corpse defilement (19.11-16)
	Ashes and water for purification (19.17-19)
C. Deliberate sinner to be cut off, utterly cut off (15.30-31)	C. Unclean person shall be cut off from the congregation (19.20)
Judgment of deliberate sin referred by Moses to God, the answer to stone the sabbath-breaker (15.32-36)	
D. Remember the law throughout their generations, by the fringes on the corners of garments (15.37-41)	D. A perpetual statute (19.21-22).

Thematically section VI comes in four parts which parallel the four parts of section VIII so the two can be easily combined:

Combined Structure of the Two Parts of the Third Legal Rung

A	Holy things for priests and Levites
B	Purification from unintended sin
C	Intention: deliberate sinners cut off
D	A statute for ever

The structure of these chapters reinforces the importance of biblical defilement. The first and third rung are given over to the theme and command the pattern. Their teaching is that defilement is the negative side of how the world is. Half of the duties of priests are included in this section, cleansing, separating, judging, forgiving, remitting, condemning. The rest of the priests' duties are given in the central crossbar where the blowing of the trumpet announces the call to arms, times of rejoicing, the assemblies in gladness to celebrate the appointed feasts, the sabbaths, new moons, the first and the seventh months (IV, X). When the trajectory round the pattern of the book is done, we will have gone from the first injunction (to put lepers outside the camp [5.1-5] because the Lord dwells with his people), to the second injunction at the end (to avoid blood defiling the land because the Lord dwells with his people, ch. 35, on the other side of the same rung). The completion of the circuit fills in the meaning of which the rites taken one by one were bereft.

The meanings run round all six legal sections so that the first rung completes the messages of the third; they have to be held in the mind simultaneously. In the comprehensive reading, the brief remarks on voluntary and involuntary sins in the third rung (15.24-31) are illustrated by the story of the people who, not being certain what do about the sabbath-breaker, refer his case to Moses, who himself does not know how to determine guilt and refers it to the Lord (15.32-36). The question of uncertain guilt is taken to a climax by the exhaustive commentary on inadvertent homicide in the last rung (35.16-24). One might happen to kill a person involuntarily, throwing a stone but not seeing that someone is in the way, killing without enmity, killing unpremeditatedly, without lying in wait. It is almost as if a single passage on intentional sin had been split in two parts, just for the sake of balancing the two halves of the book. Read as a hotch-potch no general principle emerges, but read as a parallelism in which due weight must be given to the concluding clauses, the laws generously provide arrangements to protect the slayer from the anger of his victim's kin even if it is not yet certain whether his transgression was deliberate or not (35.24-32).

According to the rules of purification in Leviticus and Numbers anyone, including specifically the stranger, is entitled to the benefits of purification and to the protection of the local city of refuge. Who is intended by the word for 'stranger' is all important. The people of Israel counted as protected strangers living on the land of God, and when they were in Egypt they were protected strangers themselves, guests or wards of the Egyptians (Lev. 25). Whether the old sense applies, or whether the editor of Numbers is making a play between the old sense and the later sense, (the non-Jewish convert), is the question, and the likeliest answer is that Numbers is trying to incorporate both meanings by attributing to Moses fairness to all well-intentioned people in the land. Jacob Milgrom says that the extension of the rules of purity to the *gērīm* cannot mean that they are obliged to observe all the minutiae of ritual and ethical prohibitions: most likely the *gēr* is limited in his obligations to refrain only from those violations which engender ritual impurity (Lev. 17.15).[1] The reasoning is flawless as far as it goes. But if the *gērīm* are Samarians, and if they claim to have been practising the same religion, (as they do according to Ezra), then why not extend all the ritual prohibitions to them too? To accord to non-Jews in the same community the obligations and privileges of purification would protect them from arbitrary despoilment and murder. The same laws which make the Jews safe, make the stranger safe, very important in a community about to divide itself on the basis of pure descent, and possibly about to exclude Samarians.[2]

3. *Other Systems of Defilement*

The tight construction of the legal sections upon the complementary themes of defilement and blessing means there is nothing haphazard about the Bible's teaching on purity and defilement. The Bible classes together defilement of corpses, idolatry and all lies, deceits, false witness and bloodshed. They are taboos of the Lord. When the taboos are observed, the people are pure, the land is pure, they are separated

1. Milgrom, *Numbers*, p. 400.
2. See Chapters 11 and 12 where this is discussed in more detail.

to the Lord in peace and prosperity. At one superficial level this resembles 'taboo' everywhere. The Polynesian word applies to a defined action which, if performed, unleashes terrible and automatic reprisals, a sacred prohibition. In its effect it is like a contagious disease, except that it can work without contact, so more like an airborne infection which strikes some and leaves others unharmed. A taboo is part of a differentiated cognitive system.

The biggest difference is that other taboo systems place each person in the order of the universe, marking birth, rank, gender, achievements. From a backward-looking perspective taboo sums up the person's heritage, looking forward it delimits future possibilities. The taboo system carves out a hypothetical space in which each peculiar identity must be respected. The way that a taboo system works depends on the differentiations that it marks. In some cultures the taboos correspond to the main divisions of society. In other cultures organized by competitive principles, individuals discover and announce their own taboos, and powerful individuals oblige others to conform to their private system.

The compliance that we find between the taboo system and the social system is a logical outcome of the credibility of the taboos. Belief is secured at one level by commitment to the social order in which the taboos are embedded. Committed to a system of individual competition, it is entirely plausible that the taboos of unimportant persons have less dangerous effects than the taboos of the powerful. To anyone committed to an individualist system, the taboos of a hierarchy look ridiculous, but to one committed to the enveloping cosmic structure of a hierarchy, the personal taboos of the individualist culture seem idiosyncratic superstititions[1]. However, the more that we study and compare taboo systems around the world, the less the defilement laws of Judaism seem to have in common with them.

1. At another level the symbolic elements of the taboo structure derive *prima facie* acceptability from the physiological meanings that it establishes within the culture itself. For Judaism the inherent dangerousness of blood and corpse contamination is imparted in infancy. God's taboo on corpses makes no hard demands on credibility; the body is trained to respond with disgust to putrefaction. That other religions should venerate relics of saints' bodies, or use bones for divination, is intuitive proof of their error. V.W. Turner called this the 'orectic pole' or the physiological set of meanings, as distinct from the ideological or moral set (V.W. Turner, *The Anthropology of Performance* [New York: P & J Publications, 1986], pp. 174-75).

Taboos necessarily operate in time and space. Since taboo is a control system, it is easy to know whom it empowers, and whom it disempowers. The clues to the uses of taboo are found in local theories about its spatial range. The quasi-judicial enquiry that looks into a case of breach generally refers to some theory of how far the effect of the taboo can reach. If someone has died, can it be because he broke a taboo? Did this baby die because of the adultery of someone who took salt from its mother's cooking? How long after the breach can the power of the taboo still do harm? Can a person flee from the effects, and how far should they travel? Is it plausible that this school boy in Kinshasa failed his exams because his uncle in the village 500 kilometres away broke a taboo? Do persons take their taboos with them wherever they go, like the taboo on eating one's totem animal? Does travel dispense? In each community a local theory of plausibility will draw spatial limits to the powers of sorcerers, to the curse of ancestors and to the effects of broken taboos. First the forensic plausibilities are worked out in judicial challenge and riposte, then the spatial limits become codified. But the biblical codification of impurity does not generate a personal theodicy or interpersonal accusations. The widow whose son falls ill asks Elijah if he has come to remind her of her sin (1 Kgs 17.18); the direct connection she makes between transgression and punishment is usual in taboo systems. However, in the Bible it seems to work mainly at the national level, as when the kings of Israel are blamed for unleashing the punishments which destroyed their kingdom. If gathering wood on the sabbath was the breach of a taboo in the usual sense, the congregation would have no need to stone him in punishment; his transgression would have its dire effect on him quite soon.

The spatio-temporal model of defilement for Judaism has been well worked out by biblical scholars. Degrees of defilement can be assessed by the time period that has to elapse before the end of purification,[1] by the scale of sin offering required, and by the spatial area which is deemed to have been attacked. Within the tabernacle three spatial limits are distinguished: individual inadvertent sins only defile the altar, which is outside the shrine; communal inadvertent sins defile the shrine; but wanton sins attack the Holy of Holies.[2] In other words, there is an outer area attainted by a common degree of defilement, not

1.   Rehfeld, 'Deuteronomistic Time'.
2.   Milgrom, *Numbers*, pp. 445-48.

too difficult to annul; an inner area, attainted by more severe defilement; and an inner, inner area, the sanctuary itself which is defiled by deliberate sinning. Milgrom's tunnel diagram illustrates the correlation of spatial proximity with severity of defilement. However, it is only the abstract model of the system, and in itself does not give an idea of what kind of control it represents. We are driven to conclude that it has not been codified in order to operate as a control.

The action surrounding an alleged defilement normally unfolds an inexorable pattern of accountability, with severe penalties of downgrading and exclusion justified in the name of purity. In other religions, once a defiling act has been committed, tragic events are unleashed which must be explained in the light of the deed.[1] This is why the analysis of taboo has to give some account of how the symbol enters the practical world as a driving force. Unfortunately, what can be done routinely for other purity systems is very difficult for the Bible. If biblical defilement ever was part of a machinery for mutual coercion, little or nothing is said about that aspect. There is a reasonable doubt about whether Early Israel was defilement-minded. The signs we have noticed in Chapter 3 of an out-and-out individualist culture in the time of David and Solomon are suggestive. Hierarchy musters loyalty to the community by defilement threats, and so does the enclave, but in an individualist culture personal loyalty is secured with personal inducements and personal threats; there is less squeamishness about open coercion and so less need for oblique techniques of persuasion. The individualist culture of Early Israel is unlikely to have been defilement-minded at all. A good example is in the book of Joshua, where the Gibeonites deceived the people of Israel into vowing their safety; when the deceit was discovered, the vow still held, so the Gibeonites were allowed to stay, but as hewers of wood and drawers of water (Josh. 9). We do not hear of them being treated as a hereditarily defiling group, which would be expected elsewhere.

The defilement system described in Leviticus and Numbers protects the sanctuary, it does not organize social categories. Admittedly, it separates priests from laity, but only in respect of access to the sanctuary. Once we start to notice that the biblical system of purity is different, its relative simplicity strikes the eye. Comparatively speaking, it is remarkable how little use the Bible makes of the symbolizing

---

1. M. Douglas, 'Risk as a Forensic Resource', *Risk* (Daedalus, Fall, 1990), pp. 1-16.

potential of the human body. Even at an abstract level, the body is so
much more than a container that it has a huge range of possible symbolic resources. The lateral contrasts of the right and left hands,
which are referred to in the biblical accounts of seating precedence,
have no effect on biblical defilement. Up–down relationships are
unexploited. Only one model of the body is used, and that, apparently
carried to obsessive lengths, is the model of the defective container. In
this system of taboos there is one unique possibility of defilement, the
breach of the body's physical integrity. Emissions which are part of
the normal bodily functioning do not defile. All the biblical emphasis
is on the breakdown of the defences of the skin, the possible failure of
the apertures to contain body fluids which should be contained, or to
prevent entry through the mouth of the wrong foods. This simple
formula based on Leviticus 12–15 may not strike the Bible reader as
peculiar without a comparative context. It is worth knowing, therefore, that elsewhere left and right are often complementary poles
which have to be kept apart. In other parts of the world a wide range
of the body's emissions are accounted dangerous. Saliva which is not
named as polluting in the Bible is very polluting in Hinduism.[1] Again,
the biblical system of impurity, apart from discriminating against
outsiders' approach to the tabernacle, is an entirely egalitarian system
in which every one is equally polluted by the same physical functions
and malfunctions.

Perhaps the most mysterious thing about the biblical system of
defilement is that its pattern of concentric circles is so cerebral. It
seems to work at the cognitive level, whereas defilement theories
usually work because they keep someone out, or let someone in, and
because there is some general agreement about the inclusions and
exclusions. Control is not the driving force of biblical pollution theory. So what is it doing so prominently in law sections of the book of
Numbers? Before we offer an explanation, first consider the way that
intention is treated. In most systems of defilement, the bad thing happens and the events follow regardless of intention, but this applies to

---

1.   Jeremias (*Jerusalem*, p. 153 nn. 23 and 24) refers to a discussion of defilement by the spittle of an Arab which prevented a high priest from officiating on the
Day of Atonement, and says: 'It is highly unlikely that a high priest would have felt
himself so defiled by the spittle of a Sadducee that he could not officiate on the Day
of Atonement'. In other words, it was not the spittle that was defiling in itself but the
spittle of an outsider.

some biblical defilements, but not to all. Intention is a mitigating factor in assessing guilt.

4. *Inadvertency*

Most functioning taboo systems have a fund of latitude and here the Bible is no exception. Taboo-breaking may be deliberate or inadvertent, but the system would not work without remission for inadvertent breach. Since taboos emerge as part of a community's effort to make a life in common they are a weapon against the faint-hearted, the neglectful, those cool in their ardour for the shared principles. But community life would be made impossible if it involved continuously bringing neighbours to book, continously accusing and imposing fines. The burden of taboo has to be bearable if its content is to be credible. Somewhere, blaming has to come to an end. The idea of forgivable inadvertency contributes this to the system.

Some taboos, quite dangerous in their breach, may be broken unknowingly. A person may come under the nefarious control of a spirit by doing something quite impossible to avoid, such as walking over the hidden grave of a dog; the offence will be known when the spirit inflicts whatever illness or misfortune is in its power. It catches its unwary victim by causing miscarriage, smallpox, or debt; the symptoms indicate which spirit was offended; the shrine priest of that spirit will know how to propitiate it. A religion equipped with a pantheon of capricious spirits who may cause harm to undeserving mortals is wonderfully benign and good for stopping blame, but it can only flourish in a community not oppressively concerned with conformity and cohesion. A taboo-system that allows for a large amount of unintentional taboo-breaking will also have an array of reconciling remedies. Conversely, if there ever were a community with an entirely rational, coherent set of punishing taboos to account for every disaster by making someone bear responsibility, it would not only be hard to live in, but plausibility problems would emerge with each challenge to the political yoke. Yes, the yoke that imposes the taboos would be political. Thanks to the doctrine of inadvertency the victim of misfortune can be released from trouble without being made to feel guilty. Thanks to the theory of inadvertency, misfortune is only lightly coupled to the moral law, and explanation does not always need to involve responsibility.

In the region of Mesopotamia, Assyria and Canaan, in the postexilic period and earlier, ideas of taboo, oath and curse were all implicated together in the explanation of misfortune. In these polytheistic religions each deity and demon had its lists of taboos or oaths which could be unwittingly infringed, causing pain and loss to the transgressor.[1] It was important to consult specialists in advance of any action to know which days of the month had been tabooed or made unpropitious in this way. The Babylonian king was so hedged with taboos that he had to take specialist ritual advice for every minor action.[2] When the exiles returned to Judah they made a clean sweep of unholy, unpropitious days by establishing their pure calendar. Part of the work of clearance involved specifying precisely what taboos mattered to their God. The first injunction in section II of Numbers is to put lepers outside the camp—not only lepers, but anybody contaminated by corpse contact (5.1-4). This is the Lord's first taboo. His worshippers must have nothing to do with death, nor with dead bodies. The God of Israel is the God of life, all the other gods are dead, and moreover, their officiants consult them in graveyards and raise the ghosts of the dead for their abominable rites. The very pretension that these dead things are living is a lie. As deception is their hallmark, so lying is a breach of the taboos of the living God. Anyone who breaks the taboo of the living God will die. So it is fitting that the first law section should immediately name the taboo on corpse-defilement, and go on to bring all the other transgressions under the single heading.

Numbers and Leviticus present a paradox in so far as they legislate against impurity without designating any social category as inherently impure or liable to contaminate others. Biblical purity reserves access to the tabernacle to the priesthood but otherwise the principles of purity are the same for all, and no class is purer than another class. The usual driving force of a taboo system is exclusion, both exclusion from community and exclusion of lower ranks. The Judaism of Leviticus and the book of Numbers is not among the exclusive religions, nor do its commands weigh heavily on its congregation. Purification is easy, and open to all who wish for it. In Numbers it is clear that good intention is the prime condition. The stranger in the

1.   Geller, 'Taboo in 'Mesopotamia, a review article', *JCS* 42.1 (1990), pp. 105-117.

2.   R. Labat, *Un Calendrier Babylonien des Travaux des Signs et des Mots* (1965).

land who wants to be included in the blessing of the Lord only has to become aware of his transgression, to repent and to bring sin offerings to be cleansed. If he says he wants to share in the worship of the Lord, he cannot be turned away. Although Deuteronomy refuses outright to allow Ammonite or Moabite to approach the altar (Deut. 23.3), Numbers makes no such rule, and no distinction of birth, except for the priesthood. Its purity laws apply universally, to the people of Israel and to the stranger (Num. 19.10).

Enough has been said to emphasize that this view of purity, unconnected with social discrimination, is curious. In a book where every sentence is weighed, nothing is careless; why did they elaborate such a doctrine? What was it for? It is risky to speculate. But there is a possible speculation which would make sense of the biblical purity code. Let us suppose, as very easily happens, that there was a populist theory of ritual contagion; that the people were hostile to immigrants, foreign settlers, itinerant journeymen and landless labourers of no local tribe; that there was a popular move to blame them for defiling the land. Some priests would cite old sources to condone the populist discrimination against foreigners; some politicians would be tempted to fan popular anger and direct pollution ideas to political purposes. But other priests would deplore harnessing the idea of God's purity to mundane and unacceptable ends. What could they do? They could write a Bible which provided a non-discriminatory theory of defilement.

The central idea is that the redactor, a hierarchist, and a brilliant poet, is also a person of his times, with strong political concerns, with anti-xenophobic and anti-government views. This speculation will be taken up again in chapters on Balaam and on the daughters of Zelophehad, but the case will need considerably more preparation.

Chapter 8

ISRAEL, THE MYSTIC BRIDE

1. *The Laws for Women*

This is definitely not the kind of book in which the editors have stuffed a bit in here and a bit there, as the thought occurs to them. It is constructed with fine artifice. This being so, it is peculiar that the redactor should have decided to include among the laws just two sets of laws for women. One is ch. 5, the law for a woman suspected by her husband of adultery, but unconvicted, and the other is about the vows of a woman, which is the last chapter in the major legal section on the law of offerings and feast days (ch. 30). And lastly, the whole book concludes with Moses giving the law for heiresses. These three places in Numbers where a law concerning women is described have been traditionally taken to refer directly and exclusively to how women should be treated at law.

What makes it odd to restrict these injunctions to their judicial sense is their incompleteness as laws for women. The book does not pretend to give a complete list of the domiciliary laws. Women's inheritance when there are brothers as heirs is not touched on, nor their dowry or its relation to the marriage endowment, nor the question of providing for them in case of divorce or widowhood. The book is not likely arbitrarily to pick out a few laws among many that affect women. It is not arbitrary in any other respect, so why would it be arbitrary about women? To treat the stories and the laws about women as if the poet had suddenly lost the thread of what he was saying is a variant on the appeal to editorial nodding. The fact that in each of the first two cases 'the woman' is given in the singular cannot be taken as a mere stylistic flourish. A law could equally be phrased either way: whether it says 'If a man vows a vow' (30.2), or 'If a woman makes a vow to the Lord' (30.4), or 'If any man's wife' is unfaithful to him (5.12): singular or plural it means the same. But if it is not a law book it may mean 'a woman', and not 'women'. In a book of this kind, legal pragmatism can only take the interpretation a part of the way.

The impressive poetic structure of Numbers leads into the deepest level of meanings. The arrangement of the legal studies through the book and their systematic interweaving with major political issues shows that if it is a law book in any sense, it deals with constitutional law. The constitution is for the society of the descendants of Abraham. This suggests a bold interpretive move by which every mention of a law concerning women in Numbers might be taken to refer, not to 'women', but to 'a woman', Israel. The law sections on women make much better sense as shifts from the local to the general situation of Israel in relation to their Lord. The prophet had told Israel: 'thy maker is thy husband' (Isa. 54.5).

The case of the woman suspected of adultery seems at first to be an incongruous item, wedged between the command to put lepers outside the camp and the laws for the Nazirite. At second reading, it turns out to be well ensconced among relevant laws about keeping faith, as we saw earlier. It is also a pertinent example of unproven guilt, which matches the section with its pair, where the unproven intention of the man slayer is the topic (Num. 35.9-34). Now that we are beginning to get a sense for how intricately Numbers is organized, we are encouraged to probe further into why this case is here in the first of the law sections, and to suspect that the faithless woman may be Israel.

2. The Unfaithful Wife

The prime instance of unfaithfulness, for which every other instance is a figure, is idolatry. Milgrom notes that in the description of the woman's suspected unfaithfulness the word for her transgression is *ma'al*. It is the only time the term 'is used outside the sacred sphere of the *sancta* and oath violations, where the object of *ma'al* is invariably the Deity'. He goes on to remind us that the unfaithful wife is a recurring prophetic image for Israel's infidelity to God. Milgrom cites Hos. 2.4-22, Jer. 3.8ff. and Ezek. 23.37 on Israel as the sinning wife.[1] *ma'al* is used in priestly texts for idolatry, extended to straying after other gods.[2] The combination of what looks like ritual instructions with prophecy of national shame and punishment would be an

1. Milgrom, *Numbers*, p. 37.
2. Milgrom, *Numbers*, p. 37.

instance of the form of writing which we noted earlier as typical of the Hebrew style, associative digression within a canonized stock of reference.

Such a reading would fit well the pattern of the rungs, since section II is paired with section XII, which starts off on idolatry. Idolatry of the people of Israel is equated with harlotry, in the priestly work (Lev. 17.7; 20.5-6) as well as in the prophets. Let us consider how well this works for interpreting the rite of the water of bitterness, and then consider the other Numbers laws for women.

The ceremony is for a woman whose husband suspects her of adultery without proof. The woman has to be taken before a priest, and to drink the words of a curse mixed in water with the dust of the floor of the tabernacle. If she is wrongly suspected, she goes away free. The husband must stop being jealous. If we interpret the rite straightforwardly as a law, the book of Numbers is telling the husband that without evidence he cannot take action against her; only the Lord knows and the question of guilt has to be left with the outcome of the ordeal. If she is guilty, the Lord will punish; if he does not afflict her, the husband must assume she is innocent and quell his jealous suspicions. That is what the chapter seems to teach.

Adriana Destro's analysis[1] of the rabbinic elaboration of the law is very fascinating, since the rabbis took the same biblical text and gave it a very different gloss. It seems that the 'rite of the wayward woman', *sôtâ*, was the subject of much rabbinical reflection. It was thought to be a rite that had fallen into disuse in very remote times. At the end of the Mishnah tractate of *Soṭah*, it is declared that the rite 'came to an end', 'ceased', was declared 'impracticable'.[2] So the Mishnah tractate is about the memory of a lost rite. It is not absolutely clear whether the rite was ever performed. But the commentary upon it would be very acceptable to those upholding conjugal fidelity in the period from the second century BCE to the second century CE, when women's relationships were brought under increasingly severe surveillance.

The procedures established for the rite allow for the woman to be admonished, and ordered by the husband not to speak to her suspected lover. If she still persists, 'goes to a secret place' with him, and

1. A. Destro, *The Law of Jealousy, Anthropology of Sotah* (Atlanta, GA: Scholars Press, 1989).

2. Destro, *Law of Jealousy*, p. 2.

'remains with him long enough to commit impurity' (*m. Soṭ.* 1.2), she must take the test. She is brought before the Supreme Court in Jerusalem, 'and subjected to all the severity that this court uses in cases of capital importance' (*m. Soṭ.* 1.4). The judges try to persuade her to confess; if she does so, she loses her right to her marriage endowment. It is striking that though it is an ordeal that will settle her guilt or innocence, she is treated as if guilty without the verdict of the ordeal: the priest will take hold of her clothes and strip her to the waist, and disarrange her hair. To make her ugly they change her white clothes for black, and remove all her jewellery to increase her shame.[1] Supposing she was innocent? Where is the role of God's judgment? There is nothing in the text of Numbers to warrant this assault based only on the suspicions of the husband.

The instructions on how the rite should be performed suggest a very prosaic bias. The rabbis were not so interested in the theme of Israel, the mystic bride, as in the provisions for holding a wayward wife to account. The Numbers text is admittedly playing out its theme at several levels. At one level there is the human husband and his rights, at another is the Lord's dealing with his betrothed, his jealous passion and his right to be enraged against Israel. The law is about jealousy, which also means zeal, or passion. Phinehas, when he speared the Midianite princess and her lover, was commended for his zeal for the Lord (Num. 25.11). Milgrom says that 'the same word (*qana'a*) in Arabic and Syriac means "become intensely red" and refers to the visible effects of anger on the face. God becomes "impassioned", that is aroused, when Israel flirts with other gods, as in Exod. 20.5 and 34.14.'[2] And note also: 'They have provoked me to jealousy' (Deut. 32.21).

We must note that the jealousy of the Lord is more easily assuaged than that of a human husband. He is more kind, more forgiving, ready for a second betrothal, a renewal of vows and a new beginning of the marriage. The prophets who used the metaphor of Israel as the betrothed insisted endlessly on the Lord's forgivingness:

> Behold I will allure her, and bring her into the wilderness, and speak tenderly to her. I will give her vineyards there... and she shall answer there, as in the days of her youth, and as in the day when she came up out of Egypt (Hos. 2.14-15).

1. Destro, *Law of Jealousy*, p. 5.
2. Milgrom, *Numbers*, p. 216.

It may be a coincidence that the first words of Numbers are 'In the wilderness', but it is not safe in so carefully contrived a composition to assume that a reference to the prophets is fortuitous. Note then that the harlot in Hosea is sometimes Samaria whom her loving husband will one day draw back to himself, and sometimes both Samaria and Israel (Hos. 5.3; 6.10).

These interpretations of the first text on a law for a woman will strengthen the case for the same sort of reading for the law of vows. But first it will be interesting to compare the rite for a suspected adulteress with the rite of purification from bloodshed in ch. 19.

3. *The Water of Purification*

The ceremony for preparing the water of purification is similar to the rite for the woman suspected of adultery who has to drink the dust mixed in water with the words of her curse. One is a drinking rite, the other a sprinkling rite, but in different ways both rites recall the scene in Exodus when Moses, finding the whole congregation dancing round the golden calf, breaks it, grinds it to powder and mixes it with water and makes them drink it (Exod. 32.20). Moses might have been performing an ancient ritual of purification by making the sinner swallow the sin, in which case Numbers' ritual of purification memorializes such a rite by turning the red gold colour of the metal calf into the blood colour of the live heifer, thus assimilating the antique swallowing ceremony into the doctrine of blood as rationalized in Leviticus. These speculations must stay as speculations, perhaps always, or at least until the structures of Exodus and of Numbers are systematically studied by Hebrew scholars.[1] But whatever they once were, the origins of the rites described do not explain what they are doing in this book.

The rite of the waters of purification may be an archaic exorcism only partly assimilated into the Judaic ritual system[2]. It is in some

---

1. This episode takes place immediately after a dialogue between Moses and the Lord who threatens to destroy the whole people because of their rebelliousness and is persuaded to desist by Moses, who taunts him with how the Egyptians would jeer and reminds him of his promises to Abraham, Isaac and Israel (Exod. 32.11-14), which exactly parallels the dialogue in Numbers (Num. 14.11-19). Evidently a close comparison with Exodus will help a full exegesis of Numbers.

2. Milgrom, *Numbers*, pp. 438-49.

ways like a sin offering, which also has what Milgrom calls 'a decontaminating effect'. But unlike the sin offering it is not a sacrifice, the animal is slaughtered and burnt outside the camp and neither the animal nor its blood is offered on the altar. The whole animal is burnt, blood and all, its ashes are collected and kept for mixing with running water for sprinkling when a purification is required.

Milgrom's strategy in dealing with this rite in his commentary on Numbers is to relate each element either to the usual sacrificial rites of Israel, or to their failure to correspond to this model. So to the question, 'Why is it a cow?' he answers that a female animal is the required sin offering for private individuals in Leviticus (Lev. 4.27-28, 32). 'Why bovine?' Because it is the biggest and so would provide the largest source of ash for the mixing. 'Why a red cow?' Because the redness was deemed to intensify the blood in the ash, a magical element from the code of exorcisms. 'Why is the blood burnt?' Why is the defiled person not obliged to leave the camp? Why does it defile the cleanser, while cleansing the defiled? He says because of its origin as an exorcism, not as a sin offering.

To the final question, why do we have an archaic exorcism retained from pre-Israelite times in the liturgy of Judaism, Milgrom answers very reasonably that there would have been a popular demand for a protection against the effects of blood defilement. Indeed, the idea of blood is so central in the symbolic structure of the Bible that one would expect nothing less than high drama to absolve from blood pollution. Faith in the regular sacrifices might not have been strong enough. Because life is in the blood (Lev. 17.10-16) the people of Israel are forbidden to eat it: fresh, running blood in living beings belongs to the Lord; dry, caked, putrefying blood of corpses is abhorrent to the Lord. From sacrificial victims the blood is poured out, the blood is sprinkled and daubed on the altar, the blood is burnt. Something spectacularly different would have to be done to purify from blood contact: hence the archaic ritual which is not a sacrifice and yet which has to some extent been assimilated to the sacrificial system.

Milgrom considers that a thoroughgoing monotheism is incompatible with the power of demons. He finds that exorcism implicitly raises the issue of demons to be exorcized. Who are they? What is their relation to the One God? Did he not promise to drive out all demons from the land (Zech. 13.2)? Milgrom sees a conflict between dealing

with demons on any terms, and the pure monotheism of Judaism. He
has the theological problem on good authority. Rabbi Yohanan ben
Zakkai was asked by a heathen some probing questions about the
efficacy of rites; it appeared to the heathen that there was something
distinctly magical about sprinkling a corpse-contaminated person with
a few drops of water mixed with the ashes of a red cow and declaring
him to be cleansed. The rabbi, answering that he who is defiled by
contact with a corpse is possessed by a spirit of uncleanness, implied
that exorcism is the appropriate form for the rite. But his disciples
were not satisfied. Neither for them, nor for the rabbi, nor for
Judaism, Milgrom says, was it conceivable that any rite could be
inherently efficacious. The rabbi then gave his students the full theological explanation:

> 'The corpse does not have power by itself to defile, nor does the mixture
> of ash and water have the power by itself to cleanse. The truth is that the
> purifying power of the red cow is a decree of the Holy One. The
> Holy One said: I have set it down as a statute, I have issued it as a
> decree. You are not permitted to transgress My decree. "This is the law"'
> (Num. 19.1).[1]

This splendid declaration is more enigmatic than it appears at first.
Does the denial of inherent efficacy apply to everything, or only to
religious realities? It could be a version of realism in which demons
are real enough but can act demoniacally only by the same power and
under the inscrutable will of God that permits any kind of effective
action. Corpse defilement would be dangerous in exactly the same way
as the power of fire to burn or the power of water to drown, only by
the decree of God.

Milgrom believes that the rabbi's saying, that the corpse does not
have power of itself to defile, makes a break with pagan magic. When
Milgrom concludes 'the break with paganism is complete', he seems to
refer to a break with a magical theory of symbolic efficacy. That
there ever was such a theory is dubious. But beyond theorizing, there
is always likely to be a hope, and even a faith that the Lord can do
miracles and that the Lord will accept blessings, allow charms, and
give signs of his interest or his compassion. And there are always
likely to be some who will jump straight to the idea of direct efficacy
of signs in procuring benefits. Most religions teach that the world is

---

1. *Pes.K.* 4.7.

constituted with the deity's power to allow and disallow as the main source of energy and action and that the deity is the prime reality. If cutting out that material interpretation of the doctrine is the break with paganism, it is surely never complete. There is no evolutionary trend that makes some religions more magically minded than others, as we saw in our discussion of a religious typology.

Numbers requires the lustral water mixed with the ashes of the red cow to be always available for purifying from contact with corpses or shedding of blood. But Milgrom forgets that the demand for purification which he rightly calls 'popular' is generally politicized, and we have to decide whether the editors of Numbers are giving a populist doctrine. Numbers explicitly says that the sojourner is eligible for the waters of purification (Num. 19.10). Who was he? Generally excluded from the temple, here are non-Jews being included in ritual purifications and even required to do them, like Jews. On this enormous topic the sojourning anthropologist would like a more politically sensitive biblical commentary. To say that the word *gēr* means a landless labourer or an alien is tantalizing: why were there so many landless labourers and aliens that special ritual provision had to be made for them? Why does Leviticus say that they must be loved (Lev. 19.34); or why do Numbers and Exodus say that they must observe the Passover (Num. 9.14; Exod. 12.48)? Who were they: compulsorily settled immigrants from Assyria, Ephraimites or other various sons of Abraham who had been dispossessed of their lands by returnees backed by the edicts of Ezra/Nehemiah?[1] A reputedly ancient rite may well have been resuscitated in a priestly attempt to mitigate the exclusionary effects of popular xenophobia. It is possible that the sprinkling with the ashes of the red cow had never been a rite before they wrote about it. If the priests wanted purification to be within everyone's reach at all times, it would be easier and much less costly for a defiled person to be aspersed with a few drops of the water of purification than to bring a ram or a sheep to be sacrificed at the altar.

4. *Israel's Cup*

The idea that consecrated blood that has passed through consecrated fire has power to purify is well within Judaism's array of purificatory

---

1. Smith, *Palestinian Parties*, p. 138.

ideas. It may not be necessary to look for the meaning in an archaic magic ordeal. By reading two puzzling laws together we get a better understanding of each. The first is the rite for the woman suspected of adultery; we assume she is Israel. The offence is sexual, adultery of Israel is idolatry. The curse which the priest writes down means that if she is guilty she will lose her reproductive power: her thigh (her genitals) will rot and her body fall away (5.20-22). Then he washes the written curse into the water of bitterness and she must drink it. Read this with the ceremony of purifying by sprinkling the ashes of the red cow. These two ceremonies cannot be treated on the same basis as the instructions for the right number of beasts to offer in sacrifice. When sprinkling ashes in water or drinking water with dust in it are filed in the reader's mind as ritual actions of the same type as anointing the altar with the blood, or displaying the bread offering on it, the puzzle becomes why they are not part of the scheme of sacrifice. However, if the sprinkled ashes of the red cow are endowed in this religion with power to purify, the explanation comes from the rest of the religion, and will not depend either on sacrifice or on equivalent practices in Mesopotamia or Egypt, fascinating though they are.

Here it is maintained that both ceremonies are about Israel; they are not to be understood at the level of ritual performances, or legal prescriptions, but rather they are classic meditations on creation and redemption. The symbols they draw on come out of the great textual store from which the Bible is built. The water of bitterness is a mixture of running water and the dust from the floor of the tabernacle. The form of the test recalls the cup of Samaria which Israel had to drink in the verse from Ezekiel in which Samaria's fate is given as an example of what will happen to Jerusalem:

> You shall drink your sister's cup, which is deep and large...
> You have gone the way of your sister; therefore I will give her cup into your hand. Thus says the Lord God...
> A cup of horror and desolation is the cup of your sister Samaria; you shall drink it and drain it out, and pluck out your hair and tear your breasts (Ezek. 23.32-34).

The woman taking the ordeal has to drink the words of the curse:

> The Lord make thee a curse and an oath among thy people, when the Lord doth make thy thigh to rot and thine abdomen to swell (Num. 5.21).

Compare:

> And you shall become a horror, a proverb, and a byword among all the peoples (Deut. 28.37).

> I will make them a horror to all the kingdoms of the earth, to be a reproach, a byword, a taunt and a curse... (Jer. 24.9; 29.18, 22).

> You shall become a horror, an execration, a curse and a taunt (Jer. 42.18).

These miscellaneous curses and execrations on Israel are for idolatry, the ultimate defilement.[1] The rite of taking a handful of dust from the floor of the sanctuary is suggestive of the power of the Lord to renew and forgive. For the sanctuary at Jerusalem was the centre of the world, and this dust came in later ages to be regarded as the dust of the initial creation of humankind on the sixth day.[2] The parallel of ashes with dust invites us to interpret the red cow also as standing for Israel, whose blood is used to wash her own defilements. The red cow ceremony is a sprinkling not a drinking, but the idea of drinking is in the background, with the lurking echo of Moses' grinding the golden calf to powder and giving it to drink to the sinning congregation in Exod. 32.20. If these rites are to be read in the straight judicial sense, the Lord is terrible indeed, and the curse on the suspected woman would be a terrifying judgment. But if they are to be read allegorically, the implications are totally different. If the woman is Israel, the terror goes out of the curse, for we know that for his betrothed he is compassionate and forgiving. In a sacred literature which can say, 'Like a heifer, Israel is stubborn' (Hos. 4.16), the store of background texts for these interpretations would not have been esoteric or inaccessible to the worshippers. By not reaching into this allegorical level of meaning the God of Judaism was made more harsh, and the sacred texts came to lack any sense beyond that of simple moral precepts.

---

1. For a supporting interpretation of this rite see M. Fishbane, 'Accusations of Adultery: A Study of Law and Scribal Practice in Numbers 5.11-31', *HUCA* 45 (1974), pp. 25-43.

2. N. Sed, 'Le symbolisme zodiacal des douze tribes', in *Etudes Juives: la mystique cosmologique juive* (Mouton: Appendix, 1981), pp. 239, 293-317.

5. *In the Days of her Youth*

It would help the reading of the laws in ch. 30 about a woman's vows if it could be agreed that the unnamed woman in the laws of Numbers is no private person, but Israel. This chapter begins with a man's vows and goes on to specify the extent to which a woman's vow is binding. If she is unmarried and her father hears the vow she makes and immediately speaks his disapproval, it is cancelled, and likewise if she is married and her husband hearing it formally disapproves; but if either the husband or the father hears the vow and says nothing, she is bound and must bear the consequences. This hardly seems to be a fit conclusion for a section of laws for animal sacrifice. If ch. 30 is a law for women it would be difficult to account for its place in the poetic structure of the book as we have found it. Unlike the other law sections in which the constituent laws can be shown to have clear connections not only within but between parallel sections of a rung, this one about women's vows has nothing obvious to do with the cultic laws of offerings of chs. 28 and 29. However, we have observed that Numbers is not a book of domestic law, and we expect that the last piece of law is capable of carrying the peroration for all the laws.

We recognize now that the book is planned on a grand scale, with every rhetorical artifice. It deals with fundamental constitutional issues. We also know that the twelve sections are paired into rungs, and that the direction of reading goes round in a ring with the concluding verse of the last legal rung matching the opening verse of the first legal rung: the Lord dwells in the midst of his people (5.3 and 35.33-34). The second section of a matching pair has a weightier, more final, conclusion because it concludes both a section and a rung. If we reread the endings of the three legal rungs we find that they all refer to the permanence of Israel's commitment to their God. Section VIII says in its last two verses: 'it shall be a perpetual statute for you' (19.21); section XII starts its peroration with the command, 'this shall be a statute and an ordinance throughout their generations' (35.29). Section X needs a peroration, and we can expect from form shown so far that ch. 30 provides it with a grand peroration on the vows of a woman, she being Israel.

The law of a woman's vows is located in the series of laws about the main feast days and the calendar of sacrifices because in the Bible the Lord deals with his people as a husband, or a father. We know what a vow means for indissolubility and permanence. In section II, on breaking faith, we learnt that Israel's covenant with God is a vow of the most solemn and indissoluble kind. At the same time, knowing that Israel is in the role of erring wife for whose repentance her husband is lovingly waiting, ch. 30 about a woman's vows is comforting. God is the husband who heard the woman's vow, and who, if he disapproved of it, had instant power to cancel its effects. The reading suggested by the placement of this chapter is that if Israel has been making evil vows to false gods, or making covenants against his commandments, she will be spared the consequences of breaking them, if only she would repent.

If Numbers is more of a constitutional document about the affairs of Israel in their relation to God, there is more reason to doubt whether this passage should be read as if it were giving the law for the vows of particular women. The rabbis read it in that spirit, but more plausibly the woman would be Israel, portrayed by Hosea and Exekiel as a young daughter, 'living in her father's house' (which is the temple in Jerusalem): 'And there she shall answer as in the days of her youth, as at the time when she came out of Egypt' (Hos. 2.15, and see Ezek. 23.1-4).

Chapter 30 starts off by describing a woman who has made a vow, 'being in her father's house in the days of her youth' (30.3). Israel is excoriated by the prophets as the whoring wife. The vows in question are evidently the vows of Israel or the vows of Samaria, her sister. Chapter 30, making a peroration for all the ordinances in the section, is making clear, by citing Hosea, the range of its theological reference. Working both at the judicial and the theological level, if the woman suspected by her husband is any woman and this is the law for what to do about the suspicion, then the ordeal takes out of human hands both the test of her innocence and the sentence if she is guilty. At that mundane level, the solution is just. At the eschatalogical level, the suspected woman is Israel and her fate in Numbers is placed in the context of the mystic bride. Then the message is even heartening. The two sets of laws concerning women set Israel's destiny back into the context which the prophets had announced for her: she has made vows to new husbands and defiled herself, but the Lord, her first husband, has heard her vows and made them void at once, she will not have to bear the consequences, and he is mercifully willing to take her back.

Chapter 9

Twelve Tribes in Marching Order

1. *Inclusion and Exclusion*

Factions strive to capture the moral high ground with a rhetoric of inclusion and exclusion. Their leaders outbid each other to claim for their own the noblest principles, and to blacken the other side with defaming accusations, especially of treachery by alliance with outsiders.[1] If the enclave is a religious sect the high ground to be grabbed is theological. In the course of the argument the nature of godhead gets redefined, purified, made more inaccessible, more punitive to enemies, and at the same time, more human, loving and attractive to loyal followers. Inclusion in the community of the elect comes to mean more and exclusion is justified by the doctrine of defilement.

The problems of inclusion that preoccupied Judah at the time of the redaction of Numbers are graphically described in Ezra/Nehemiah. To the north stood Samaria, formerly the Northern Kingdom of Israel, at that time also a province of the Persian empire, richer, more numerous and powerful than Judah. Samaria's clever governor, Sanballat, could have plausibly lodged with the Persian government a claim to take over Judah. Ezra and Nehemiah rejected Sanballat's overtures of friendship. Ezra and Nehemiah suspected other foreign enemies of having the ear of the Persian government: on the eastern border Ammon, Moab, and on the south Edom. They also implied that there was some kind of alliance between these hostile foreign powers and the people of the land, a category which they referred to as 'the adversaries of Judah' and whom they accused of conspiring with Judah's enemies. This political context we will discuss more systematically in Chapter 11. Briefly, the government of Judah could justifiably feel surrounded with enemies and could plausibly accuse of treason

1. M. Douglas, *Risk and Blame* (London: Routledge, 1992).

anyone who wanted to ally with the surrounding foreign states. The policy preferred by the governors of Judah was a sectarian turning away from the nations, exactly the policy Max Weber attributed to the priests after the exile. The idea that the priestly editors of Numbers would have sided with the government party in its exclusionary policies is not supported by the text of their book. On the contrary view here being developed, the editors did not at all condone the government party's exclusivity.

They were hierarchists and heirs to an old tradition which they were engaged in recording. In this tradition the people of Israel were not coextensive with Judah. Israel for them, as for the prophets, included all the sons of Jacob as heirs to the promises made by God to Abraham, Isaac and Jacob. Judah and Samaria both turned to idolatry, but both the sons of Joseph and the sons of Judah had a right to be counted in the congregation if they would repent and have atonement made for their sins. Backsliding was the normal experience of religious history, idolatry was a matter of intention, purification was available, and the definition of the congregation of Israel did not depend on ethnic or territorial political factors. Their classification of the congregation would include all the descendants of Abraham, including Edom, on condition of giving up idolatry. Though obviously political, the question of whom to count as an ally was bound to be seen as theological. Is the promise for all the sons of Abraham? Or is it for all the sons of Jacob? Or is it only for the sons of Judah? And if it is for the latter, who is to count as a son of Judah? Is it only the remnant returned from Babylonian exile? It is difficult to see how the priestly editors could have evaded the political questions. For the whole promise to be reserved to the few would stick in some theological gullets, quite apart from the claims of those excluded who had always thought themselves heirs of Abraham. There were 'the people of the land' whom the people of Israel were not supposed to marry (Ezra 9.2), and the strangers, sojourning in the land of Judah. Ezra would exclude them, but Numbers would not exclude any of the sons of Jacob. With these heavy issues in mind, we scrutinize the story sections knowing it to be unlikely that the frequently repeated lists of the twelve sons of Jacob are recorded in a book like Numbers only for antiquarian decor.

2. The Twelve Tribes

The book of Numbers gives several listings of the tribes descended from the sons of Jacob. They are not all the same. When the Lord tells Moses to make a census of the people of Israel, he uses the same list as that given in Genesis (46.8-27). When Moses actually counts he follows the same Genesis list, but not in quite the same order. After the census is done Moses receives instructions for how the tribes are to be disposed around the tabernacle, which is also to be their marching order. Numbers' official list is the marching order, repeated on three occasions, all in the opening section of the book, chs. 1–4.

Three Lists of Jacob's Sons, Genesis and Numbers

Who came to Egypt: Gen. 46.8-27	Listed by God: Num. 1.1-17	The count: Num. 1.20-43	Marching order Num. 2.1-31
Reuben	Reuben	Reuben	Judah
Simeon	Simeon	Simeon	Issachar
Levi	Judah	Gad	Zebulun
Judah	Issachar	Judah	Reuben
Issachar	Zebulun	Issachar	Simeon
Zebulun	Ephraim	Zebulun	Gad
Gad	Manasseh	Ephraim	Ephraim
Asher	Benjamin	Manasseh	Manasseh
Joseph	Dan	Benjamin	Benjamin
Benjamin	Asher	Dan	Dan
Dan	Gad	Asher	Asher
Napthali	Napthali	Napthali	Naphtali

All the first three lists start with Reuben and Simeon, the two eldest sons. In the Genesis list, Levi is there, but in the first Numbers list he is gone and never appears again, because Moses has to number the Levites separately. The gap left by Levi would reduce the total to eleven tribes, but already in the second list for commanding the count Joseph has died and his family has two branches, Manasseh, the elder, and Ephraim. Thereafter there will always be these twelve tribes. In the actual count, the third list, Gad has taken the place of Judah and is listed with Reuben and Simeon to form a block which in the official list will take second place to the one led by Judah.

The Official Order

Judah, Zebulun and Issachar (placed on the east);
Reuben, Simeon, Gad (placed on the south);
Ephraim, Manasseh, Benjamin (placed on the west);
Dan, Asher, Napthali (placed on the north).

In the official list the twelve tribes are listed in four blocks of three, each with a leader, each block placed at one of the four orientations of the square around the tabernacle. When the leaders of the tribes make their offerings to the altar they come forward in the same official order (ch. 7), and when the people of Israel set out on their journey they march under their respective captains in that order (Num. 10.13-28).

THE FOUR QUARTERS OF ISRAEL

NORTH

Dan Asher Napthali

Levites

WEST

Ephraim
Manasseh
Benjamin

TABERNACLE

Judah
Issachar
Zebulun

EAST

Reuben Simeon Gad

SOUTH

Diagram 7

The official order in itself is intriguing. Why is Reuben on the south when he lived on the east? And why is Gad, another east bank tribe, listed with him on the south? Evidently geographic position is not being projected. And why is Ephraim, the remainder of the Northern

Kingdom of Israel, placed on the west? Since the list shows changes made to the first listing from Genesis, we have to go to where Genesis first names the twelve sons of Jacob (Gen. 29; 30; 35), and from there on to the Genesis list of the sons of Jacob who came with him to Egypt at Joseph's behest (Gen. 46.8-27), and finally to Jacob's blessing (Gen. 49.3-27).

First I present the list of their birth order and the ranking of their mothers. The two wives of Jacob are Leah, the elder, and Rachel, the beloved. Leah, though not loved by her husband, is prolific; Rachel only produces two male children of her own, the two youngest of all the sons. Her daughter, Dinah, whose name is not mentioned in Numbers, has only indirect effect on the tribal order of precedence. Indirectly her seduction by the prince of Shechem, traitorously avenged in blood by her brothers Simeon and Levi (Gen. 34) caused the latter to be cursed by Jacob. In the listings birth order evidently has an influence, as well as mother's status.

Birth Order of Sons of Jacob

Leah	Rachel's servant	Leah's servant	Rachel
1. Reuben			
2. Simeon			
3. Levi			
4. Judah			
	5. Dan		
	6. Napthali		
		7. Gad	
		8. Asher	
9. Issachar			
10. Zebulun			
			11. Joseph
			12. Benjamin

The list of those who came to Egypt (Gen. 46.8-27) overrides birth order so as to treat the sons of each wife together with the sons of her maid as a single unit. This corresponds to the inheritance and house governance rules in many polygamous peoples, for example in the Southern Bantu cattle complex. Leah's sons, in birth order, are followed by Leah's servants' sons in their separate birth order; then follow Rachel's two sons who are actually younger than her servants' sons who follow after. The rule is quite simple: children of servants do not rank. God's list makes a variation on showing that the servants' sons do not count: it gives all the full heirs first, in order of birth and mother's rank, and then jumbles up the four sons of servants without regard for mother, mother's mistress's rank, or birth order. This should be a warning to the reader of Numbers, as it would be obvious to a contemporary in Judah, that mother's rank is significant for the Genesis story and we should be prepared to find that it partly governs the placing of tribes around the tabernacle in Numbers. Dan and Napthali, the two sons of Rachel's servant, stand on the north, with one of the children of Leah's servant, Asher, between them. That makes it clear that the north is for the children of servants. Among servants' sons neither mother nor relative age explains the positions, for Napthali is older than Asher, who is only his half brother.

The other list in Genesis appears in Jacob's deathbed oration (Gen. 49). In this list Judah is named fourth, as he is fourth according to birth order. But on that occasion his three elder brothers are cursed by their father: Reuben, Simeon, and Levi: Reuben because he slept with his father's concubine and Simeon and Levi because they dishonourably attacked the king of Shechem when their sister Dinah was seduced by his son (Gen. 34). This important incident reflects the relations of the sons of Judah and of Joseph (whose capital city was Shechem). It is not forgotten in Numbers and will be discussed in the last chapter. The curses account for why Judah comes first in the order of the host around the tabernacle in Numbers: his elder brothers have been disgraced. That in itself is a reason for recalling Jacob's last words to his sons for reading Numbers. And more significantly for the fifth-century political scene, those tribes that Jacob cursed had been long since swept away by wars, and only those two sons to whom he gave an obvious blessing are left. The story of how the Lord placed them around the tabernacle is the first of the reminders in the Numbers' stories that the prophecies have come true and the curses and blessings are fulfilled.

Levi has no place among the inheritors of the land, and the other two of the cursed sons of Leah, Reuben and Simeon, stand on the south, joined by Leah's servant's child, Gad. So the diagram makes it clear that cursed and low-ranking sons can stand together, on the north and the south, regardless of their birth place in the family. On the east and west, children of one mother, in correct birth order, face each other, Judah and his full brothers on the east, Ephraim and his brother and uncle on the west. By divine command the descendants of

Rachel and Leah have been placed on opposite sides of the tabernacle, facing each other.

All twelve tribes, with the exception of Levi, are treated throughout Numbers as the heirs of the promises: none is formally disinherited. Cursed or blessed by Jacob, sinners or good men in the Genesis story, whatever their ancestors did, and whatever they do to confirm their sinfulness in the course of the book of Numbers, by the end of the story they will have all had their portion of the promised land assigned to them.

3. *The Sons of Levi*

The meaning of their positions becomes clearer by analogy with the other diagram drawn by Moses at the Lord's instructions. The tribes of men able to bear arms form the outer ring around the tabernacle. The Levites and their families form the inner ring.

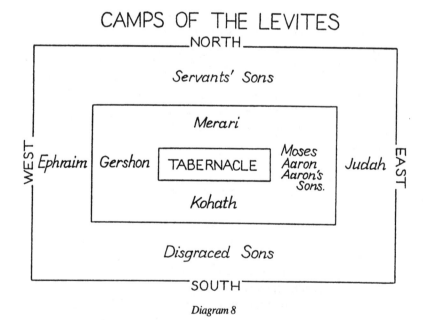

Diagram 8

On the east in front of the tabernacle are the brother leaders, Moses and Aaron and the sons of Aaron (Num. 3.38). They are aligned with Judah and his brothers, sons of Leah. Facing them on the west is the eldest Levite family, Gershon (Num. 3.23), encamped behind the tabernacle, aligned with Ephraim and the other descendants of Rachel's full sons. The alignment of Judah with Moses is no accident: the same east/west axis which counterpoises Judah and Joseph similarly counterpoises the leading families of the Levites. Moses and Aaron confront Gershon, the senior family of Levites, whom they have superseded, as Judah confronts and supersedes the son of Joseph on the diagram, and as the kingdom of Judah has superseded the kingdom of Israel in history. To the south the Kohathites are encamped, parallel to the disgraced sons of Jacob. In the north encamps Merari, the most junior family of Levi (Exod. 6.14).

The diagram of the Levites who will not inherit that land is in parallel with the diagram of the heirs. The disposition of the Levites has to be read at the same time and in the same way as the disposition of the warrior tribes. The meanings held in the inner and outer squares mutually control each other: the east means the place of the rising sun (Num. 3.38). It means the place of Moses and Aaron (and Aaron's sons), and also the place of Judah, a concentration of spatial analogies and sacred reference. There is nothing neutral or insignificant about being placed on the east in this diagram. Aaron and his issue are definitively separated from the other descendants of Levi and put in first place. Nor is the rest of the placement neutral. Gershonites, after all, were the senior family of Levites, but they are in the west; there can be no question of their later trying to pull rank over Aaron's descendants for the diagram shows where Moses himself long ago said they had to stand. Aaron and Moses in strict genealogical terms have supplanted Gershon's position of the eldest son, just as Judah has moved up ahead of the northern kingdom, here represented by Joseph's children. The hierarchical and hereditary nature of the priestly organization is fully engaged in this diagram.

Kohath was the very family from which Aaron and Moses descended, their closest kinsmen. By giving to Moses and Aaron the eastern position in the camp and sending the other families of Kohath to the south, the Kohathites are made spatially equivalent to the disgraced sons of Jacob. The irony of history is here, since they are going to be disgraced as the story unfolds. They have also been displaced in the succession, since their prestigious brothers do not count as their junior siblings. The spatial symbolism around the tabernacle anticipates the rule that applies to all the Levites who are not sons of Aaron, that they work under the oversight of the latter (Num. 4.17-20). Korah should have been the next senior line after the exaltation of Aaron's branch of the Kohath family. When they are given their place of encampment round the tabernacle it is not Korah but the son of Uzziel who is named as 'the head of the fathers' house of the families of the Kohathites' (Num. 3.30). At the midpoint of the book Korah will sin; overriding his right of succession within Kohath is like taking his sin into account before he ever did anything wrong. God's worry that the Kohathites might not survive will be justified, and his wish that they do survive will be fulfilled: they are going to survive to be counted in the census before the end of the book (Num. 26.57-62); but Korah has already been downgraded before he has uttered a subversive word. One understands why some commentators feel sympathy for Korah, son of Kohath—a born loser, the dice were loaded against him.

The placing of the Levite families around the tabernacle is followed by the allocation of their tasks. On the east, Moses and Aaron have charge of the tabernacle itself; on the west, Gershon handles the tabernacle tent and the hangings (Num. 3.25-27). This in itself shows by analogy that the placing of Ephraim on the west is not a move to shun or disinherit his people. On the south Kohath looks after the ark, the table, the lampstand, sanctuary vessels, the altars and the hangings (Num. 3.31-32). It is an honour, not a mark of servitude, that Kohath has the duty of carrying the ark on their shoulders. The act of carrying a burden is a metaphor for Moses' relation to the people of Israel. When, in the next story section, the leaders presented six wagons and twelve oxen for the work of the tabernacle (Num. 7.3-9), Moses distributed them between the other Levite families, but refused to give any to the sons of Kohath, because their charge was to carry the holy things themselves (Num. 4.15). On the north, Merari has what must surely be the servants' jobs, picking up and carrying the frames, the bars, the pillars, the sockets, pegs and cords (Num. 3.36-37), less honourable tasks than carrying the holy things and the ark itself.

Why should the sons of Merari be given the menial tasks? On the one hand, they could have been, as Frank Cross has suggested, the remnant of the Mushites, the priests of a local cult, who had to be somehow absorbed into the Levitical genealogy.[1] In that interpretation, placing them on the north among the servants and giving them the less esteemed tasks would indicate second-class citizenship.

Part of the explanation of why some person or topic should be placed as it is placed in the book has to refer to the requirements of the rhetorical structure. Another suggestion compatible with the first would connect with Nehemiah's effort to introduce order into the affairs of the temple. He counted 392 sons of Solomon's servants among the personnel to be organized (Neh. 7.60). These would be the right class of temple attendant to be placed on the north of the tabernacle, parallel with the sons of Jacob's servant concubines. The system of parallelism works top to bottom, right to left and left to right, each way the analogy is read gives meaning to the other side. The servants' sons standing on the north for both civil and religious ranks provide a kind of spatial pun, each exemplar making the meaning for its pair. Taken by themselves, we might not be sure that we are right to interpret the positions of Dan, Asher and Naphtali as the servants' quarters, and not quite sure whether the sons of Merari are given menial tasks, but when they are put in parallel, the point is clear.

4. *The Hierarchical Vision*

Referring again to the political tensions in Jerusalem prevailing at the time of editing, the diagram of places around the tabernacle might seem to support the government policy of separatism since it puts Ephraim in an inferior status to Judah. However, certain considerations undermine that conclusion. First, a hierarchy has to have a first place, but the next place is not without honour. Secondly, the tribes are all there, standing peacefully in a pattern divinely ordained: that does not sound like support for a policy that would exclude one of them. Thirdly, in this book none of the tribes is accused of the defilement of worshipping false gods. When they make their gifts to the tabernacle, though they go up in the official order, their gifts are exactly the same, monotonously listed, one after another, for the whole of ch. 7. Such a laborious list would not be spelt out for nothing. Standing there together, name by name, presenting their gifts in turn, item checked against item, spoon against spoon, clearly no one

---

1. Cross, *Canaanite Myth*, p. 206.

of the princely givers ever lost a birthright.

At first sight the equality of gifts to the tabernacle suggests defer-
ence to the egalitarian principles enshrined in the enclave culture. But
on reflection, in view of the political controversies of the time, and
remembering that the priestly editors were secure of their position in
a hereditary hierarchy, the interpretation should probably be more
political than cultural. Hierarchy is historically minded, more traditionalist, more interested in reconciliation with and inclusion of past
members. It has less worry about conspiracy, more confident that others will be eager to share the benefits of the superior constitution. The
book of Numbers betrays its hierarchical leanings at many points.

We have been alerted to the hierarchical structure of the placement
of the Levites around the tabernacle. The placement of the arms-
bearing men is based on political realism, for the dominant tribes are
both those blessed by Jacob and those whom the course of history has
brought out on top, Judah and Ephraim. We should continue to watch
what the sons of Jacob do on the story rungs. Only certain tribesmen
are distinguished by name in the stories. The named ones are descendants of the sons whom Jacob cursed, Reuben, Simeon and Levi, and
the descendants of the sons to whom he gave major blessings: Caleb of
the tribe of Judah, and Joshua, of the tribe of Ephraim, son of Joseph.
As we witness their fortunes in the story, we find that the named
descendants of the cursed ancestors sin again conspicuously, and the
named descendants of those whom Jacob blessed emerge as heroes,
until finally Joshua, the man of Ephraim, is commissioned to succeed
Moses. The two heroes of the forty years' in the desert, a man from
Judah and a man from Ephraim, lend support to the policy of brotherly behaviour to Samaria.

Near the end of the story there is a second formal census, where
Moses does not use the official list, but counts them in the same order
that the Lord gave for the first count, which suggests that the official
marching order is a deliberate innovation peculiar to Numbers and so
inserted into the tradition for editorial purposes deemed central to the
theme of the book. The second census, in ch. 26, harks back to the list
of Gen. 46.8-27, with small differences: Gad has replaced Levi, as in
the official list; the order of the last three sons is unchanged, but
Manasseh is counted before Ephraim, as he would have been before
Jacob reversed the status of his two grandsons.

Reuben, Simeon, Gad;
Judah, Issachar, Zebulun;
Manasseh, Ephraim, Benjamin;
Dan, Asher, Napthali (Num. 26.50).

The second census after the plague was expressly made in preparation for war. The sons of Reuben, Gad and half of Manasseh asked for permission to settle in the fertile country on the east of the Jordan. Moses consented on condition that they should fight with their brethren to win the promised land (ch. 32). If they had refused to fight, Moses' reference to God's anger (Num. 32.6-15) amounted to a threat. The episode makes the point that Moses counted Reuben, Manasseh, and Gad as one with their brethren in responsibility and in their share of the promise. Moses did not allow the curse of Jacob on Reuben to make any difference to his land rights.

In the fifth-century confrontation of Samaria and Judah the equivalent question would be whether Ephraim had forfeited his birthright as one of the sons of Jacob. If not, how could his descendants be refused membership of the community? The book of Numbers deals with the question comprehensively. In the matter of survival, and in the matter of political hegemony, Judah is unique. Judah's position on the diagram is part of the rhetorical strategy for demonstrating that Jacob's curses and blessings came true. His first three brothers have been downgraded. Since all of the tribes had a claim to their common patrimony in the promised land, the list would start with the eldest brothers, Reuben and Simeon. Jacob originally cursed them, but Moses does not discriminate against them.[1] They did wrong, and even now, under Moses' command, they do wrong again, as we shall see in the next chapter, but their sinning on the journey to the promised land does not disqualify them from standing in the final line-up of the tribes for the distribution of land. Jacob's prophecies have become prominent in interpreting the lists of his sons as they receive their

---

1. The last line-up of the tribes is when Moses under divine instruction tells the people who is to be in charge of the division of the land (in the last legal section, 34.13-29). Because Reuben, Gad and half of Manasseh have had their choice, the list is correspondingly short: Judah, Simeon, Benjamin, Dan, Manasseh, Ephraim, Zebulun, Issachar, Asher, Naphtali. The name order seems close to that in Josh. 13–19, where the land is finally divided up.

positions around the tabernacle in the first section. Following the argument through the trellis of parallel sections will show that his blessings and curses underpin the structure of the book.

Chapter 10

JACOB'S PROPHECIES:
TWO STORY RUNGS

1. *First Story Rung*

We now return to the literary structure, and focus on the two story
rungs. The last chapter showed how the diagram of the sons of Jacob
standing around the tabernacle records the historical effect of his
curses, reflected in their positions. One should notice that though the
curses of their father were effective and though the descendants of the
cursed sons were destroyed, the curses were implemented by the military power of enemies, not by Jacob's other sons. This interpretation
is strengthened by the exploits of the sons of Jacob in the story rungs.

As the law rungs formed a structural unit, so the four story rungs
can be taken as a quatrain, with four themes:

> A. Heirs counted, three categories, setting out, the cloud,
>   B. Internal revolts punished, all three categories
>   C. Turning point, crisis flowering rod
>   B1. External enemy vanquished
> A1. Journey accomplished, land apportioned to heirs

The four story sections that run in parallel across the plan of the book
make two rungs: section III pairs section XI, section V pairs section
IX.

They are like rungs in the sense that they run across the story, with
each right-hand side set of stories completed or complemented on the
left. The common theme of section III and section XI is reciprocity.
But there is a great deal of other action going on in section XI, which
evidently has the responsibility of providing a conclusion for all the
stories told so far, in the same way as law chapter 30, on women's
vows, concludes the previous law sections.

Diagram 9

TWO STORY RUNGS

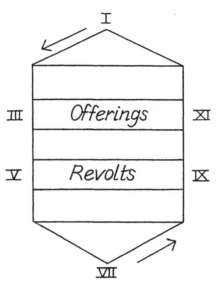

First Rung: Reciprocity:
Gifts to the Lord and from the Lord

Section III
The gifts of the captains to the tabernacle (7.1-83)
Dedication of the altar (7.84-89)
The lamp stand (8.1-4)
Purifying the Levites for their service in the tabernacle (8.5-17)

Levites a gift from the Lord to Aaron (8.18-26)

Passover on 14th day of first month of second year (9.1-14)

Cloud to guide them for all their settings out (9.15-23)

Section XI
War against Midian to avenge Israel, victory, spoils, order to slaughter the Moabite women who seduced the men of Israel (31.1-18)
Purify yourselves and your captives (31.19-20) and purify metals by fire and the water of separation (31.21-24)
Tribute of livestock and captives to the Lord (31.25-48); free offering of jewellery to the tabernacle (31.49-54)
Reuben and Gad fight alongside Israel and are granted their land on the east of the Jordan (32)
Moses summarizes all their settings out (33.1-49)

The two parts of the first rung are connected by the theme of gifts to the Lord and from the Lord. The first part is a whole chapter about the gifts the chieftains made to the tabernacle, followed by the dedication of the altar, with much about purifying of the Levites who are to give their service to it, and finally the Lord makes a gift of the Levites to Aaron. Matching that theme at the other end of the rung is the levy of prisoners and livestock, the voluntary giving of war booty to the tabernacle by the captains, and much about purification. There are other links to watch. Section III has the dedication of the altar, and section XI starts with the call to avenge the idolatry caused by the wiles of the Moabite women. The ending of section III is the account of how the cloud stayed over the tabernacle and guided the people as to when they were to stay and when they were to set out, while the ending of section XI is Moses' summary of their stopping points and their settings out. Leaving out details which do not fit, the bold structure would be as follows:

Section III	Section XI
gifts	gifts
purification	purification
Passover	Reuben
Cloud for setting out	Settings out reviewed

The beginnings and endings pair off better than the middle part which links up with the rest of the book in ways unconstrained by the demands of parallelism. Section XI winds up the conclusion of section III, together with all the rest of the stories, an entirely satisfactory conclusion. The promise about the cloud for their guidance for all their settings out has been fulfilled, as have all the other promises.

2. *Second Story Rung*

In the next story rung sections V and IX do not show an obvious, line by line, linked internal structure. There are dense and fairly obvious correspondences, but the order of linking is irregular. Both are journeys through the desert, both are replete with miracles and punishments. Murmurings punished in section V are similar to requests granted in section IX. The two sections, be it remembered, are divided by the story in section VII of the catastrophic confrontation of Korah and the captains against Moses and Aaron, ended by earthquake, plague and fire, and the year's promise eventually renewed by the sweet miracle of Aaron's blossoming rod.

Second Story Rung

Section V	Section IX
A. Tribes set out with the cloud, arrive in Paran (10.11-28)	A. Arrive in Zin, death of Miriam (20.1)
Moses' request for guidance from Hobab (10.29-32)	
Guidance of the Cloud (10.33-36)	
B. People's complaint (11.1-3)	B. Requests, for water, miracle at Meribah (20.2-13)
B1. Complaint for meat (11.4-35)	
	C. Request to Edom (20.14-21)
B2. Miriam's and Aaron's complaint, shaming of Miriam (12.1-16)	A1. Death of Aaron (20.22-29)
B3. Spies' false reports (13–14.10)	C1. First armed victory against Canaanites, at Hormah (21.1-3)
C. God's curse on Israel (14.11-38)	B1. Request for food and water, fiery serpents (21.4-9); well of water (21.10-19)
	C2. Victories against kings Sihon and Bashan (21.20-35)
B4. Disobedience and defeat at Hormah (14.39-45)	D. God's blessing on Israel by the mouth of Balaam (22–24)
	B2. Idolatry of the people, sacrilegious deed and deaths of Cozbi and Zimri (25)
	D1. New census (26)

At the end of section V God has been so angry that he wanted to wipe out his people, but cursed them instead; in section IX, through Balaam, he renews his age-old blessings on Abraham and Jacob's blessings on Judah. Section V is doom-laden, full of divine anger and violence against the people; section IX deals with similar incidents in a mood of divine forgiveness. For Israel the curse is matched with subsequent blessing and the destruction is turned against her enemies.

3. *The Crises*

To show this change of mood between the two halves of the book it is worthwhile comparing the crises that arise in each section. The first revolts in section V come in 11.1-35. The chapter starts with a short self-summary (11.1-3):

A. The people's unspecified complaint,
    B. the Lord's anger,
        C. fire,
A1. Moses prays to the Lord,
    B1. the Lord responds,
        C1. fire is abated.

Then follow immediately the details of the second rebellion, much more complicated since it is Moses who complains of the people, and God who seems to be about to help them:

A. The people's complaint for food, weeping for Egypt, loathing manna, asking for flesh to eat (11.4-10),
A1. Moses complains of the burden, asks God for help (11.11-15);
    B. God responds,
        C. Moses to choose 70 elders (11.16-17) who receive spirit (11.25-30)
    B1. God responds, promises to provide flesh (11.18–23)
        C1. God sends quails (11.31–32)
            2. punishment follows, a great plague (11.33).

The third, Miriam's revolt, is of the same structure as the first:

A. Miriam, supported by Aaron (Num. 12), claims spiritual authority,
    B. the Lord's anger,
        C. she is punished with leprosy,
A1. Moses intercedes.
    B1. God responds,
        C1. punishment mitigated, she is put outside the camp for seven days.

Fourth, there are two revolts, or one in two stages:

A. False reports of the promised land spread by scouts (13), results in the people murmuring against Moses, and weeping for Egypt (14.1-5)
A1. Joshua and Caleb calming the people, threatened with stones (14.6-10a).
    B. the Lord's anger, threatens to destroy the people (14.10b-12).
A2. Moses intercedes with God (14.13-19)
    B2. God responds (14.20-21)
        C. Curses all the adults, 40 years in the wilderness, (14.22-38)

Finally, the fifth revolt follows on the people hearing their fate and mutinously fighting the Canaanites: their penalty is automatic and immediate.

    A. The people weep, decide to go up to the hill country
       without cloud's guidance (14.39-40)
    A1. Moses warns them of Amalekites and Canaanites (14.41-43)
       B. they respond disobediently (14.44)
           C. Israel's soldiers routed by the Canaanites to
             Hormah (14.45)

One should notice that all except the first of the episodes in section V end punitively for the people of Israel. In section IX, because the halfway point of the book is passed, we can assume there is a new generation. The people make similar complaints; what counted as mutiny before is now counted a reasonable request, and God grants it each time. First, they complain of there being no water (20.2-5), Moses brings water out of the rock at Meribah (20.10-13).

The episode at Meribah provokes the Lord's anger against Moses for not trusting in him (20.12; 27.14); he therefore was not allowed to enter the promised land. Under the analysis by rungs the lack of trust in section IX demands to be matched with Moses' request to Hobab to guide them in section V. When Moses asked Hobab, the Midianite, his brother-in-law, to be their guide (10.29-32), it was already a shift from the general pattern of compliance established in the first story section. It was certainly somewhat strange under the guidance of the cloud to ask for guidance from a human. The story of Hobab should not be read without the story of the destruction at Hormah, and the latter has to be read in the light of Moses' warning to the soldiers not to go out because the Lord will not be with them, and repeated, because they should not depart when the ark of the covenant is not with them. The ark follows when the cloud moves, and the cloud has specifically been given to them for guidance (Exod. 40.34-38; Num. 9.15-23). So why did he want Hobab? The suggestion here is that the editors used Hobab in the structure of parallel rungs to give advance warning for how to interpret the otherwise enigmatic Meribah episode. Even Moses did not trust enough in the Lord's promises.

The second crisis is to do with Israel's relations with the neighbouring kingdoms:

A. Canaanite king captures men of Israel (21.1)
    B. Israel asks for victory and promises to destroy
      their cities (21.2)
        C. The Lord harkens to their request (21.3a)
A1. Israel destroys Canaanite cities at Hormah (21.3b)

This cancels the ignominious defeat the armies of Israel suffered at Hormah in the matching section V.

The third crisis has a more complicated denouement:

A. the people complain of food, water and manna (21.4-5)
    B. God sends fiery serpents to chastise them (21.6)
A1. people repent, Moses intercedes (21.7)
    B. God mitigates the punishment by the bronze serpent
      (21.8-9)
        C. The Lord brings them to a well (21.16)

After a long interruption of the narrative for the Balaam episode, the people sin again, making the fourth crisis:

A. The people seduced by Moabite women sacrifice to Baal
    (25.1-3)
    B. God responds, commands execution of the leaders (25.4)
    1. Moses gives the order (25.5)
      C. Plague (25.9)

Perhaps the command was carried out; the record does not tell us. While the people were weeping and presumably repenting, a man of the Simeonites and a Midianite woman named Cozbi committed an offence in the inner room of the tent of meeting. It was so heinous that it provoked Phinehas, grandson of Aaron, to spear her and the man through the abdomen. It must have been something very shameful, as Phinehas's act turned God's wrath away from the people of Israel who would have otherwise been quite consumed by the plague (25.10-11).

A. The people weeping (25.6)
    B. the offence of Zimri and Cozbi (25.6),
      C. summary punishment by Phinehas (25.7-8)
      C1. plague kills 24,000 (25.9)
    B1. God's anger turned away by Phinehas's deed (25.10-11),
A1. A covenant of peace for Israel, a perpetual priesthood for
    Phinehas and his descendants because he made atonement for
    Israel (25.12-18)

These two crises ought to be treated as one, the apostasy due to the Moabite temptresses and the sin of the Midianite princess, Cozbi. They are not only connected in time and place but the last provides the whole series with its conclusion. It would have been clearer if we had written it thus:

> A. Israel sacrifices to Baal
>   B. Leaders to be punished
>   C. Moses gives the order of execution
>   D. The people weeping
> A1. Offence of Zimri and Cozbi
>   B1. Execution of offenders by Aaron's grandson
>   C1. Plague
>   D1. Covenant of peace

All the crises on the second side of the rung end in victory or blessing: at Meribah water comes out of a rock, though God is angry with Moses (20.10-13), the second ends when Israel wins the war against the Canaanite king (21.3), the third ends with God taking them to a well (21.16), the series culminates with the covenant of peace (25.12-13).

Note the disparagement of manna matched in the two sections:

> Oh, that we had meat to eat! We remember the fish we ate in Egypt for nothing, the cucumbers, the melons, the leeks, the onions, and the garlic; but now our strength is dried up and there is nothing but this manna (section V, 11.4-6).

Compare section IX:

> And why have you made us come up out of Egypt, to bring us to this evil place? It is no place for grain, or figs, or vines, or pomegranates, and there is no water to drink (20.4).

> Why have you brought us up out of Egypt to die in the wilderness? For there is no food and no water, and we loathe this worthless food (21.5).

The verbal repetition signals an intention to pair the two sections. We are justified in noticing the way the patterns of complaint develop. On the first side of the rung, in ch. 11, the cause of complaint is first remedied with quails, but then the punishment falls heavily; on the second side, in ch. 21, punishment is first applied, then remitted and then the request for water granted. We should also notice that while the political implications in section V are internal to Israel, in section IX they are external. The persons involved in the revolts in section V correspond specifically to the categories which were picked out in the numbering at the beginning: the captains, the Levites, and the congregation. When the issue is food or water, the murmuring is by the congregation; when the issue is spiritual leadership, the sons of Levi do the murmuring (Aaron and Korah); when it is the conduct of the wars and journeys, the murmuring is by the captains supported by the congregation at large. In section IX the various revolts are all by the congregation; the Levites and the captains have been subdued already.

To understand the sense of this development we should attend again to the structuring of the book in four quarters. Each quarter contributes its burden to the whole: the first states God's plan for his people and the conditions for its fulfilment, the second introduces the complications of their wilfulness, the third has made the turn into the second half of the book and introduces foreigners, and it leads to the fourth triumphal quarter in which the Canaanites are subjected.

There is also an inverted match in the middle of each of these two sections, God's curse in the one balanced by his blessing in the other. In the first section a tremendous curse on the people of Israel, a formal curse condemning them to forty years of wandering, is matched by the divinely inspired blessings that pour out of the mouth of Balaam. The two legal rungs examined earlier have God's curse balanced by his blessing; the pattern of curse matched by blessing in one of the story rungs is balanced by the pattern of blessing and curse in the legal rung, making an even more complex elaboration of the overall pattern. Balaam will have another function too. The blessings he gives restate the promises to Abraham, and revive (and also revise) Jacob's deathbed blessings. He fits in here, after the first of the victories of Israel against the Canaanites. An instrument of the Lord, for after he has spoken the military exploits of Israel go from glory to glory. For the Numbers poet he is an instrument of the rhetorical structure used with consummate skill. We will need to give a whole chapter to Balaam.

4. *Reuben, Simeon and Levi*

The forty years begun and the forty years ended are clearly marked by the repetition on each side of the midpoint of the words of God's curse. First the Lord declares that all those who rebelled will die in the wilderness, the whole generation of them; only their children will survive to enter the promised land, with two exceptions, Caleb the son of Jephunneh and Joshua the son of Nun (14.36-38). When they come out and are numbered once again, the point is made:

> There was not a man left of them, except Caleb the son of Jephunneh and Joshua the son of Nun (26.64-65).

The two conspicuously virtuous heroes of the scouts' crisis are respectively from the tribe of Judah and the tribe of Ephraim. That these tribes are eventually to be the two survivors of the horrors surrounding the destruction of the Temple and the return from Babylon makes the mythic parallel between the sojourn in the desert and the exile in Babylon.

Jacob on his deathbed cursed the first three of his sons, Reuben, Simeon and Levi. Korah is a grandson of Levi, and the sons of Peleth with whom he conspires are of the tribe of Reuben: they rebelled together against Moses and Aaron (section VII, 16.1-3). The only one of the cursed tribes who has done nothing to disgrace himself yet is Simeon. Anyone familiar with mythic structure will be waiting after the rebellions of Korah and Reuben for Simeon to fall into disgrace. When it turns out that the man who was speared in one thrust with a Midianite woman was a Simeonite the waiting is over: Simeon and Levi have now been paired as brothers in wickedness, as in Jacob's curse: 'Simeon and Levi are brothers, weapons of violence are their swords...I will divide them in Jacob and scatter them in Israel' (Gen. 49.5-7). When Simeon's disgrace is matched both with Korah's rebellion and with Aaron's connivance at the revolt of Miriam, the tally of sins by the offspring of the cursed brothers Reuben, Simeon and Levi is complete. However, none of these misdeeds will prevent their tribes from being mustered for the inheritance at the end.

In the book of Numbers the Levites are definitely convicted of disaffection. Quite apart from the role of Korah, the bad priest who was sent to hell, there is the story of Aaron and Miriam's revolt. The episode of her shaming is so dramatic that one tends to forget that her rebellion was supported by Aaron. The balance between sections V and IX, and the complete list of Jacob's cursed sons require that Aaron's complicity with Miriam be recorded in section V, and both of their deaths in section IX. As the pattern of other rebellions emerges, Aaron is squarely placed in the record of rebels, revolting on his own behalf, an encroachment into the inviolate sanctuary to be compared with the encroachment of Korah in the next section. Aaron's words, or rather the words that he and Miriam say together at her instigation, anticipate the words that Korah will use:

> Has the Lord spoken only through Moses? Has he not also spoken through us? (12.2).

Korah is going to say against Moses and Aaron:

> For all the congregation are holy, every one of them, and the Lord is among them; why then do you exalt yourselves above the assembly of the Lord? (16.3).

So already, in ch. 12, there has been a revolt of the high priest himself. The Lord instantly forgives Aaron. (Or does he? It is not said why Aaron is not allowed to see the promised land.)

Only certain tribesmen are distinguished by name in the stories. They are descendants of the sons whom Jacob cursed, Reuben, Simeon and Levi, and the descendants of the sons to whom he gave a conspicuously favourable blessing: Caleb of the tribe of Judah, and Joshua, of the tribe of Ephraim, son of Joseph. As we witness their fortunes in the story, we find that the named descendants of the cursed ancestors sin again conspicuously, but are not excluded from inheritance. The named descendants of the blessed ancestors emerge as heroes, until finally Joshua, the man of Ephraim, is commissioned to succeed Moses, making ready for the book of Joshua. The fact that the heroes of the forty years in the desert were a man from Judah and a man from Ephraim supports the thesis that Numbers is preaching a consistently brotherly message to Samaria.

In Numbers all the sons of Jacob share the destiny of Israel. God is very forgiving. Perhaps only hierarchical priests could envisage so much forgiveness. The enduring brotherhood of the twelve sons is carried not only in the lists and the stories, but in the whole structure of the story sections. Whatever they do, all their sins and backslidings make no difference to the list that Moses finally draws up for the partition of the promised land. This is well known, but its importance for the interpretation of the book has not been observed.

Chapter 11

ISRAEL DEFILED: MIRIAM
AND HER BROTHERS

1. *Miriam*

Miriam is a beloved heroine in Jewish traditions, but no cause for her high standing shows in the commentaries on Numbers. Like turning poetry into limping prose, it is not difficult to underestimate her part, which anyway only takes a few lines. The story in ch. 12 says that she led the first of the revolts against Moses' spiritual authority, and her follower was no less than Aaron. First the two of them 'spoke against Moses because of his Cushite wife' (12.1), and second they asked whether the Lord spoke only through Moses, and had he not spoken through them also and heard them (12.2). That is the sum of their offence.

It was not Moses who responded, but the Lord himself who called the three of them to him in the pillar of cloud. A major infraction and a major act of divine retribution is signalled by the pillar of cloud. The Lord's words give solemn witness to the precedence of Moses, and he challenges them: why were they not afraid to speak against 'my servant Moses'? He departs in anger, and when they look round, behold, Miriam's skin is leprous, white as snow. Aaron begs Moses to intercede with the Lord for her, confesses that they sinned, foolishly, and begs for her not to be as one dead, whose flesh is half-consumed (12.12). Moses cries out to the Lord to heal her on the spot. Evidently his word was heard and the request instantly granted (how could it not have been after a demonstration of support from God's two chosen leaders?). Miriam is then put through the ritual for a leper who has been pronounced clean by the priest: she has to stay outside the camp for seven days.[1] We cannot doubt that the brief moment is very

---

1. Lev. 12.4-6.

important from the fact that Moses himself, when he doubted whether Pharaoh would listen to him, had his hand turned leprous, white as snow, and instantly healed by the Lord. The miracle of Moses' leprosy takes place in Exodus (4.6-7), in the same context in which he has found that his rod could be used as a serpent. Rod switched into serpent and back again, leprosy switched on and off, the two signs make the analogy of the hardships of Israel in Egypt with their hardships in the desert.

Miriam was publicly humiliated. But we have come far enough in reading Numbers to ask seriously whether Miriam figures here as the historic person, or whether she is a rhetorical symbol, a string for allowing allegorical connections to be made. Her strange story makes more sense if she is representing the people of Israel.

One should note that in the Numbers' story Miriam's genealogy was highly specified. Numbers does not explicitly say that she was the same girl who proposed to Pharoah's daughter that she would find a nurse for the Hebrew baby in the bulrushes, and then returned with their own mother (Exod. 2.4-9). Nor does Numbers say that Miriam was the same as the prophetess who led the other women in singing a hymn of praise after the Israelites had crossed the Red Sea safely (Exod. 16.20). The one piece of background Numbers provides for Miriam is that she was the sister of Moses and Aaron, three children of the same mother (Num. 26.59). This woman was suddenly disgraced, afflicted with leprosy, put outside the camp while the whole congregation postponed their march for the period of her purification. What had she done to deserve that ignominy? When Moses interceded on her behalf, God likened the case to that of a daughter who has so offended her father that he has spat in her face (Num. 12.9-14). That is very strong language. What had she done that Aaron had not also done? They had both asked for a share of the spiritual leadership. Why did he escape with no more than a private reprimand while she underwent such a public shaming?

Feminist criticism would attribute the asymmetry between Miriam's and Aaron's punishment to a general prejudice against women in public life. Her case would be a sign of the despised condition of women in the Bible.[1] But is it plausible that a book of this genre, with the large-scale philosophical agenda we are tracing, can afford to take

1. M. Bal, *Death and Dissymmetry: The Politics of Coherence in the Book of Judges* (Chicago: University of Chicago Press, 1988).

time to drive home a lesson on female inferiority? Remember that the priestly editors were part of a hierarchical culture, which would dispose them to honouring women as embodiments of the principle of hierarchy itself. Thoroughgoing hierarchists believe that gender polarity means that women are only inferior in an inferior context, and that their role is to represent the whole against sectional interests. It would be a mistake to disregard this story's links with the rest of the book for the sake of interpreting Miriam's fate as typical patriarchal oppression. Public shame was heaped on Miriam, but the book of Numbers says nothing directly to explain why she was picked for her role.

Apart from wanting to share the spiritual leadership, Aaron and Miriam had also said something to Moses about his Cushite (sometimes interpreted as Ethiopian) wife (12.1). One tradition has interpreted the remark about Moses' wife[1] as a kindly intervention reproaching Moses as a husband for neglecting his wife for his public duties. Clearly this has nothing to do with her punishment. Some scholars have taken Aaron's and Miriam's remark as a racist taunt to Moses for having a foreign wife. According to Frank Cross a rhetorically irresistible contrast between the black skin of the Ethiopian woman and a leper's skin 'white as snow'[2] will be the reason why she was turned into a leper.[3] Even if this expresses Numbers' anti-racist leanings, such colour coding may make the punishment fit the crime in one sense, but the relative severity of the punishment is not merited by the offence. The structural analysis of black and white, Cushite and Israelite, is too haphazardly unconected with the rest of the Bible to take the burden of explaining Miriam's fate. Another rabbinical tradition chooses passing on gossip for the reason why Miriam was punished, a simple and minor weakness, hardly enough to warrant the penalty. All the explanations undervalue the implications of leprosy in Leviticus and Numbers.

The interpretation I shall offer fastens on three aspects of her story. Two of these are political: one, based on her relationship to Moses which has been read as an objectionable parallel with the divine sister-

---

1. Milgrom, *Numbers*, the rabbis make 'no objection to her Cushite origin, but, on the contrary, defend her, claiming that Moses refused to have sexual intercourse after his descent from Sinai' p. 93, citing Sifre to Numbers 99.

2. A form of leprosy (2 Kgs 6.27, Exod. 4.6).

3. Cross, 'The Priestly Houses of Early Israel', in *Canaanite Myth*.

wife of the Pharaohs; the other, her double relationship to both Moses and Aaron, which recalls Genesis's treatment of Dinah and her two brothers, Simeon and Levi. The third, theologically the most profound, is that her leprosy must be discussed in the light of leprosy as the ultimate defilement, the figure of idolatry and betrayal, cited at the head of the essay on broken faith in Num. 5.1-4.

2. *Sister of Moses, Queen of Heaven*

We want to know why a woman leader of a revolt against Moses was his own sister. Was the nature of her punishment significant? Why did her revolt involve Aaron? Why was she punished, and not he? In this genre we cannot ignore the lateral reading, and moreover, for any puzzle in this book we have learnt by now to ask routinely what it has to do with Judah's situation confronting neighbouring territories in the fifth century. We have also learnt not to ignore the repeated listings of the sons of Jacob. Miriam's story must be set in the framework of the rest of the book. There are two political points here: one focuses on why Miriam was Moses' own sister, with reference to the current worship of fertility goddesses; and one on the parallel between Miriam, sister of Moses and Aaron, and Dinah, sister of Simeon and Levi.

In the Bible a woman is often a metaphor for Israel. The prophets commonly present the people of Israel as the erring wife who has betrayed her husband or as the wife sought by her loving lord.[1] The principle that has worked well for Numbers on the vows of women, ch. 30, and for the woman suspected of adultery, ch. 5, should also be applied to the sister of Moses and Aaron. Reading Miriam's story through the structure of the work, we notice that it is told in section V and her death is the first event to be announced in section IX, 20.1. Thus she connects the two sides of the second story rung. Looking across that rung we find that her shaming is matched in section IX by the publicly indecent death of the Midianite princess, Cozbi. Miriam and Cozbi are paired, two conspicuously well-connected women encroaching on the holy things. In section V Miriam encroaches on

---

1. Isa. 54; Hos. 2.1-3; 5.

the divine prerogative and is made a leper, and in the opposite section Cozbi defiles the tabernacle precinct and is summarily killed.

Miriam	Cozbi
Moses' and Aaron's sister; (26.59)	Daughter of Zur, head of a chiefdom in Midian (25.15)
Wanted a share in Moses' prophetic role (12.2)	Seduced a man of Israel near the tent of meeting (25.6)
Punished with leprosy (12.10); Moses interceded (12.13)	Cozbi punished with death (25.8)
Miriam's living shame (12.10-16)	Cozbi shamed in death (25.16-18)
The Lord angry, as if her father had spat in her face (12.14a)	The Lord's anger nearly consumes the people (25.8)
Miriam's punishment remitted to seven days outside the camp (12.14b-16)	Phinehas's deed stayed the plague (25.11)
Moses commended, spiritual leadership confirmed (12.6-9)	Phinehas commended, confirmed in priesthood (25.13)

The sequence through sections V and IX goes with mounting violence from Miriam smitten with leprosy to Cozbi slain, and from there on to the mass slaughter ordained for the deceiving Midianite women in section XI (Num. 31.15-16). The reader's eye is now trained to see the three stories about feminine defilement as belonging to a square of four sections (or two rungs).

DEFILING WOMEN

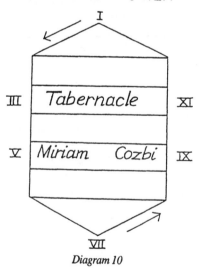

Diagram 10

In section III, which makes the initial statement for the two rungs, no women appear at all, still less any defiling women. It is about gifts to the tabernacle, consecration of the tabernacle, purification and dedication of Levites to the service of the sanctuary. As an opening statement it expands the theme of the inviolable purity of the sanctuary which has been stated in section I. This beginning indicates that the three women's stories have to do with desecration of the tabernacle.

A. sanctity of the tabernacle, chs. 7, 8, 9
B. a woman of Israel encroaches on priestly prerogative, ch. 12
C. foreign women seduce Israel to idolatry, ch. 25
D. punishment of foreign women, ch. 13.13-18

Compared with what happened to Cozbi and to the Midianite women, Miriam got off lightly: she was only half-consumed, and that for a short time.

An anthropologist, Edmund Leach, proposed that the claims of Miriam, though rejected, are a residue in the Bible of 'a strain of religious thinking in which the idea that the deity might be partly female was relatively acceptable'.[1] However, the lateral reading supports the contrary thesis: the claims of Miriam were made public in Numbers in order to be publicly rejected because Israel rejected that strain of religious thinking. It is true that female deities were worshipped throughout the region surrounding Israel, and equally true that in some empires God was thought to be incarnate in the kings. But the distinctive feature of biblical doctrine at the time of the editing is to have rejected a king, also king gods, queen goddesses and goddesses of all kinds. When Judaism, in the last decades of the monarchy, adopted the 'Yahweh-alone' movement, it categorically rejected idols, magic, divination, sorcery, soothsaying, cults of ancestors and ghosts, and any gods but one. Judaism then began definitively to distinguish itself from the surrounding religions. Popular rival cults were outlawed. Jeremiah's anger against the cult of the 'queen of heaven' testifies to the reality of the threat in postexilic times:

1. E.R. Leach, and A. Aycock, 'Why Did Moses Have a Sister?', in *Structuralist Interpretations of Biblical Myth* (Cambridge: Cambridge University Press, 1983), pp. 33-57.

> Do you not see what they are doing in the cities of Judah and in the streets of Jerusalem? The children gather wood and the fathers kindle fire, and the women knead dough, to make cakes for the queen of heaven (Jer. 7.17-18).

In ch. 44 Jeremiah attributes all the horrors of defeat and exile to the false worship, particularly blaming the men who knew that their wives had been offering incense to other gods. He describes a dialogue in which the people of Judah retort that while they worshipped the queen of heaven they prospered and that it was only when they left off burning incense, making cakes with her image and pouring libations for her that they were consumed by sword and famine. To which Jeremiah replied with God's threat that he will give them a sign, he will destroy Egypt's Pharoah. The worship of the queen of heaven was evidently widespread and menaced the precarious, emergent monotheism of Judah.

Who was the queen of heaven that the people of Judah worshipped? According to Susan Ackerman she was probably a syncretist goddess who combined the already syncretized characteristics of east Semitic Ishtar and west Semitic Astarte.[1] Being Moses' sister would cast Miriam in one of these roles pre-set for vilification. Numbers, by putting on record God's rejection of Miriam's claim to be as good as Moses, would empower the denunciation of women's fertility cults. For the women of Israel were continually succumbing to the temptation to pay cult to Ashtoreth. Why else should they be continually being rebuked for it? There are 40 references to Asherah, and wooden poles put up in her honour.[2] As if it were not enough to be a false religion, the rejected cult was vilified by being associated with the ultimate defilement, sexual perversion (1 Kgs 14.22-24).

Miriam's punishment of leprosy is a strong pointer on how to read her story. The corruption of the body is the regular image of the false religions. If she earns this affliction she must be associated with the enemy, the false gods of death. The leprosy described by Aaron as a living death tells us to look for the most profound and all-encompassing meaning. The plot, the materials from which it was

---

1. S. Ackerman, 'And the Women Knead Dough: The Worship of the Queen of Heaven in Sixth-Century Judah', in P. Day (ed.), *Gender and Difference in Ancient Israel* (Philadelphia: Fortress Press, 1989), pp. 109-22.

2. *The New Oxford Annotated Bible* (Oxford: Oxford University Press, 1973), p. 438.

woven, the burning issue of monotheism at the time of the compilation, all indicate leprosy as the condign punishment for her case. It is not because she is a woman, but because she is Israel. Miriam presents a model of what Balaam and the women of Moab did, a model of Israel seduced by false gods. The danger of religious apostasy was at the top of the priestly agenda. Israel's temptations to religious syncretism, the frenzied attacks on kings for false religion, and the filth imputed to foreign cults, these supply enough explanation of why Miriam was silenced. Her father spat in her face because there was never going to be room in Israel's religion for a divine king, still less for a cult of a fertility goddess, a goddess of love, sister to a king/deity. By ensuring that the reader knows that Miriam is the leader's own sister, the poet marked her out as a major symbol of Israel's broken faith. Yet God forgave her; as soon as Aaron asked for forgiveness, he instantly transmuted her sentence to the seven days outside the camp required of anyone cured of leprosy and pronounced clean by the priest. As the prophets said, this is how the Lord would forgive Israel if they repented.

3. *Simeon and Levi*

Placed by the pattern of the stories in parallel with Cozbi, Miriam is also linked with the man of Israel who was slain with Cozbi. He was Zimri, son of Zalu, a leader of the Simeonites (25.14). We noted earlier a sense of completion when his name appeared. History has once more repeated itself, as it is wont to do in the multi-layered time-space of myth. In Genesis Jacob's first three sons sinned; now the leaders of the tribes descended from them have sinned again. The offences committed in the story of Numbers take the reader directly back to Jacob's deathbed scene.

a. Reuben
    Seduced his father's concubine, was disinherited in Gen. 49.4, and in Numbers his descendant joins Korah's revolt against Moses's leadership and effectively against the whole divine plan, since these rebels regretted ever having left Egypt (16.1-2, 13-14)

b. Simeon and Levi
   Jacob denounced Simeon and Levi together as brothers in cruelty,
   fierce in anger and treacherous conspiracy (Gen. 49.5-7)

Jacob prophesied that Simeon and Levi would be scattered in Israel,
and here are their descendants, far apart on two sides of the first story
rung of the book of Numbers. Aaron, the grandson of Levi, treacherously joins Miriam's plot to dislodge Moses from the leadership; and
on the other side, Zimri, the Simeonite, behaves so badly with a
Midianite woman that the Lord sends a terrible plague to wipe out all
the people. In the original Genesis story these three eldest sons were
eliminated from the succession to Jacob. In default, the leadership of
Israel fell to Judah. The words of Jacob's blessing on Judah, 'Your
father's sons shall bow down before you' (Gen. 49.8) transfers to
Judah the hegemony which Joseph's dream of his brothers bowing to
him seemed to confer on the house of Joseph (Gen. 37.5-11).
Numbers upholds the leadership of Judah in the pattern of the tribes
around the tabernacle, but there is nothing about any tribes bowing
down to any others.

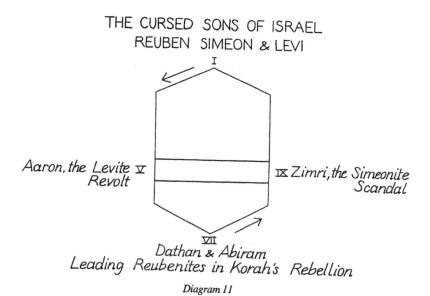

THE CURSED SONS OF ISRAEL
REUBEN SIMEON & LEVI

I

Aaron, the Levite V
Revolt

IX Zimri, the Simeonite
Scandal

VII
Dathan & Abiram
Leading Reubenites in Korah's Rebellion

Diagram 11

In this space, this conjuncture of three names opens a deeper reference. Numbers has reproduced the pattern of the three disgraced brothers: in the generation of Moses, Jacob's children, Simeon, Levi and Dinah, are represented by Zimri, Aaron and Miriam. In reassembling the first actors' descendants Numbers invokes the solemn scene of Jacob's death. Sitting up on his bed, his feet on the ground, Jacob tells his two sons who were afire with zeal for Israel's honour that he can never forgive their attack on Shechem. At the beginning, the book of Numbers places all the sons of Jacob in obscurity except legitimate Judah confronting powerful Ephraim. This pattern, repeated in the official order, signalled to politically minded readers in the fifth century that the book was about contentious issues of the day. Zimri's story placed here confirms the reading of this ordering as a reference to the contest between Judah and Samaria. For why was Jacob so angry with Simeon and Levi? The answer takes us back to their onslaught on the people of Shechem in the story of Dinah (Gen. 34). And who was Shechem? The name is that of the capital city of Samaria, richer and more numerous and more powerful than Israel.

Simeon and Levi were not obviously in the wrong;[1] zealous for the honour of their people, they had been outraged by the seduction of their sister. Their father Jacob had concluded a unique pact with Hamor, the king of Shechem: the pact was not just to share the abundant pastures and to exchange wives, but also, amazingly, for Hamor's people to be circumcised in the one faith, 'to be one people' (Gen. 34.22). After the new allies had honourably carried out their part of the contract and been circumcised, Simeon and Levi fell treacherously upon them, killed the men and sacked the city of Shechem. Jacob reproached them bitterly. His words would do well for the predicament of Israel in the time of the Second Temple: their act had made him, Israel, odious with the people of the land. He prophesied that the whole house of Israel would be destroyed because of this. To which the brothers replied, self-righteously, that it was not right that the son of the house of Shechem should treat their sister Dinah as a harlot. Evidently in Jacob's judgment her harlotry could be forgiven, but the breach of covenant could not.

Vengeance for the honour of Israel was meritorious, as the Lord

---

1. J. Pitt-Rivers, *The Fate of Shechem, or the Politics of Sex, Essays in the Anthropology of the Mediterranean* (Cambridge: Cambridge University Press, 1977).

twice proclaimed in Numbers.[1] Dinah had been seduced, called a
harlot by her brothers, and so was Israel habitually castigated by the
prophets for harlotry. The brothers' crime in their father's eyes was
in breaking a solemn covenant. The charge of harlotry applied to a
people implies idolatry. No question here as to whether the story of
Dinah is about a woman or about a corporate group: Dinah was a
figure of Israel. Long before the exile it would have been judged
meritorious to attack Samaria.

> For now, O Ephraim, you have played the harlot, Israel is defiled
> (Hos. 5.3).

Samaria was a harlot. In many fifth-century circles the avenging zeal
of the brothers would have been judged right. Ephraim, instead of
being reckoned a brother sharing in the same covenant, was counted
as a stranger, an enemy. But Numbers always counts Ephraim as a
member of the congregation of Israel. The Genesis story of Simeon
and Levi's slaughter of the men of Shechem accumulates meaning as
the centuries unfold.

After he has cursed Reuben, Simeon and Levi, Jacob gives Judah a
long, complex blessing. Enigmatic it may be,[2] but the blessing
definitely promises Judah power, kingship, and authority (Gen. 49.8-
12). Jacob makes short blessings for the next six of his sons, Zebulun,
Issachar, Dan, Gad, Asher, Napthali. Joseph's blessing is as long and
enigmatic as Judah's and also promises him power and prosperity,
Benjamin's is brief and unpropitious. When he has finished giving
instructions about his own burial, Jacob draws up his feet on to the
bed, and dies. From the fifth-century perspective the deathbed blessing
on Joseph is a blessing on Ephraim, because Ephraim is all that is left
of Joseph's house. Ephraim has also had an earlier separate blessing
(Gen. 48.14-20) in which Jacob foretold that he would be the senior
house of Joseph. After saying, 'In thee shall Israel bless, saying, God
make thee as Ephraim and Manasseh', he set Ephraim in front of
Manasseh (Gen. 48.20). Then in a veiled aside Jacob made a special
bequest of Shechem to Joseph:

---

1. Num. 25.10-11; 31.1-2.
2. Aaron Wildavsky considers all the blessings by Jacob on his sons to be
spiked with unfavourable double meanings (*Assimilation*).

Moreover, I have given to you, rather than to your brothers, one mountain slope [Hebrew, *šĕkem*, shoulder, slope of a hill] which I took from the hand of the Amorites with my sword and my bow (Gen. 48.22).

So Jacob tried to cover the original breach with Shechem even at the very end. His anger gains new interest in Numbers' cross-referencing the names of Simeon, Levi and their sister. The Numbers poet is saying, in terms that would be easily understood by his contemporaries, that the story of Dinah and her treacherous brothers is still with us, in the same way as the story of the wandering in the desert is still with us, and the exile in Egypt. Furthermore, Jacob's blessings all come true, as well as his curses. It would be dangerous to disregard his homily.

The diagram that God drew with the tribes standing around the tabernacle in chs. 1–4 says allegorically that they are all heirs to the promises made by God to Abraham. This is the central lesson of Numbers. Now we understand the frequent enumerations of tribes. The repeated lists of names are not unessential embellishment but the core. The story of Shechem adds a powerful corollary: anyone who covenants to worship the God of Abraham, whether or not descended from Abraham, is not to be attacked as the men of Shechem, but treated as an honourable ally. There is one more corollary: what about the peoples descended from Abraham but not keeping the same faith? These would be the Arab peoples descended from Ishmael and from Esau, Jacob's own brother. Numbers takes up the latter point.

4. *Jacob and Esau*

Immediately after the miracle of water out of the rock at Meribah (20.14), Moses sent a brotherly salute to the king of Edom, politely asking for safe passage through his territory. The request was met with point blank refusal, twice (Num. 20.18, 20). What did Moses do? Did he fight? Did he complain? What he did was to take the people of Israel the long way round. If we are in doubt as to what to make of this, a pattern of further encounters of the same kind guides the reading. After Edom's refusal and threat of attack, Aaron dies (20.23-29). Then follow three attacks on Israel by Canaanite kings. In one of these the same pattern of request and refusal is repeated:

Israel Requests Passage

Edom		*Amorites*
1st request 20.14-17	2nd request 20.19	Only request 21.21-22
Request refused 20.18	Second request refused, 20.20	Request refused 21.21-23
Threatened attack	Threatened attack	Threatened attack 21.23
	Israel retreats 21.21	Israel fights, victorious. 21.24ff.

Between the requests to Edom there is an attack on Israel by Arad, a Canaanite king in the Negeb (21.1). Israel vowed a vow to the Lord; the vow is like a sacred contract in which Israel asks for this enemy to be delivered up and promises in return to destroy them utterly (21.2-3). The ensuing military engagements with the king of Arad and King Basham of Og (21.33-35) each end in victory for Israel and complete destruction for the Canaanite enemies. Israel's vowed bargain is fulfilled on both sides of the transaction.

On the other hand, Moses' peaceful response to Edom, made conspicuous by his armed victories in the other cases, recalls Genesis and another earlier episode in Jacob's story. Edom is Esau, the older brother whom Jacob supplanted in the matter of the blessing and birthright and who planned to kill him (Gen. 27.41-42). Later, when the brothers meet, Jacob is afraid because Esau comes out in force; Jacob concedes to Esau's show of arms by sending gifts, the brothers embrace, Esau forgives Jacob the old wrong and they part with exchange of gifts (Gen. 33.1-16). So when Moses greets Edom with a message from 'your brother Israel', when he humbly accepts Edom's rebuff, when he concedes to Edom by going round his territory, he is re-enacting the patriarch's encounter with his brother. At the same time, the bloody victories over the Canaanites fulfil Noah's thrice-repeated prophecy (Gen. 9.25-27) that Canaan would be cursed and a slave to his brothers.

Moses's respectful behaviour towards Edom fulfils other prophecies, those of God to Abraham, Isaac and Jacob, that their descendants would be his people. The book of Numbers at this point shows that the reckoning is complete, the vows have been honoured, God's plan for Israel is fulfilled. The story is about to introduce Balaam, the prophet whose mouth lets out the same stream of ancient prophecies which we have been discussing. It would not have been very difficult to read the lesson of these patterned encounters for the politics of the day. However, there is more to the story of Miriam than a political homily.

5. Flesh Half-Consumed

Miriam's leprosy has to be taken seriously. Leprosy is the figure for false gods, idolatry and death. Its full meaning in Numbers needs a parallel commentary on leprosy as dealt with in Leviticus. In default of this commentary, we can only hold to the poetic structure for guide in plunging into more profound theological depths. From what we have seen so far of the principles of composition, it cannot be a trivial point that when Aaron asks Moses to intercede for Miriam, he describes her leprous condition as 'flesh half-consumed, as a foetus putrefied in the womb' (12.12). Observe that her half-consumed flesh matches the flesh of the quails which had only been half-eaten, because the Lord smote the people with a plague, 'while the flesh was yet between their teeth, before it was chewed' (11.33). The metaphors of 'flesh' and 'consuming' make further links between two parts of the fifth rung. The word used here for 'meat' and for 'flesh' are the same; likewise the word for burning and the word for eating. Some elaborate verbal play is being deployed in the story sections and why Miriam was described as one whose flesh was half-consumed becomes an important question.

Although the pattern of the book is based on the five horizontal rungs and the one vertical link, this main armature is not the only compositional form used. Rings of transforming metaphor spread across the four story sections. Each is announced by three repetitions of a key word from whose imagery a flow of verses takes off in a spiral of transformations carrying over several rungs. We have seen how efficiently the frame of twelve sections holds the book together in parallel halves. Another lighter structure runs across and between the firm armature, rings of metaphor which do not provide a rigid framework. They do not compare in strength of holding power to the strict halving and quartering of the twelve sections. Rather, the pattern of cross-referencing key metaphors makes verbal pyrotechnics all over the text. This secondary principle of rhetorical organization needs a good knowledge of Hebrew language to be elicited. Yet its surface embroidery over the other structure is clear enough from the English translations. The play upon 'consuming fire' and 'flesh consumed' will illustrate how these metaphors create a web of concordances to sustain the meaning of Miriam's leprosy.

To recapitulate: in section V the first rebellion of the people rouses the anger of the Lord, which is transformed into a consuming fire (11.1-3). In the second revolt, the Lord sends quails for the people to eat (11.31), but while the flesh is still between their teeth (half-consumed) his anger is roused and he sends a plague (11.33). In the third revolt Miriam is turned into flesh half-consumed (12.12). The fourth revolt is ended with the curse of forty years and the fiery glory of the Lord appears (14.10-13) as he is about to disinherit them. Summarizing the play with this metaphor in the first set: the people complain and the fire of the Lord consumes the people; the people ask for flesh, and are about to consume it, but the Lord's plague consumes them; his anger makes Miriam like half-consumed flesh. Then the play upon flesh half or fully consumed is temporarily dropped to be picked up again and inverted in the other section of the same rung: the people half consume the flying winged flesh (quails). In section IX flying fiery serpents consume the people's flesh. Then Moses makes a bronze flying serpent to cure the people who were bitten.

Section V
1st set, on consuming fire:
    A. People complain at Taberah
            C. Fire of the Lord consumes 11.1
    A1. People cry out
        B. Moses intercedes 11.2
            C1. Fire abated 11.3

2nd set, on flesh consumed:
    A. People weep for flesh in Egypt 11.4-15
        B. Moses complains 11.10-15
            C. God sends winged flesh 11.31
    A1. People halfway through consuming flesh 11.33
            C1. God's wrath kindled, sends plague 11.33

3rd set, Miriam half-consumed:
    A. Miriam complains to Moses 12.1-2
        B. Moses meek, 12.3
            C. The Lord angry in pillar of cloud 12.4-9
            1. Miriam, her flesh half-consumed, 12.9-12
        B1. Moses intercedes, 12.13
            C2. Lord relents, penalty modified, 12.14-15

Section VII

In the climax of Korah's rebellion, after the earthquake has swallowed the rebels of Korah's household (16.32), the people fled, 'Lest the earth swallow us up' (16.34), and 'Fire came forth from the Lord and consumed the two hundred and fifty men offering the incense' (16.35). Then follows the dramatic scene in which Aaron saves the people and stops the plague by making atonement with holy fire from the altar. The poetic structure by making parallels with different kinds of swallowing and consuming has made a place for a similar metaphoric play upon fiery serpents in the next section.

Section IX

A. people complain for food in Egypt (21.4-5)
    C. God sends fiery winged serpents to chastise (21.6)
A1. Fiery winged serpents bite and kill the people
    B. People repent
        1. Moses intercedes
        C1. Bronze winged serpent saves the people

Across these two sections the two themes weave chiastically: winged flesh for the people to consume crossing over with winged fire to consume the people, in both cases only half-consumed. Given the artfulness with which this trail is laid, the bronze serpent in Numbers suggests itself for a parallel to the molten calf in Exodus. These passages place the molten serpent in the context of fire. The winged fiery serpents which were biting the people's flesh have replaced the winged flesh which the people were biting in section V. The bronze serpent does not consume, and it is held up in an act of benediction. The bronze serpent concludes the sequence which started with the burning bush in Exodus, and the rod-serpent of Moses' miracle before Pharaoh; and since serpent is associated with divination, it makes ready for the true oracle of Balaam, in which the Lord says: 'There is no enchantment in Jacob, no divination in Israel' (Num. 23.23). Finally, in the third quarter, the burning anger of the Lord, which has been kindled against the people of Israel and been diverted before it has consumed them altogether, is turned against the Canaanites and the enemy; Moab and Heshbon are consumed with fire (21.28, 30).

The fire metaphors are free poetic forms, connecting up the sides of the book that have been separated according to the stable structure of parallel sections. Whereas the alternating of law and story interrupts, the fire metaphors give continuity. One can compare them to a jazz musician's improvisations on the main melody. They are like musical improvisations which take off from an existing form, depart from it a little, return and innovate upon it. Once they have been invented, they create the terms upon which the rest of the music will grow. So it is with the fire metaphors in the book of Numbers. These rings of metaphors with their witty inversions enhance the fixed structure by working within the form already laid down.

The primary pattern of the book holds the message of the covenant: the promises to Abraham, Isaac and Jacob, and the demand that the people be entirely committed to the cult, its holy feast days and the aniconic god. Many things seem difficult in the text if interpreted without reference to the secondary poetic structures of fire and flesh. In their presence, Miriam's story affords a glimpse of theological reflections on life and death. Leprosy in the Bible is equated with idolatry, and idolatry is equated with death; here is Miriam, suspended miserably between living and dying, her flesh half-consumed. Later in the story Aaron is to stand triumphantly between the living and the dead, the midpoint between the consumed and the not consumed. The context is after the rebellion of Korah, when the congregation murmured against Moses and Aaron for killing the people. Responding to this last attack on Moses's spiritual authority, the Lord appeared in glory, and told Moses and Aaron to get out of the way so that he could consume the congregation of the people of Israel. But Moses told Aaron to make atonement for them with fire from the altar. Aaron's greatest moment in the whole Bible is when, boldly swinging the censers with God's holy fire, he caused the plague to abate. Surrounded by the dead on one side, and by the living on the other, by fire he cancelled the moment of weakness when he followed Miriam in challenging Moses. Looking back down the story from this vantage point, after following all the permutations of consuming winged serpents and winged meat for consuming, the theme is too central theologically for Miriam, with her flesh half-consumed like one dead, to be a woman who is publicly disgraced. She is indubitably passionate, impulsive, vulnerable Israel. No wonder she is such a revered and beloved figure in Jewish tradition. When she was put outside the camp like a leper that has to be cleansed, the people of Israel postponed their journeying until she was brought in again (12.15).

NOTE ON SERAPHIM AND FIERY SERPENTS

David Goodman

The passage Num. 21.4-9 contains a number of interconnected uses of the Hebrew root *nḥš*. It refers to four terms:

1) *han-nĕḥāšîm haś-śĕrāpîm*
2) *han-nāḥāš*
3) *śārāp*
4) *nĕḥāš nĕḥōšet* (*nĕḥāš han-nĕḥōšet*)

Note also the assonance with *nḥš* in the use of the word *nēs*, 'standard, pole' and the common verbal root *nšk*, 'to bite' in the context of the serpents.

> From Mount Hor they set out by the way to the Red Sea, to go around the land of Edom and the people became impatient on the way.
> And the people spoke against God and against Moses, 'Why have you brought us up out of Egypt to die in the wilderness? For there is no food and no water, and we loathe this worthless food.'
> Then the Lord sent fiery serpents (*han-nĕḥāšîm haś-śĕrāpîm*) among the people, and they bit the people, so that many people of Israel died.
> And the people came to Moses, and said, 'We have sinned, for we have spoken against the Lord and against you; pray to the Lord, that he take away the serpents (*han-nāḥāš*) from us.'
> And the Lord said to Moses, 'Make a fiery serpent (*śārāp*), and set it on a pole; and every one who is bitten, when he sees it, shall live.'
> So Moses made a bronze serpent (*nĕḥaš nĕḥōšet*), and set it on a pole; and if a serpent (*han-nāḥāš*) bit any man, he would look at the bronze serpent (*nĕḥaš han-nĕḥōšet*) and live (21.4-9).

This serpent is referred to again in Isaiah's account of Hezekiah's reforms:

> He removed the high places, and broke the pillars, and cut down the Asherah. And he broke in pieces the bronze serpent (*nĕḥaš han-nĕḥōšet*) that Moses had made for until those days the people of Israel had burned incense to it; it was called Nehushtan (*nĕḥuštān*) (2 Kgs 18.4).

The name *nĕḥuštān* apparently derived from *nāḥāš* is a hapax legomenon. The three clear root meanings of the root *nḥš* are well-attested in other Semitic languages:

1. serpent (app. onomat.) [Ar. cogn]
2. to practise divination, divine, observe signs [Aram. cogn.]
3. copper, bronze [Ar., Eth., Ph., Palm.]

The word *nāḥāš* 'divination, enchantment' is found twice in the Hebrew Bible. Both of these occurrences are in Numbers, and both in relation to the Balaam story:

> For there is no enchantment (*nāḥāš*) against Jacob, no divination (*qesem*) against Israel (Num. 23.23).

and in the plural absolute form:

> When Balaam saw that it pleased the Lord to bless Israel, he did not go, as at other times to look for omens (*nĕḥāšīm*), but set his face toward the wilderness (Num. 24.1).

The idea of 'flying serpents' occurs in Isaiah in several contexts. First in an imprecation against the Philistines:

> Rejoice not, O Philistia, all of you, that the rod (*šēbeṭ*) which smote you is broken, for from the serpent's root (*miš-šōreš nāḥāš*) will come forth an adder, (*ṣepaʻ*) and its fruit will be a flying serpent (*śārāp mĕʻōpēp*) (Isa. 14.28).

In this passage, the word *ṣepaʻ* is a biblical hapax legomenon of an unknown root, and is thought to be loosely associated with *ṣipʻōnī*, which is found in several biblical passages and considered to be a kind of venomous viper. A parallel of these two words referring to snakes is found in a passage in Jeremiah:

> 'For behold I am sending among you serpents, adders (*nĕḥāšīm ṣipʻōnīm*), which cannot be charmed (*lāḥaš*) and shall bite you', says the Lord (Jer. 8.17).

The word *lāḥaš* is not common and is usually found in the context of snake-charming:

> The captain of fifty and the man of rank, the counsellor and the skilful magical and the expert in charms (*ū-nĕbōn lāḥaš*) (Isa. 3.3).

Note the reference in Isaiah (59.5), and to the flying serpent:

> An oracle on the beasts of the Negev.
> Through a land of trouble and anguish, from where come the lion and lioness, the viper (*ʼepʻeh*) and the flying serpent (*wĕ-śārāp mĕʻōpēp*), they carry their riches on the backs of asses (Isa. 30.6).

The most famous association of the idea of 'seraphim' and 'flying' comes in Isaiah's vision of the divine throne:

> Then flew one of the seraphim (*min haś-śĕrāpīm*) to me, having in his hand a burning coal (Isa. 6.6).

A fuller description of the seraphim is given earlier:

> Above him stood the seraphim (*śĕrāpīm*; each had six wings: with two he covered his face, and with two he covered his feet, and with two he flew (*yĕ'ōpēp* (Isa. 6.2).

The Numbers passage seems to strike a difference between the two expressions: *han-nāḥāš* and *nĕḥāš nĕḥōset*. In Num. 21.9, is it the *nĕḥāš nĕḥōset* which is on the pole/standard whereas *han-nāḥāš* bites the people. Similarly it seems that *śārāp* in 21.8 is intended to be synonymous with *nĕḥāš nĕḥōset*. The passage appears then to be a part of a derivation of the historicity of the presence of *śĕrāpīm/nĕḥāšīm* in the Temple.

There is some curiously witty reference present here, revolving around the three possible interpretations of the root *nḥš* and presumably must also include *nĕḥūštan*.

Chapter 12

BALAAM AND BALAK: A POLITICAL SATIRE

1. *The Story*

God is not a man, that he should lie, or a son of man, that he should
repent. Has he said, and he will not do it? Or has he spoken, and will he
not fulfil it? (Num. 23.19).

These words, given to the foreign prophet, Balaam, state the underlying message of Numbers: what God has said will come true. And the
book will tell you just what he said. As I have argued so far, the substance of the book is a major theological statement about the ancient
promises, about the congregation included in them, about defilement
and the role of intention in defining sin. By now we know that though
Numbers uses its chiastic structures and parallels to embellish the text,
turns themes around and does somersaults with curses and blessings, it
never loses control of its project. We should not be slow to recognize
the story of Balaam (Num. 22–24) as a play within the play. It is a
whole story nested within a whole story, the smaller referring to the
larger, and the larger referring to the life of the day. That the story is
a satire is generally agreed, but who is being satirized, and why, is not
usually discussed. The interpretation I will offer continues the vein
already started: the book of Numbers is being edited in an enclave
culture, a community rife with factions. Criticism of authority is all
too likely, but a carnival of turning right-way-up into upside-down is
unlikely, though possible in a hierarchy. One should remember that
Numbers is compiled by members of a priestly hierarchy, and that I
have argued throughout that the editors would not have been
politically neutral. The story of Balaam satirizes the colonial
governor, ruling with a big stick.

The story begins with King Balak seeing the victories of the armies
of Moses in the plains of Moab and feeling threatened. He sends messengers with fees in their hand to engage a master magician to put a

magic curse on Israel. Balaam, on receiving their message, does not go with them at once, but says that he first must consult the Lord. (Apparently, uniquely in the Bible, but essential to the story, the foreign prophet recognizes the same Lord as Israel.) In the night God tells Balaam not to go with the king's messengers, and not to curse the people, because they are blessed (Num. 22.12). Everyone who read Numbers would know who blessed them. The covenants between God and Abraham are blessings, the angel of the Lord blessed Abraham (Gen. 22.17), God blessed Isaac for Abraham's sake (Gen. 26.2-5; 24). The reference to the foundation stories for the great blessings on Israel should take the interpretation of this story back to Genesis.

Next morning Balaam declines to go with the messengers and they duly report back to Balak. He sends more messengers of nobler rank and promises all kinds of honour if Balaam will just come and curse this people for him (Num. 22.17). To this Balaam gives the exemplary answer of a God-fearing man:

> Though Balak were to give me his house full of silver and gold, I could not go beyond the command of the Lord my God, to do less or more (Num. 22.18).

But we can already tell that he has weakened, for he tells them to stay overnight so that he can consult the Lord again. In the night the Lord comes to him and gives him these instructions:

> If the men have come to call you, rise, go with them; but only what I bid you, that shall you do (Num. 22.20).

Evidently they do ask him again in the morning, for he saddles his ass and goes with the princes of Moab. God is angry with him; why he is angry is not revealed to us. One traditional interpretation is that God could read Balaam's heart and knew that Balaam was secretly determined to get the fees for cursing Israel, as proved later in the story. This would make everything that Balaam says about his obedience to the will of God a set of lies. After he sets off, accompanied by two servants, the ass sees the angel of the Lord barring her path and refuses to budge. Neither Balaam nor his servants nor the Moabite princes see the angel. Three times Balaam beats the ass and three times she tries to avoid the angel which she sees standing there with a drawn sword. Finally she has recourse to the age-old donkey's protest: she lies down under him. Her master furiously strikes her again and threatens to kill her. The animal's mouth is opened and she uses human speech to say reproachfully:

What have I done to you, that you have struck me these three times?

Balaam is apparently not surprised that she should speak, and enters into an argument with her:

Because you have made sport of me. I wish I had a sword in my hand, for then I would kill you.

But the ass reproaches him again, reminds him of her life-long record of faithfulness, implying that only something very extraordinary has stopped her from obeying him this time. But he rejects her excuse (22.30); whereupon the angel of the Lord reveals himself and asks Balaam why he has struck his ass three times. He, the angel, says that she turned aside three times because she saw him (the angel). To cap it all, he adds if the ass had not done so, he would have killed Balaam, and, ultimate surprise, he would have spared the ass (22.33). Balaam makes abject apology, but we know the end of the story so we know that he is not sincere. In the upshot, the angel lets Balaam go on with his journey, but he repeats the words of the night before: Go with the men, but only the word which I bid you, that shall you do (22.35).

Balaam goes on, meets King Balak, and warns him that he is only going to speak the words that God puts into his mouth. Balak takes Balaam to some point of vantage, prepares a sacrifice, and Balaam goes on to a hill alone to meet God, who puts his word into his mouth. Three times commanded to curse the people of Israel, three times Balaam utters a magnificent blessing (23.7-10, 18-24; 24.3-9). Three times King Balak is angry, and the last time Balaam answers him again in the words of his greeting, that he would not, for any amount of gold or silver, be able to go beyond the word of the Lord (24.13). This happens to be true, since God speaks through him. Before going home he gives three more oracles, all in high poetry, in the same vein, praising and blessing Israel and foretelling the downfall of Moab, and other enemies of Israel (24.15-24). The story ends with each of them going back to his own place (24.25). Much later we learn from Moses that he taught the women of Moab to deceive the men of Israel, and for that was killed on the field of battle (31.8, 16).

Balaam uttered blessings on Israel, but has received nothing but execration from posterity, both Christian and Jewish. He has gone down in history as the corrupt magician, the perfidious prophet who would have sold Israel to the armies of Moab, had it not been that God circumvented his wiles. Joshua gives no credit to Balaam for having said blessings:

> Then Balak the son of Zippur, king of Moab, arose and fought against Israel; and he sent and invited Balaam the son of Beor to curse you, but I would not listen to Balaam; therefore he blessed you; so I delivered you out of his hand (Josh. 24.9-10).

And Deuteronomy likewise insinuates that he did say something against Israel, to which God refused to listen:

> They hired against you Balaam the son of Beor from Pethor of Mesopotamia to curse you. Nevertheless, the Lord your God would not hearken to Balaam; but the Lord your God turned the curse into a blessing for you, because the Lord your God loved you (Deut. 23.4-5).

But as far as we are told, Balaam never uttered any curse. Peter counted him among false prophets:

> They have followed the way of Balaam, the son of Beor, who loved gain from wrong doing, but was rebuked for his own transgression; a dumb ass spoke with human voice and restrained the prophet's madness (2 Pet. 2.15-16).

Jude wrote:

> Woe to them! For they walk in the way of Cain, and abandon themselves for the sake of gain to Balaam's error, and perish in Korah's rebellion (Jude 11).

In Revelation Balaam is denounced among others dwelling near Satan's throne:

> Balaam, who taught Balak to put a stumbling block before the sons of Israel, that they might eat food sacrificed to idols and practice immorality (Rev. 2.14).

When did he do this teaching of Balak? We are never told. The only exception is Micah who links Balaam to the greatest prophets of Israel (Mic. 6.3-5).

Balaam's behaviour in the story is enigmatic, to say the least. Commentators have argued as to whether he is to be regarded as a saint or as a sinner, and whether the moral ambiguity is to be attributed to different historical layers in the editorial process.[1] But

---

1. Milgrom, *Numbers*, pp. 469-71.

the complete change of style suggests that the moral standing of the central figure is not the main issue.

To listeners or viewers in the fifth century BCE (one must add viewers because it is such a natural for performance) the character of Balaam would have been obviously bad from near to the beginning. We miss the clue if we do not pay attention to the words: 'This people are blessed'. If the people of Israel are blessed by the Lord, nothing that anyone can do in the way of magic or cursing can undo the blessing. When Balaam goes to consult with the Lord after the second relay of messengers has come to persuade him to go with them, all that we hear of the conversation is that the Lord said, Go, but if you go, you will only do what I put in your mouth. Take this seriously, and it means, Go, if you must, but you will never be able to make a curse (Num. 22.20). Normally, given the meaning of blessing and cursing, the conversation between Balaam and the Lord would have taken the form of Balaam asking if the people of Israel are really blessed. And if they are really blessed, would the Lord consider lifting his blessing for a few days? Or we can surmise that Balaam would have been too clever to dare such a gambit with the Lord. But when he reports back that he will go with the men to King Balak, anyone knowing what a blessing entails would recognize his deceit and his love of gain. His evil moral character is not in doubt. The important matter lies elsewhere.

The story is set apart from the rest of the narrative of Moses in several ways. It is staged in a charmed world governed by three-times-three: the men invite Balaam to go to Moab three times, the ass turns aside three times, she is struck three times, the king invites Balaam to curse three times (22.36-37; 23.13, 27), and he blesses three times, while a fourth blessing has three parts (24.15-24). By these means we are alerted that this is an exceptional insertion in the book.

There are strong echoes from the story of Micaiah who always prophesied evil to the king of Israel (1 Kgs 22.9). There is the close similarity between the beginning of Balaam's dealings with Balak and the beginning of Elijah's dealings with King Ahazia, also at war with Moab in 2 Kings 1. In both cases the bad king sends his messengers to the prophet, in both cases the prophet twice refuses to go with them and when, the third time, he does go, the king who sought to employ him comes to a disastrous end. The story also has perverse echoes of Elisha's delivery of the king of Moab into the hands of Israel (2 Kgs

3.13-27). The style of those narratives is epic, but Balaam's story reads as a humorous sketch. If God seems to behave capriciously, telling Balaam to go with the men and then being angry with him when he goes, it may be that something has been taken for granted, something omitted because the Lord's action has had to be compressed by the three-by-three fairy tale conventions. Balaam certainly behaves badly to his faithful ass. Apart from beating her, and conversing with her, it must be absurd to threaten a mare with death by the sword because she is making her rider ridiculous (22.29). Nothing in the story is so peculiar as the donkey's gift of speech. The only other animal to use human speech in the whole of the Bible is the serpent in the garden of Eden; but this time the speaking animal is working with God. Her dignified protest contrasts with Balaam's fury. She does make Balaam a figure of fun. To be sitting on an animal which lies down is embarrassing, but when the animal turns round and rebukes her master in human speech, that begins to be farce; and when the master angrily enters into dialogue with her, that is broad slapstick. The angel of the Lord tells Balaam that his life has been saved by his God-fearing ass: what an undignified rescue for the famous sage. On this reading Balaam is a comic figure, and the story is a satire. Who is the butt of the satire?

2. Balaam's Prophecies

Someone is being parodied, someone who negotiates with kings, who claims to speak in the name of the Lord, but who disovers that he can do nothing except as the instrument of God. Who in this pantomime would Balak be? The name Balak could mean destruction. A conquering emperor, Nebuchadnezzar or the king of Persia, is a likely candidate. If we know where to look for the king, who is the model for the prophet who came from afar? The name Balaam could be interpreted as 'lord of the people': a likely candidate would be the governor of Judah, who came all the way from the king of Persia's court. Who is the female animal who has carried him uncomplainingly, and whom he beats and threatens with a sword? Would it be the patient people of Israel? This will seem plausible when we consider what prophecy-laden words God put into Balaam's mouth.

Just before Balaam comes on the scene, Israel's armies have routed the Canaanites at Hormah (21.3), destroyed King Sihon, and taken

Jazer and Bashan. Now camped on the border of Moab, their menacing presence has made King Balak afraid (22.3). After the Balaam episode there are various intervening materials in Numbers before we hear of his death. The military story picks up again when God calls the people of Israel to make war on the Midianites, they slay five kings of Midian, and also Balaam (31.8). His prophecies come right in the middle of Israel's victorious campaigns against the Amorites and the people of Canaan. Israel is taking by arms the land that God promised when he blessed Abraham and Isaac in Genesis.

We should not expect to find anything random or careless about Balaam's prophecies. The first blessing he utters repeats comprehensively the words of God's promises to Abraham and Jacob: he sees 'a people dwelling alone, and not reckoning itself among the nations: who can count the dust of Jacob or number the fourth part of Israel?' (Num. 23.10; Gen. 28.14). Balak complains that he hired Balaam to curse his enemies, and he has done nothing but bless them (Num. 23.11).

Next time Balaam utters an amalgam of the blessings of Jacob on Judah and Joseph:

> The Lord their God is with them, and the shout of a king is among them. God brings them out of Egypt; they have as it were, the horns of the wild ox. For there is no enchantment in Jacob, no divination in Israel; now it shall be said of Jacob and Israel, What has God wrought! Behold, a people! As a lioness it rises up and as a lion it lifts itself; it does not lie down till it devours the prey and drinks the blood of the slain (Num. 23.21-24).

When Balaam opens his mouth to bless the people of Israel, God puts into it the words of Jacob's dying blessings. Enough to make Balak tremble if he understood, the words are a straight repetition of Jacob's blessings on his sons:

> Judah is a lion's whelp; from the prey, my son, you have gone up. He stooped down, he couched as a lion, and as a lioness; who dares rouse him? (Gen. 49.9).

The reference to 'horns of the wild ox' come from Moses' blessing on Joseph:

Let these come upon the head of Joseph, and upon the crown of the head of him that is prince among his brothers. His firstling bull has majesty, and his horns are the horns of a wild ox; with them he shall push the peoples, all of them, to the ends of the earth; such are the ten thousands of Ephraim, and such are the thousands of Manasseh (Deut. 33.16-17).

The Moabite king now takes Balaam to have a third try from the top of Peor that overlooks the desert. Balaam lifts up his eyes and sees Israel camping, 'tribe by tribe', presumably in the order which has been decreed in the beginning of Numbers. He says:

How fair are your tents, O Jacob, your encampments, O Israel! Like valleys that stretch afar, like gardens beside a river, like aloes that the Lord has planted, like cedar trees beside the waters. Water shall flow from his buckets, and his seed shall be in many waters, his kingdom higher than Agag, and his kingdom shall be exalted. God brings him out of Egypt; and he has, as it were, the horns of the wild ox, he shall eat up the nations his adversaries, and shall break their bones in pieces, and pierce them through with arrows. He couched, he lay down like a lion, and like a lioness; who will rouse him up? Blessed be everyone who blesses you and cursed be everyone who curses you (Num. 24.5-9).

Another laugh for the soldiers of Israel massed on the border of Moab, for in these last words Balaam has dared to repeat in King Balak's hearing God's very first words to Abraham:

And I will bless them that bless you, and curse him that curses you (Gen. 12.3).

Again there is the lion; and again the horns of the wild ox; the valleys and gardens and waters are from Jacob's blessing on Joseph: a fruitful bough by a spring, whose branches run over the wall (Gen. 49.22).[1]

Balak now dismisses Balaam in anger, and Balaam retorts with a final oracle which curses Moab, Edom, Amalek and the Kenites, and

---

1. Eric Burrows notes that even when Balaam uses Jacob's curses they are turned into blessings. Reuben's sin, which earned the curse of his father, was to make his semen flow in his father's bed; Jacob cursed him for a watery effusion, an outpouring of water; in Balaam's mouth the same curse associates Reuben with some proto-zodiacal forerunner of Aquarius, a star seen as giant water-pourer, source of fertility. The strife and misdeeds that Jacob condemned are turned by Balaam's words into beneficent stars, a move very congenial to the style of Numbers which brings the quarrelling brothers into a harmonious group around the tabernacle (*The Oracles of Jacob and Balaam* [Bellarmine Series; London: Burns Oates & Washbourne, 1938]).

foretells the destruction of the Assyrian empire. In the same speech he gives the famous messianic prophecy:

> A star shall come forth out of Jacob, and a sceptre shall rise out of Israel; it shall crush the forehead of Moab and break down all the sons of Sheth (24.17).

Reading Balaam's prophecies without close attention to the cryptic words in Genesis 49, the first interpretation is that Balaam has simply repeated the messianic prophecy to Judah. Jacob said:

> The sceptre shall not depart from Judah, nor the ruler's staff from between his feet (Gen. 49.10).

This is traditionally read as the prophecy of David's kingdom. But Balaam has not repeated it word for word. Jacob actually said the sceptre was for Judah, and reserved a different blessing for Joseph; Balaam has said that the sceptre was in Israel, comprising Joseph and Judah. For the anti-separatist party that would be a highly significant change. Jacob was even-handed in blessing the two houses, Joseph and Judah, but Balaam has combined the blessings on the two houses into one. This is not a slip on his part. One of his rhetorical turns is to name both Jacob and Israel, the one whenever he names the other:

> Come curse Jacob, come denouce Israel! (Num. 23.7).
> He has not beheld divination in Jacob, nor has he seen trouble in Israel (23.21, repeated in 23).
> How fair are your tents, O Jacob, your encampments, O Israel (24.5).

When Balaam uses the word Israel it is never in contrast with Judah. Israel, in his speeches, means Jacob's progeny. The blessing that falls from his mouth is a blessing for the whole of Jacob, that is, for the whole of Israel.[1] Balaam never mentions Judah, but he always puts Israel and Jacob together.

Zechariah prayed for a joint triumph to include both Judah and Joseph, but always distinguished them: whenever he said one name he followed with the name of the other:

> You were a curse among the nations, O house of Judah, and house of Israel (Zech. 8.13).
> The brotherhood between Judah and Israel (Zech. 11.14).

---

1. H.G.M. Williamson's chapter on the usage in Chronicles of the word 'Israel' supports the analysis offered here (*Israel in the Book of Chronicles* [Cambridge: Cambridge University Press, 1977], ch. 7).

Zechariah continually kept Judah and Joseph in balanced apposition:

> And I will cut off the chariot from Ephraim and the horse from Jerusalem (Zech. 9.10).
> And I will strengthen the house of Judah and I will save the house of Joseph (Zech. 10.6).

For him the pair are as complementary as bow and arrow:

> When I have bent Judah for me, filled the bow with Ephraim (Zech. 9.13).

Zechariah looked forward to the day when all the nations that came against Jerusalem 'would even go up from year to year to worship the King, the Lord of hosts, and to keep the feast of tabernacles' (Zech. 14.16). All the nations! Numbers has enough to do to keep the door open for the twelve sons of Jacob.

3. *Ezra/Nehemiah in Factional Perspective*

The Balaam episode is a political lampoon against someone in authority with a big stick. There are plenty of reasons why the Numbers poet should want to lampoon the governor. Two morals in the Balaam story cover the whole case. The dominating theological theme of Numbers is that God controls events. King Balak wrongly thought that he could divert the effects of the curses and prophecies by buying magic, Balaam wrongly thought he could deceive God. At the time of his speaking the blessings, Balaam had lost control over what he said, he was only an instrument of God. Later he tried to earn his money from Balak by seducing the people of Israel to the worship of Baal, but though he sinned and met his due punishment neither what he did nor what the Israelites did made the smallest dint in the realization of God's plan. The second moral is about the unity of Israel: by his mouth God says how beautiful is the order of their camps, all their camps, because Balaam has seen them from three aspects. All his blessings are for Israel as a whole. Although Balaam succeeds in dividing them through the wiles of the Moabite women, the Lord treats them as a single unit. To priestly eyes the failure of the governor would be the same as the failure of Balaam, not to have recognized God's angel barring the path with a sword.

A good place to start justifying the theory of Balaam as a political parody is the quotation from Numbers made by Nehemiah himself.

The colonial governor uses the hiring of Balaam to curse Israel to justify a rule that 'Ammonite and Moabite should not come into the congregation of God for ever' (Neh. 13.1). The reference is not to Numbers but to Deuteronomy (23.3), where it is said that Ammon and Moab did not meet Israel with bread and with water but hired Balaam to curse Israel. Deuteronomy earlier had said that Esau and Moab dealt hospitably with the people of Israel, claiming that the king of Heshbon should also have been equally generous in giving them bread and water (Deut. 2.26-29). In the Numbers' story Moses did offer to pay for water if Edom would grant them safe transit through that kingdom, but Edom refused (Num. 21.14-21). No mention of expecting bread and water from Moab is found in the Numbers' account of Moses' encounter with Moab, who was not even invited to grant them safe passage and provisions. One can surmise that if he had been given the option Balak was so frightened that he might well have accepted, but Moses did not offer to treat with him and so he called on Balaam's magic instead. Nehemiah has distorted scripture by selecting the exclusionary rule from Deuteronomy, and leaving out Deuteronomy's account in ch. 2 of the pacific encounters of the people of Israel with Esau, Moab and Ammon. In Deuteronomy Moses says that he was explicitly instructed by the Lord not to disturb Esau's people because he has guaranteeed their land to them (Deut. 2.5), and not to disturb the children of Lot (Ammon and Moab) because he has given them their land for a possession (Deut. 2.19).

The discrepant versions of Israel's encounters with their neighbours may be a sign of the factions within the temple community. The stories were presumably being reworked to justify the boundary around the congregation. Deuteronomy's position is unclear, since it was critical of Ammon and Moab in 23.3, where it is said that they did not meet Israel with bread and water, but in 2.29 praised Edom and Moab for doing just that. Nehemiah would exclude Ammon and Moab, as would Numbers if the hostilities in the stories are anything to go by. The book of Ezra would draw the boundary to exclude the 'adversaries of Judah and Benjamin', even though they claimed the same faith and asked to be allowed to help in rebuilding the temple. Who were they? If they were deportees sent by the king of Assyria into Judah as part of his transfer of populations when he conquered the Northern Kingdom, they could well be Samarians. This is how the following passage could be read:

Let us build with you, for we worship your God as you do, and we have been sacrificing to him ever since the days of Esar-haddon, King of Assyria, who brought us here. But Zerubbabel, Jeshua and the rest of the fathers' houses in Israel said to them: You have nothing to do with us in building a house to our God; but we alone will build to the Lord, the God of Israel, as King Cyrus the king of Persia has commanded us (Ezra 4.2-3).

Several interesting things appear in this statement. For one, the claim to brotherhood in religion was blocked by reference not to a religious source but to the king of Persia. For another, the rejection was held to be the beginning of the conspiracies against the government that caused 'the people of the land' to be counted as 'adversaries of Judah' (Ezra 4.4-5). Thirdly, the passage claims that the rejection of these people living in Judah was made by 'all the fathers' houses in Israel'. On this topic the book of Ezra has poor credibility: the rejection may have been made by Zerubbabel and Jeshua, as claimed, but probably not by the rest of the fathers' houses of Israel, only by those who came back from exile.

Williamson explains the policy of rigid exclusion as a tactic necessary for maintaing the provincial government's good standing in the eyes of the Persian authorities:

Positively, they maintain that they alone are the true and legitimate successors of Israel, and that their exclusive claims and rights have been upheld by the very highest Persian authorities; to admit others to their company would jeopardize their legal privileges. Negatively, they regard all foreigners as potentially threatening... they ran the danger of being quickly swamped by the larger numbers of those whose aims and ideals were incompatible with theirs. Unattractive as much of this may seem to us today, it is not hard to sympathise with the fears of an embattled and financially weak community as they sought to maintain against overwhelming odds the distinctiveness and purity of what they believed God had vouchsafed to them.[1]

We have mustered reasons for thinking that Numbers would not exclude Samaria, and also reasons for supposing that the Numbers editors were out of sympathy with government policy. The accounts in the Ezra/Nehemiah source of how the returned exiles refused intermarriage with the people who had always been living in Judah and how they dispossessed them of their lands, and how they did it in the

---

1.   H.G.M. Williamson, *Ezra and Nehemiah* (Old Testament Guides; Sheffield: JSOT Press, 1987), p. 90.

name of religion, would repel any contemporary with a universalist
view of Israel's destiny. Ezra's description of how he established the
hegemony of the returned remnant and his exaggerated sanctimony
would make him an easy target for satire, and Nehemiah would be
even better.

Commentators on Ezra/Nehemiah have been perplexed about the
dating of events in the two books. The contradictions and obscurities
are thought to have been introduced by a later hand. However, knowing that the book is an unreliable source for dating does not prepare
the reader for the sleight of hand that presents deeds of the returning
exiles as actions of the whole congregation. Knowing that this text is
full of obscurities helps to explain how those who had signed Ezra's
covenant to put away their foreign wives came to be thought of as the
whole congregation, and the rest as dissenters, and later as agents of
abomination. After they had built the house of God,

> the people of Israel, the priests and the Levites, and the rest of the
> returned exiles celebrated the dedication of this house (Ezra 7.16)... On
> the fourteenth day of the first month the returned exiles kept the
> Passover... the passover lamb was eaten by the people of Israel who had
> returned from exile, and also by everyone who had joined them and sepa-
> rated himself from the pollutions of the people of the land to worship the
> Lord, the God of Israel (7.19-21).

Ezra has a document from Artaxerxes, the king, empowering him to
appoint magistrates and judges, and giving him authority for life and
death, banishment, imprisonment or confiscation of property, to be
used against anyone who 'will not obey the law of your God' (Ezra
7.25-28). To carry out his responsibilities, Ezra gathers around him
'leading men from Israel', that is leading men who had come with him
from Babylon (7.28).

Shortly after they arrived in Jerusalem the problem of foreign
marriages is introduced. Certain of the leading men complain to the
governor that the people of Israel, lay and clerical, have not
'separated themselves from the people of those lands' and insist that
officials and leading men are foremost transgressors.

The text would need to be ambiguous if it was to make the story of
coercion acceptable to posterity. We are sometimes given the impression that it is all the people of Israel who are joyfully celebrating the
renewal of the cult in Jerusalem, and sometimes told clearly that the
congregation is exclusively composed of the returned exiles (Ezra

6.19-20; 8.35). Nehemiah says that 'all the congregation of them who were come again out of the captivity' celebrated the Feast of Booths (Neh. 8.17-18), and immediately afterwards that 'the children of Israel were assembled with fasting, in sackcloth, and with earth upon them. And the seed of Israel separated themselves from all foreigners and stood and confessed their sins and the iniquities of their fathers' (Neh. 9.1-2). We have only this statement to back the notion that they were separating themselves from foreigners, not from 'the people of the land' (in the sense of the people of Judah who had never left). But it seems a fair reading that only the party of the returnees are being called the 'seed of Israel', and only they enter into a covenant to 'separate themselves from the people of the lands unto the law of God' (Neh. 10.28), and only they make an oath not to 'give their daughters to the people of the land nor take their daughters for their sons' (v. 30).

The scene is a standard accusation of defilement. The accusers are the group allied with the returnees, with the backing of the government of Persia. The accused are presumably the local adversaries who are holding on to the land of the returnees, and are unsound on religious doctrine. If they do not prove their loyalty now, they will be excluded from the congregation, downgraded in their civil status, and lose their land. This is how defilement is used as an accusation the world over. It is a rare account of the declaration of a new taboo by a powerful group which draws a boundary of purity around itself. This is the normal use of defilement in other religous codes of purity. The historic meeting was the point of choice: hereafter a hereditary caste system was going to be sustained by a doctrine of defilement by birth, and there will be no choice for those born on the wrong side of the line.[1]

Num. 33.50 gives instructions for dispossessing completely the inhabitants of the land of Canaan. These pre-Israelite pagans are to be driven out, their stone idols and melted images and their high places to be destroyed. But by the time of redaction many generations of the sons of Jacob had been inhabiting that land; some would have no doubt gone over to pagan ways, others would be traditional worshippers of Israel's God. Numbers makes a great point of intention and repentance in doctrines of sin, and tells how Moses referred accusations to the

---

1. Jeremias, *Jerusalem* pp. 216-18.

judgment of the Lord. Showing a conspicuously different attitude, Ezra/Nehemiah took it on themselves to make political judgments of defilement which would have accorded with populist hostility to ethnic variation.

The argument about the boundary of the congregation that would have been going on would also have had to be an argument about the nature of the religion and about the Jewish destiny. It would have followed on the argument of the seventh century BCE promoting the cult of 'Yahweh alone' against the syncretism and magic of Palestinian practice. Presumably it would have anticipated the controversy between the Sadducees and the Pharisees in the first century about religious universalism and nationalism.[1] It was and always will be a profound theological question, and it is unlikely that the controversy was in abeyance while the Pentateuch was being put into its final form. If there was conflict on these issues in the Second Temple community, the second destruction of the temple destroyed the records and dispersed the priests. The rabbis, when it came to their turn, assumed that the Pentateuch had little to do with politics.[2] There is still a pious convention that a timeless, ahistorical message must have been produced in some timeless, ahistorical way.

4. *Eliashib's Point of View*

What was the high priest doing while the government was redefining the congregation? Nehemiah records the good team work put in by the priests and Levites in building the wall of Jerusalem, and notes that Eliashib the high priest and his brethren did their share (Neh. 3.1). He lists Eliashib in the acceptable genealogy of priests (Neh. 12.10), though he is not in the list of priests that came from Babylon. He mentions Eliashib twice more. Once he accuses him of defiling the temple precinct for the sake of giving lodging to Tobiah, the treacherous collaborator of Sanballat (13.4-9); secondly, he accuses Eliashib of condoning the marriage of his own grandson to the daughter of Sanballat, the governor of Samaria (13.28), two subversive deeds, by

---

1. I. Epstein, *Judaism a Historical Presentation* (Harmondsworth: Pelican, 1959), pp. 95ff.

2. J. Neusner, 'Judaism in a Time of Crisis, Four Responses to the Destruction of the Second Temple', in *Judaism, A Quarterly of Jewish Life and Thought* 21.3 (1972), pp. 313-27.

Nehemiah's reckoning.[1] One should observe that Eliashib's name does not appear in the list of priests who set their seal to the covenant made by all those who had separated themselves from the people of the land (10.1-30). Nor is he named in the list of priests in Jerusalem (11.10-14), or in the lists of those who took part in the great ceremony of dedicating the wall (12.27-42).

Was Eliashib holding himself disapprovingly aloof? Did he organize a priestly protest? Did Eliashib exist at all? Well, there might have been a high priest in Jerusalem before the exiles returned. And yes, there were high priests of that name afterward. It has been suggested rather kindly that the author of the book of Nehemiah just got the generations mixed up.[2] There is reason to doubt whether the Eliashib who befriended Tobiah by giving him the temple storeroom for a lodging could be the same as Eliashib the high priest. It takes a subtle reading to make the distinction: Nehemiah uses the expression 'Eliashib the high priest' when referring to the high priest and for the temple profaner he just says 'Eliashib the priest who had oversight of the chamber of the house of the Lord' (13.4-9), so it might have been a different person. But the easier and usual reading is that it was the same person in both cases,[3] and surely the reader is meant to assume that only the high priest could give the orders for such a profanation. If there really was a dissenting high priest called Eliashib, would this story about his defiling the temple storeroom be reliable? It depends on how trustworthy a witness you take Nehemiah to be, and on whether the witness had ever had recourse to defilement accusations in the past. He might have had reason to defame the high priest, but fudged the names because he could not attack him directly. The lever for interpreting the role of Eliashib in the book of Nehemiah must be politics, not historical accuracy.

Priests who did not support the faction of the newly arrived governor could well feel that they were dangerously superseded by those who were in favour. Ezra and/or Nehemiah (for this purpose it does not matter which came first or when they came) took it on themselves to read the Bible to the congregation (Neh. 8.5) and to interpret it.

---

1. Cogan argues that there would certainly have been in Jerusalem a community that admitted Samarians to their number ('"For we, like you, worship your God": Three Biblical Portrayals of Samaritan Origins', *VT* 38 [1988], pp. 286-92).

2. Williamson, *Ezra and Nehemiah*, pp. 62-63.

3. Soggin, *History*, p. 278.

Organizing tithes and the rota of priests and Levites for the service of
the temple had been a charge for the king in Solomon's day, but at no
time would it not be an encroachment on the domain of the priesthood, as ordained by Moses in Numbers, to declare holy days and festivals, to institute new ceremonies and revive old ones. And who was
supposed to declare an act defiling? In several places in Numbers it is
taught that humans cannot judge of guilt or innocence: even Moses did
not know whether the sabbath woodgatherer had sinned (Num. 15.32-
36); only the Lord can know whether the woman suspected of adultery has defiled herself (Num. 5). Numbers' dissertations on intentional and inadvertent sinning in ch. 15 take on a new relevance in the
light of self-interested accusations of defilement launched by the
returnees against the people of the land.

The impression the governors give is that during the exile the cult
had fallen into desuetude, priests and Levites scattered, no tithes paid,
no sacrifices, no memory of the law, not even the sabbath observed.
This is plausible, as the temple had been destroyed and the impression
that has gone down into history is of the cult in abeyance. We return
to the question of historical reliability. Balaam's guilefulness is simplicity itself compared with the skilful snares spread by Nehemiah. He
is shifty about dates, apparently meticulous about names but not mentioning certain names, implying deviously that the party that came out
from Babylon are all that was left of the seed of Israel. He insinuates
defilement without directly accusing the high priest of profaning the
temple. The only things that Ezra and Nehemiah are absolutely clear
about are their takeover of the promises of Abraham for the exclusive
benefit of their supporters, and following from this claim, their
exclusionary stance against the people of the land and against Samaria,
Ammon and Moab. If there were priests and scribes in Judah in the
period of the exile, if they identified with the calumnied Eliashib, and
if they felt sympathy for the people of the land, they could be
expected to be incensed.

It is not likely that the priests in that small community kept apart
from the bitter politics of the day. The book of Numbers reads con-
vincingly as a priestly riposte to the doctrines promulgated by the
government party. The story of Korah's alliance with the Reubenites
in rebellion against Moses and Aaron, followed by Aaron's glorious
double vindication, could be written to deal a blow against the pretensions of the priestly party in harness to the secular authorities. Why

does Numbers repeat so often the laws that have been stated in Leviticus and Exodus? It would be in order to emphasize the point that Aaron had been given supreme authority in matters to do with the temple. It is Aaron, the high priest, who keeps charge of the rods, not the governor. Nehemiah boasted that he reassembled the personnel of the temple, set them in their stations, appointed treasurers over the storehouses, persuaded 'all Judah' to bring in the tithe of oil, grain and wine to the storehouses (Neh. 13.10-14), and made proper provision for the Levites (10.32-39). Nehemiah seems to have done it all without consulting the high priest.

This interpretation of Numbers, as a theological work to defend truth and justice from perversion, is proposed in the hope that scholarly curiosity will be aroused, and even that substantiation may follow. The style of Numbers, its controlled passion, its sustained scope and balance, suggest a powerful, urgent motive. Consider again its central theme, the inheritance: the land that has been promised, the sons of Jacob as the inheritors, the final injunction that 'every one of the tribes of Israel shall cleave to the inheritance of their fathers' (36.9), the insistence on 'everyone of the tribes of Israel' and their prominent numbering and renumbering in the right order. It is difficult not to read this as a response to the political situation. On the one hand the returnees want their lands; on the other hand, the people of the land have been working them for fifty odd years and want to keep them. Something is going to happen to transfer the land from the present occupiers to the new arrivals, because the latter are backed by the power of Persia, and when that happens something is going to be quoted from Holy Scripture to justify the transfer. If he wants to protest, the priest poet will have to speak out. He does: the book of Numbers is how he says it.

Nehemiah is a natural butt. One of the strange things about his political history is that it is written like a private confession to God. The way he dramatizes himself, his sanctimoniousness and self-glorification, are ridiculous. He thinks he can do anything, he admits he beats people up (Neh. 13.25), he makes out he knows what God wants, but he does not. Balaam works well as a skit on Nehemiah, stupidly berating and beating the ass on which he rides. With this reading the animal has to be a female, because she stands for Israel. The people of Israel recognize the Lord better than the governor. The ass sees the angel and obeys the Lord's command, whereas Balaam tries to bluster his way through. Balaam pretends to be totally obedient to God's will; unctuously he tells everyone that he only does and says what the Lord commands. He should have known that he could never change the blessing on Israel. His voice would be dripping with insincerity as he apologizes when he finally sees the angel. Although it is written that he gives up consulting omens, in the end he is discovered to be a fraud. His royal client, Balak, is angry with him. The perfect pantomime king is matched by the perfect pantomime villain. The story of Balaam could serve as Eliashib's version of Nehemiah's story.

Chapter 13

THE LAND AND THE JUBILEE

1. *The Men of Manasseh*

One of the weaknesses alleged against the editorship of Numbers is the inadequacy, even the triviality, of its ending in ch. 36. Here, instead of valediction we read how the men of Manasseh come back to Moses once again for further advice about their nieces' inheritance. Moses has already given a decision concerning the five daughters of Zelophehad in the previous narrative section (27.1-11). Apart from the untidiness of dealing with the same topic in two different places, it has seemed to some commentators to be unworthy of a major theological book that it should end with the making of a law for heiresses. But that is how it does end: Zelophehad's kinsmen were worried about the possible alienation of the family lands if daughters with no brothers as heirs could inherit, for there would be nothing then to stop them from taking their fathers' heritage with them on marriage. On a straight reading there is no conceivable reason why these women's inheritance problem should be split into two parts, with one reserved for the very last chapter. It can be a test case for the tradition for reading the Bible as a blow-by-blow account of the history of the editing, versus the rhetorical structure—or a test case for the lateral reading in a ring.

Only if the structure of the composition is to play no role in interpretation are we free to assume that this last story is there because the editors thought of it after they had finished the rest. The implication is that as they were writing the last set of laws, the papyrus still freshly cut, these men of Manasseh would have come up to them with an important point that had not occurred to them before. Just think what that interpretation does for the rest of the book. If they were so careless of the compositional unity at that point, the rest of it must be a jumble. Think what it does for the perception of the editors' role: they would be mere scribes, struggling to get everything into the record. If that was what they intended, they failed: everything is not in the record. It is not a law book, still less a complete set of the laws. How could it be? Again, if this is one last law added on to the others, how may we account for its presentation in the narrative mode? If the style of writing does not matter to the modern exegesis, is not disrespect or even contempt for the priestly editors compounded?

On this historical interpretation of the editorial process, most of the important questions to be asked of a sacred text are ruled out in advance. For example, why was it written? What impulse was strong enough to sustain the compilers through the arduous work of writing? Laws do not have to be written down, they often work better unwritten. Theology does not have to be written. Usually there is a historical reason for undertaking the pains of composition. One can ask what view the text was compiled to confound, or what consequences of policy it sought to avert. Unless a controversy about irreconcilable issues pushes an argument to assert fundamental principles about the nature of existence, the creation of the universe and the demands of the creator, the fundamentals can safely remain implicit.

Numbers has always been regarded as a serious book. Therefore we take it seriously, even to the point of examining the style. This leads to noticing that the law pertaining to heiresses is not given in the style for laws. In the vivid narrative style of a special encounter with Moses we are told that the uncles of the women complain about the probable effect of the Jubilee on their inheritance:

> And when the Jubilee of the people of Israel comes, then their inheritance will be added to the inheritance of the tribe to which they belong; and their inheritance will be taken from the inheritance of the tribe of our fathers (36.4).

This is an extraordinary complaint. The Numbers list of appointed feasts (chs. 28, 29) only deals with the annual cycle, so in Numbers there is no other mention of the Jubilee. Exodus requires a fallow year for the land in the seventh year (Exod. 23.10-11) but says nothing about a Jubilee. The law of Jubilee that the sons of Manasseh are referring to is from Leviticus which calls for the celebration of a sabbatical year when the land shall be left fallow (Lev. 25.1-7), as in Exodus, and adds a Jubilee in the fiftieth year, which it requires in addition to the seven-yearly release of slaves and remission of debts (Lev. 25.8-55; 27.1-34).

What the men of Manasseh say does not tally with what Leviticus says about the Jubilee's effect on land rights. Leviticus provides for land that has been sold to return to its original owners: all debts are to be remitted and all slaves to be freed in the year of Jubilee, and 'the field shall return to him of whom it was bought' (Lev. 27.24). To be sure, it is more complicated than that; the original owners have to redeem their sold property at appropriate rates and within a certain time.[1] Commentators have pointed out that the inheritance of heiresses marrying into another tribe has nothing to do with the law of the Jubilee.[2]

One might expect Moses to allay the misgivings of the men of Manasseh by correcting their interpretation of the law. All he needed to say was that they had got the purpose of the Jubilee wrong, and that marriage of an heiress would not mean taking away any land from her father's line of descent. Instead he takes their question seriously as if they have raised a real difficulty. He commends the house of Joseph for speaking out. Notice the naming of the house of Joseph here (36.5). To avoid the loss they anticipate, Moses counsels Josephite heiresses to marry within their father's family. He concludes his advice by reiterating the injunction about cleaving to the inheritance of their fathers. One should notice that he makes the same point four times in five verses:

i)   The inheritance of the people of Israel shall not be transferred from one tribe to another;

ii) for everyone of the people of Israel shall cleave to the inheritance of the tribe of his fathers...

iii) So no inheritance shall be transferred from one tribe to another;

iv) for each of the tribes of the people of Israel shall cleave to its own inheritance (Num. 36.4-9).

1.   There is also the difference made for selling a dwelling house in a walled city (which if it is going to be redeemed has to be redeemed within a year or not at all), compared with houses in unfortified villages which can be released in the Jubilee (Lev. 25.29-31). Without records to illustrate how these laws were applied, they are extremely difficult to interpret.

2.   P. Budd surveys several commentaries on this issue and specifically Snaith's view that Num. 36.4 assumes wrongly that the reversion of property at the jubilee concerns inherited land, whereas according to Lev. 25.8-34 it only applies to sales of property (*Numbers* [WBC, 5; Waco, TX: Word Books, 1984], pp. 388-890; N.H. Snaith, *Leviticus and Numbers* [NCB; London: Nelson, 1967], pp. 345-46).

We are left with the idea that Moses also made a mistake about the Jubilee, as well as the men of Manasseh, and that Numbers made just one more mistake. Martin Noth would solve it simply by omitting from the text of Numbers the whole of 36.4. He says that 'the reference to the Jubilee is out of place...it breaks the sequence of thought, and suggests that in the year of the Jubilee everything would remain unaltered'.[1]

2. *The Jubilee*

What does this little episode at the end of Numbers mean? Written so solemnly, the words of Moses commending the 'Sons of Joseph', repeating that the inheritance shall not be transferred, and misreading Leviticus?

The editors of Numbers generally stood shoulder to shoulder with the Leviticus editors, and it is not likely that here they were disagreeing with them or obliquely scoring a disputed calendrical point. Yet it is also probable that what has been taken for a minor discrepancy in the editor's interpretation of the laws in Leviticus is not accidental. Reference to contemporary political issues suggests another kind of explanation. The political factions in an enclave escalate the defence of their policies to the highest principles, and so the Bible would be continually invoked on both sides, for and against particular platforms.

Religion is a medium for factional challenge and riposte; the religious calendar is a conspicuous medium, a set of pins on which to peg out a whole theological position. Later in the Second Temple period the Dead Sea sect broke away from the mother-community precisely because of disagreement about calendrical calculation. As Talmon has put it,

> No barrier appears to be more substantial and fraught with heavier consequences than differences in calendar calculation. An alteration of any one of the dates that regulate the course of the year inevitably produces a break-up of the communal life, impairing the co-ordination between the behaviour of man and his fellow, and abolishes that synchronization of habits and activities which is the foundation of a properly functioning social order. Whosoever celebrates his own Sabbath, and does not observe the festivals of the year at the same time as the community in

1. Noth, *Numbers*, pp. 256-58.

which he lives, removes himself from his fellows and ceases to be a member of the social body to which he hitherto belonged.[1]

But the case is stronger than he allows: the calendar affords good ground for factional dispute. The disagreement in question was about the primordial holiness of the solar calendar which would require reckoning the sabbath from sunrise to sunrise, as the sect maintained, or the priority of the lunar calendar, as it came from Babylon, which reckoned the sabbath from sunset to sunset. Variations in the calendar are prime material for identifying factional strife.

The idea of the seven year-sabbath follows from a key principle in the Levitical pattern of appointed feasts. After every six days the people and the work animals honour the Lord by enjoying their sabbath of rest. After every six years the land enjoys its sabbath of rest to the honour of the Lord (Lev. 25.1-7). After every seven sabbaths of years there is to be a pentecostal celebration in the fiftieth year. On the tenth day of the seventh month the trumpets shall sound the Jubilee: to every man his possession shall be returned, every man shall return to his family, and liberty shall be proclaimed throughout the land to all its inhabitants (Lev. 25.8-46). Observe that even the hired servant and the sojourner shall return to his own family and to the possession of his fathers, for he also is accounted as a servant of the Lord whom he brought out of the land of Egypt (Lev. 25.35-42), and they are not to be sold or treated harshly.

A well-established seven-year cyclical pattern was widely diffused in the ancient Near East.[2] Jeremiah reproached Israel for neglecting it. His particular target of rebuke was the practice of slavery; he prophesied the fall of Judah to Babylon as the Lord's punishment precisely for not releasing their slaves (Jer. 34.8-22). The prolonged fallow period that he described as a sabbath for the land during the exile was presented not so much as a time of joy for liberated slaves but a time of punishment. Leviticus picks up this enigmatic point: the land is entitled to enjoy its sabbaths over a long period, that is while the people of Israel are absent in exile, because while they inhabited their own land they omitted to leave it fallow in the seventh year as commanded by the Lord:

1. S. Talmon, 'The Calendar Reckoning of the Sect from the Judaean Desert', in *Aspects of the Dead Sea Scrolls* (Scripta Hierosolymitana, 4; ed. C. Rabin and Y. Yadin; Jerusalem: Hebrew University, 1958), pp. 162-200.

2. C. Gordon, *Ugaritic Literature* (1949), IV, p. 57.

> The land also shall be left by them, and shall enjoy her sabbaths, while she lies desolate without them; and they shall accept the punishment of their iniquity because they despised my ordinances and abhorred my statutes. And yet, for all that, when they are in the land of their enemies I will not cast them away, neither will I abhor them, to destroy them utterly, and to break my covenant with them; for I am the Lord their God. But I will for their sakes remember the covenant of their ancestors, whom I brought forth out of the land of Egypt in the sight of the nations, that I might be their God (Lev. 26.42-45).

The desolation of the land left by the exiles is taken to be its sabbath rest, awarded to the land, and against the people, because the people of Israel did not observe the sabbaths of the land.

Although the law for the sabbatical year and the Jubilee seems hard and fast in Leviticus, in practice it was not at all clear when either fell due. Deciding to celebrate the Jubilee would be one of the functions of the high priest, but surely it would always be subject to political pressures. The date would depend partly on the calendar and partly on the date of the last one and partly on the gathering of a consensus among slave owners and negotiations about redeeming land. After the return from Babylon there was debate about when the last Jubilee was held. It should be in the year following seven sabbatical years, that is, in the fiftieth year since the last Jubilee (Lev. 25.8-12), but when would that have been? Zedekiah's proclamation of emancipation in late 588 BCE would be invoking the custom of the sabbatical year in the seventh year.[1] Mass manumission of male and female slaves was put into effect on that occasion through a solemn covenant contracted with the temple (Jer. 34.8-10, 15, 18-19). Since it was during Nebuchadnezzar's siege of Jerusalem, one can well imagine the moral and religious pressure put by the priests on the king to this end. That would plausibly count as a celebration of the Jubilee, and the next one could be dated from then. But when the siege was raised (temporarily as it turned out) the owners of the manumitted slaves forced them back into service (vv. 11, 16, 18). Jeremiah said:

> You had done right... But you turned and polluted my name, and caused every man his servant and every man his handmaid, whom you had set at liberty to return and brought them into subjection... (Jer. 34.16).

So it could be argued very plausibly that the manumission revoked

---

1. N. Sarna, 'Zedekiah's Emancipation of Slaves and the Sabbatical Year', in H.A. Hoffner (ed.), *Orient and Occident* (1973), pp. 143-49.

was not a true celebration of the Jubilee and that the obligation was still outstanding.

Then there is the more fundamental doubt about how many years should elapse between one Jubilee and the next. Leviticus appointed it for every fifty years (24.34ff.). According to Chronicles Jeremiah said the period should be seventy years:

> To fulfil the word of the Lord by the mouth of Jeremiah, until the land had enjoyed her sabbaths; for as long as she lay desolate, she kept sabbath, to fulfil threescore years and ten (2 Chron. 36.21).

Jeremiah was taken to be prophesying that the exile in Babylon would last seventy years between two Jubilees (Jer. 29.10).[1] However, if Leviticus's rule of fifty years is adopted and Zedekiah's celebration counted as valid, the fifty years of exile and sabbath for the land would run from 588 to 538. There would have been a case for celebrating it at any time after the return, just because it was obviously overdue.

3. *Peoples of the Land*

Finally, there would have been scope for dispute as to who was counted as the 'children of Israel' who would benefit from the Jubilee manumission. To us reading Leviticus so much later there might seem to be ambiguity as to who precisely has the right to this protection. At the time it may not have been ambiguous, but now two opposed interpretations are possible between the reference to sojourners in the land who count in the blessings of the Jubilee, and some other people, heathens sojourning there who, if enslaved, will be bondsmen to the people of Israel for ever (Lev. 25.44-46). If there is any ambiguity it would be in the expression 'children of Israel', and we have noted that Numbers has been at great pains to define that category. If we are agreed on who is comprised in that term, there is no ambiguity at all, for Leviticus makes the peroration to that passage repeat the rule:

---

1. The difference between fifty and seventy years shows how much latitude was there in the interpretation of the Jubilee. One can surmise that to some contemporaries the figure seventy years would have made double sense if it brought the time for the overdue sabbatical year into the period of Ezra–Nehemiah, when some major redistribution was fervently desired.

they shall be your slaves for ever, but over your brethren, the children of Israel, ye shall not rule one another with rigour (Lev. 25.46).

The rule in Leviticus is that the people of Israel are allowed to make into bondsmen the children of heathens, but not the children of Israel and not sojourners who are not heathens (Lev. 25.38-42). If they are not poor brethren who have been enslaved for debt, or if they do not subscribe to Judaism, they do not have to be released from bondage at the Jubilee. The passages are not contradictory, and the teaching is compatible with the purification rite that Numbers extends to sojourning strangers (19.10). It is, however, incompatible with the reading of Num. 33.52-56, where the people are enjoined to drive all heathens out of the land. Therein lies scope for dispute: are sojourning strangers to count as heathens? The text could be used by the government party if they wanted to separate their own people from foreign immigrants. When Ezra/Nehemiah are so righteously indignant about intermarriage with the people of the land both Leviticus and Numbers require them to specify whether the people of the land are idolators in practice, or just descended from idolators. The question of idolatry and defilement is automatically made the criterion.

As suggested in the previous chapter the question of who counted in the congregation was a hot political matter, and one that entailed theological principles. The interpretation of the 'children of Israel' is part of the interpretation of the law of the Jubilee. Moses recognizes this when in Num. 36.5 he addresses the men of Manasseh as the sons of Joseph. They would be asking if they were to be excluded from the benefits of the Jubilee. Were their lands secure if they had obtained them in repayment of debt? The men of Reuben and Gad could have asked the same thing. Together with the men of Manasseh they saw land that they liked east of the Jordan: Moses confirmed the right of Reuben and Gad to the land they had chosen and gave Gilead to the sons of Manasseh (Num. 32). If the peoples of these tribes were in the territory of Judah at the time of Jubilee, they would thus indisputably be counted as sons of Israel (as if all the previous countings did not prove it), and entitled to their land, and if they have fallen on hard times they would be indisputably entitled to the benefits of the manumission of bond slaves. What is still not clear is whether their rights to their land apply to land they might have held for over fifty years in Judah during the exile of the noble and educated families in Babylon. If they gave their daughters to the returnees they might lose all. Moses of course is not expected to know about this problem occurring in a much later era. But he advises them to be cautious in arranging marriages.

4. *Nehemiah's Limited Jubilee*

Although he never said that he was celebrating the sabbatical year, this is what Nehemiah implicitly did in his apparently successful bid to get the land restored to the returned remnant (Neh. 5.1-13). The returnees would have experienced the usual problem of exiles in getting land back and Nehemiah drew on the usual populist funds of xenophobia to justify them. Alberto Soggin says the very existence of the community was threatened by 'all the law suits which had arisen over the lands of the exiles which Nebuchadnezzar had distributed to those who had remained behind and which were reclaimed by the exiles when they returned'.[1] Nehemiah's solution was to call for a general remission of debts and slavery (Neh. 5). Widespread throughout the region there had been a custom of declaring an amnesty when a new ruler came into power. When political power has been transferred the amnesty would be applied in favour of those who supported the current ruler and against those who had opposed him; it would free prisoners and restore lands. Some land crisis is given by Nehemiah as the reason for his amnesty but he never describes it as a conflict between the returned exiles and the people of the land. The Jews have complained to him that they are in financial straits, that they have bonded their own children against their debts, and that they cannot redeem them because other men have their lands and vineyards (Neh. 5.5). The term 'the Jews' suggests the legitimacy of the long-established inhabitants of Judah and the terms of the complaint recall the problems of debtors which Leviticus's Jubilee was designed to mitigate. Nehemiah rebukes 'the nobles and the officials' and accuses them of corruption, all the while making a heavy appeal to religion. The conflict is thus between the returnees and the people who are *de facto* holding the land, and who could appeal to the fifty-year entitlement to keep it, or claim compensation for being dispossessed.

If commentators are right about the causes of the land crisis, Nehemiah is upbraiding the category he elsewhere refers to as 'people

---

1. Soggin, *History*, p. 277.

of the land' (Neh. 10.28-31), and not the people who have returned
with him and are claiming their land. Piously he points out that the
Jews are their kinsmen and charges them with selling their brethren
(Neh. 5.8), a clear enough reference to Lev. 25.42. What does this
imply? Are the people he is persuading to agree to his plan non-Jews:
that is, not men of the tribe of Judah, though kinsmen in the sense that
they are descended from Abraham? He administers to everyone an
oath before the priests in a moment of great emotional effervescence
(Neh. 5.12). It is made to sound as if the people of the land (who,
after all, had the land) were the ones who heartily agreed and took the
oath to restore everything and require nothing in return. And yet
were they even present? This all took place at a great assembly which
Nehemiah, in a telling phrase, 'held against them' (Neh. 5.7). Was it
held in the same conditions as the great assembly that Ezra (10.7-8)
held 'against' the people who had married foreigners? On that occasion all the men of Judah came, having been warned if they did not
come they would forfeit all their possessions. There must be some
reasonable suspicion that in Nehemiah's assembly the rulers used the
oath to take their lands away from the sons of Jacob who had not gone
into exile or to expropriate immigrants from the neighbouring
provinces.

5. *The Inheritance of the People of Israel*

It would be rash for a commentator on Numbers to decide that a piece
that starts under the rubric of the inheritance of the people of Israel is
extraneous. In the five verses of Numbers' problematical last chapter
(36.4-9) the law repeated four times declares that the inheritance shall
not be transferred from one tribe to another. When there is such a
heavily reiterated phrase we have come to know that the meaning of
the passage revolves around it. We have to be interested in why Moses
hailed the men of Manasseh as 'the sons of Joseph', the name that takes
us to the heart of the perplexities of the day. The story has evidently
something to do with the people of Ephraim. We should also be interested in why Manasseh's daughters were thought to be about to marry
outside their tribe. Could it be that the returnees tried to solve their
land problems by marriage alliances? The thought takes us to another
burning issue, that of intermarriage with the other tribes living in
Judah. The question is how many Ephraimites were living there at the

time of Nehemiah. There was a problem with infiltrated people from the other tribal areas, on the west as well as on the east. Nehemiah mentions among the enemies of Judah, the Ashdodites (Neh. 4.7) and complains that the modern Jewish children could not even speak their own language (Neh. 13.23). We would need to know what treatment was meted out by Ezra and Nehemiah to the peoples who were sons of Joseph, of whom there could have been many living under his jurisdiction.

The first time that the 'people of the land' appear in the book of Ezra they announce themselves as having been settled there by the Assyrian king (Ezra. 4.2), but they say that they worship the same God and ask to be allowed to share the work of building the temple. Being settled by the Assyrian government implied that they were from Samaria as Assyria colonized Ephraim by forcibly moving out the locals and settling foreign tribes there. This suggests that at least some of the people whom Ezra regarded as the adversaries of Judah were people of Samaria (sons of Joseph) living in his jurisdiction. His next sentence implies that the adversaries are 'the people of the land'. By the same stroke he has deviously implied that the land of Judah was inhabited by foreigners when 'the remnant' came back from exile. This is implausible.[1] Master of innuendo, he can also suggest that if they were forcibly settled from the land of Ephraim, the people whom he calls the adversaries of Judah are not real Ephraimites but foreign colonizers. From what we know of his policy toward those not belonging to the party of the returnees we can recognize this as a preliminary defamation of people he is going to exclude from the congregation as idolators.

In that context, the sons of Joseph would have been right to be worried; the doctrine of the Jubilee year was going to be used against them. And Moses was right too. Whatever Leviticus said about the Jubilee being a time for restitution, liberation and unification, this time it was going to be for confiscation, constraint and division. In the situation of conflicting claims to the land once owned by the exiles, Leviticus says: 'In the year of the Jubilee you shall return every man his possession' (Lev. 25.13), a blow in favour of the rights of the returnees. But Leviticus goes on to require those who are being dispossessed to be compensated, and sets the rates for compensation.

1. S. Talmon, 'Addendum to Max Weber', in *King and Cult* (Magnum Press, Hebrew University, 1986).

Ezra's method of accusing the people of the land of idolatry allowed him to repossess without reference to Leviticus, and without paying compensation. It is Nehemiah who implies that the law of Jubilee requires free restitution to the kin of debtors. As a contribution to the controversies about the land rights crisis, Leviticus ch. 25 would need a very careful exegesis. There may have been two separate crises solved in the two different ways. It is more than possible that this interpretation has got the problem and the solutions the wrong way round. But it is probably correct to read Numbers' last chapter as contributing to that debate the reminder that Moses had said that no inheritance should be transferred from one tribe to another.

6. *The Wilderness*

The piece on the daughters of Zelophehad which ends the whole book is technically a straightforward 'enjambment', a dove-tailed wedge connecting the two halves. In a sense the commentators were right to say that it is not the ending because it is the kind of ending which takes the story back to the beginning. Chapter 36 has switched its mode from law to narrative, and at the same time it has made a jump from the end of the book to the beginning again, from the old year into the opening of the new, which is in the narrative mode. The reference to the Jubilee, though it comes at the end, rightly belongs with the first section, the first New Year. It is part of the theme of land inheritance. It recalls the key notion of the land that the Lord promised to the descendants of Abraham. In the opening section Moses is told to number the men who can bear arms, tribe by tribe, according to their fathers' houses. The common historical connection between arms-bearing and territorial rights is left implicit and only brought out negatively in 18.20. Moses says that tribe by tribe the people of Israel are to cleave to the inheritance of their fathers. By coming at the very end of the book this little coda latches the end to the beginning, closing the ring.

The book of Numbers begins with the census, the congregation to be counted tribe by tribe, and when the count is over, they set forth, everyone with their families, according to the house of their fathers (Num. 2.34). The peroration of the whole book picks this up when it says four times that the inheritance of the people of Israel shall not be transferred from one tribe to another (Num. 36.7-9). To miss in this peroration the echo of the book's beginning is to miss the point of the numbering and renumbering of the twelve tribes. And from what we know of the several levels of reference that are continually deployed, we can be sure that the inheritance includes the right to be sanctified as much as it includes the right to land.

With this chapter the structure of the book is complete and the story is ended on the threshold of the new cycle. The end of the first half of the year ushers in the second half and the end of the second half points on to the next beginning of the first half. The book's arrangement in parallels presents the crisis of Korah's rebellion in the desert as the turning point between two half years. The other crises in their history each takes its place in a continuous pattern. Coming out of the desert in Numbers is like coming out of Egypt in Exodus, and like coming home from Babylon in the memory of the Second Temple community. While the Numbers community is still weeping in the desert, Israel blossoms and buds as Isaiah prophesied (Isa. 27.6); the Jewish New Year is inaugurated, time is renewed, the promises have been kept, and the Second Temple community is constituting itself. Furthermore, coming out of the fourth quarter is not an exit from the cycle of generations. When the fourth quarter is complete, the first is about to begin. The book of Numbers has brought itself to its own conclusion, with a special commendation of the sons of Joseph.

What Numbers is saying in terms of Abraham's descendants' rights to their inherited land conforms to Ezekiel's rebukes to Israel and Judah as the two harlot women: both have betrayed their husband, both are punished, and the Lord is ready to forgive both (Ezek. 23). The priests and the prophets are not preaching against one another. Both mourn the loss of the Northern Kingdom, grieve over its treachery, and yearn for Ephraim to repent and come home. Numbers is on the side of forgiveness, the inscrutability of the Lord's judgment, and the need to make purification available for whoever seeks it. The twelve sons of Jacob are one people:

> Say to your brother, 'My people', and to your sister, 'She has obtained pity' (Hos. 2.1).

BIBLIOGRAPHY

Ackerman, S., 'And the Women Knead Dough: The Worship of the Queen of Heaven in Sixth-century Judah', in *Gender and Difference in Ancient Israel* (ed. P. Day; Fortress Press, 1989), pp. 109-122.

Anderson, G.W., 'Characteristics of Hebrew Poetry', in *The New Oxford Annotated Bible with the Apocrypha, An Ecumenical Study Bible* (Revised Standard Version; Oxford: Oxford University Press, 1977).

Ardener, S., 'Sexual Insult and Female Militancy', in *Perceiving Women* (ed. S. Ardener; New York: Dent, Halsted, John Wiley, 1975), pp. 29-54.

Bal, M., *Death and Dissymmetry, the Politics of Coherence in the Book of Judges* (Chicago: University of Chicago Press, 1988).

Betz, H.D. *et al.*, *The Greek Magical Papyri in Translation* (Chicago: University of Chicago Press, 1986).

Brown, P., 'A Dark-Age Crisis: Aspects of the Iconoclastic Controversy', *English Historical Review* 88 (1973), pp. 1-34.

Budd, P., *Numbers* (WBC, 5; Waco, TX: Word Books, 1984).

—'Does the Book of Numbers have any Individuality and Integrity as a Unit within the Process of Revision?', in *The Old Testament, an Introduction* (ed. O. Eissfeldt; Oxford: Blackwell, 1963), pp. 156-57.

Bundy, E., *Studia Pindarica* (California: University of California Press, 1986).

Burrows, E., *The Oracles of Jacob and Balaam* (London: Bellarmine Series, Burns Oates & Washbourne, 1938).

Childs, B., *Introduction to the Old Testament as Scripture* (London: CMS, 1979), pp. 190-200.

Cogan, M., ' "For we, like you, worship your God": Three Biblical Portrayals of Samaritan Origins', *VT* 38.3 (1988), pp. 286-92.

Crone, P., 'Islam, Judeo-Christianity and Byzantine Iconoclasm', *Jerusalem Studies in Arabic and Islam* 2 (1980), pp. 59-95.

Cross, F.M., *Canaanite Myth and Hebrew Epic: Essays in the History of the Religion of Israel* (Cambridge, MA: Harvard University Press, 1973).

de Heusch, Luc, *Le roi ivre, ou l'origine de l'etat* (Paris: Gallimard, 1972); ET, *The Drunken King, or The Origin of the State* (Indiana University Press, 1982).

Deussen, P., *Das System des Vedanta* (Leipzig: Brockhaus, 1883); ET *The System of the Vedanta: according to Badarayana's Brahma-Sutras and Cankara's Commentary thereon set forth as a compendium of the dogmatics of Brahmanism from the standpoint of Cankara* (trans. C. Johnston; New York: Dover Publications, 1973 [1912]).

Destro, A., *The Law of Jealousy, Anthropology of Sotah* (Atlanta: Scholars Press, 1989).

Douglas, M., *The Lele of the Kasai* (IAI; Oxford: Oxford University Press, 1963).

—'Techniques of Sorcery Control', in John Middleton and E.H. Winter (eds.), *Witchcraft and Sorcery in East Africa* (London: Routledge & Kegan Paul, 1963).

—*Natural Symbols* (Hammondsworth: Penguin Books, 1970).

—*How Institutions Think* (Syracuse: Syracuse University Press, 1987).

—'A Kind of Space', *The Idea of a Home*, Social Research 58,1 (1990), pp. 288-307.

—'Risk as a Forensic Resource', *Risk* (Daedalus: Fall, 1990).

—*Risk and Blame* (London: Routledge, 1992).

Doumas, C.G., 'High Art from the Time of Abraham', *Biblical Archaeology Review* (1991), pp. 41-51.

Duckworth, G.E., *Structural Patterns and Proportions in Virgil's Aeneid: a Study in Mathematical Composition* (Ann Arbor: University of Michigan Press, 1962).

Dumont, L., *Essays on Individualism, Modern Ideology in Anthropological Perspective* (Chicago: University of Chicago Press, 1986).

Dunsire, A., 'Holistic Governance', *Public Policy and Administration* 5.1 (1990).

Epstein, I., *Judaism, a Historical Presentation* (Harmondsworth: Pelican, 1959).

Evans-Pritchard, E., *Nuer Religion* (Oxford: Clarendon Press, 1956).

Fisher, L.R., 'The Patriarchal Cycles', in *Orient and Occident, Essays Presented to Cyrus H. Gordon on the Occasion of his 65th Birthday* (ed. H.A. Hoffner; Verlag Butzon and Bercker Kevelaer, 1973), pp. 59-63.

Fishbane, M., 'Accusations of Adultery: A Study of Law and Scribal Practice in Numbers 5.11-31', *Hebrew Union College Annual* 45 (1974), pp. 25-43.

Fox, J.J., 'Roman Jakobson and the Comparative Study of Parallelism', in *Roman Jakobson: Echoes of His Scholarship* (Lisse: The Peter de Ridder Press, 1977).

Geller, M., 'The Šurpu Incantations and Lev. V.1-5', *JSS* 25.2 (1980), p. 183.

—'Taboo in Mesopotamia, a review article', *Journal of Cuneiform Studies*, 42, 1, (1990), pp. 105-117.

Gellner, E., *Saints of the Atlas* (London: Weidenfeld & Nicolson, 1969).

Gleick, J., *Chaos, Making a New Science* (London: Heinemann, 1988).

Gluckman, M., 'The Kingdom of the Zulu of South Africa', in *African Political Systems* (ed. M. Fortes and E.E. Evans-Pritchard; Oxford: Clarendon Press, 1940).

Gordon, C., *Ugaritic Literature* (1949), 4, p. 57.

Gray, G.B., *The Forms of Hebrew Poetry* (London: Hodder & Stoughton, 1915).

Greengold, C., *The Structure of Pindar's Epinician Odes* (Amsterdam: Hakkert, 1980).

Hamilton, R., *General Form in the Odes of Pindar* (The Hague: Mouton, 1974), p. 73.

Harshav, B., *The Meaning of Yiddish* (California: University of California Press, 1990).

Jakobson, R., *Questions de Poetique* (Paris: Editions du Seuil, 1973).

Jeremias, J., *Jerusalem in the Time of Jesus* (London: SCM Press, 1969).

Khare, R., *The Hindu Hearth and Home* (Durham, NC: Carolina Academic Press, 1976).

Labat, R., *Un calendrier babylonien des travaux des signes et des mots* (1965).

Laeuchli, S., *The Language of Faith: Introduction to the Semantic Dilemma of the Early Church* (New York: Abingdon Press, 1962).

Leach, E.R., and A. Aycock, 'Why did Moses have a Sister?', in *Structuralist Interpretations of Biblical Myth* (Cambridge: Cambridge University Press, 1983).

Lewis, D., 'Why did Sina Dance?', in *Creating Indonesian Cultures* (ed. P. Alexander; Sydney: Oceania Publications, 1989), pp. 175-198.

—'A Quest for the Source: The Ontogenesis of a Creation Myth of the Ata Tana Ai', in *To Speak in Pairs, Essays on the Ritual Languages of Eastern Indonesia* (Cambridge: Cambridge University Press, 1988).

Lowth, R. *Lectures on the Sacred Poetry of the Hebrews*, translation of *De Sacra Poesia Hebraeorum Praelectiones Academicae* (Boston, 1829).

Mars, G., *Cheats at Work, an Anthropology of Workplace Crime* (London: Allen & Unwin, 1982), pp. 75ff.

Meijers, D., 'The Structural Analysis of the Jewish Calendar and its Political Implications', *Anthropos* 82 (1987), pp. 604-610.

Merton, R.K. *Social Theory and Social Structure* (New York: The Free Press, 1949).

Milgrom, J., *Numbers, The JPS Torah Commentary* (Philadelphia: The Jewish Publication Society, 1990).

Murphy, R., and L. Kasdan, 'The Structure of Parallel Cousin Marriage', *The American Anthropologist* (1959), pp. 17-29.

Nahum, S., 'Zedekiah's Emancipation of Slaves and the Sabbatical Year', in *Orient and Occident* (ed. H.A. Hoffner, 1973).

Needham, J., 'Fundamental Ideas of Chinese Science', in Colin A. Ronan (ed.), *The Shorter Science and Civilisation in China: an Abridgement of Joseph Needham's Original Text*, I (Cambridge: Cambridge University Press, 1980), pp. 169-70.

Neusner, J., 'Judaism in a Time of Crisis, Four Responses to the Destruction of the Second Temple', *A Quarterly Journal of Jewish Life and Thought* 21.3 (1972), pp. 313-327.

—'History and Structure: The Case of Mishnah', *JAAR* 45.2 (1977), pp. 161-192.

—'Form and Meaning in Mishnah', *JAAR* 45.1 (1977), pp. 27-54.

—*Self-fulfilling Prophecy, Exile and Return in the History of Judaism* (Boston: Beacon Press, 1987), p. 60.

—'Judaic Uses of History in Talmudic Times', in *Essays in Jewish Historiography* (ed. A. Rapoport-Albert; Wesleyan University Press, 1988).

—'The Case of Leviticus Rabbah', in *By Study and Also by Faith* (ed. J.M. Lundquist and S. Ricks, 1990), pp. 332-388.

—*The Mishnah, A New Translation* (1988).

Noth, M., *Numbers, A Commentary* (London: SCM Press, 1968).

Ovenden, M., 'The Origin of the Constellations', *The Philosophical Journal* 3.1 (1966) pp. 1-18.

Pitt-Rivers, J., *The Fate of Shechem, or the Politics of Sex, Essays in the Anthropology of the Mediterranean* (Cambridge: Cambridge University Press, 1977).

Ratzinger, J., *Church, Ecumenism and Politics: New Essays in Ecclesiology* (1988).

Rehfeld, W., 'Deuteronomic Time', in *Proceedings of the Ninth World Congress of Jewish Studies Jerusalem: 1985*, I (Jerusalem: World Union of Jewish Studies, 1986), pp. 121-125.

Ritner, R.K., 'Horus on the Crocodiles: A Juncture of Religion and Magic in Late Dynastic Egypt', in *Religion and Philosophy in Ancient Egypt* (ed. W.K. Simpson; Yale Egyptological Studies 3; Yale Egyptological Seminar, The Graduate School, Yale University, New Haven, 1989).

Roth, W., *Hebrew Gospel: Cracking the Code of Mark* (Oak Park, IL: Meyer Stone, 1988).

Sahlins, M., *Islands of History* (Chicago: University of Chicago Press, 1985).

Schwartz, B.I., *The World of Thought in Ancient China* (Belknap, Harvard, 1985).

Schwarz, M., and M. Thompson, *Divided We Stand* (Hemel Hampstead: Harvester Wheatsheaf Press, 1989).

Sed, N., 'Le Symbolisme Zodiacal des Douze Tribues', in *Etudes juives, la mystique cosmologique juive* (Mouton: Appendix, 1981).

Segal, D.A., 'The European, Allegories of Racial Purity', *Anthropology Today* 7.5 (1991), pp. 8-9.

Smith, M., *Palestinian Parties and Politics that Shaped the Old Testament* (London: SCM Press, 1971).

Smith, W.R., *Kinship and Marriage in Early Arabia* (Cambridge: Cambridge University Press, 1885).

Snaith, N.H. *Leviticus and Numbers* (NCB, London: Nelson, 1967).

Soggin, J.A., *A History of Israel, from the Beginnings to the Bar Kochba Revolt, A.D. 135* (London: SCM Press, 1984).

Stern, M. 'The Period of the Second Temple', in *A History of the Jewish People* (ed. Ben-Sasson; London: Weidenfeld & Nicolson, 1976), pp. 185-306.

Swetz, F., and T.I. Kao, *Was Pythagoras Chinese? An Examination of Right Triangle Theory in Ancient China* (Pennsylvania State University Press, University Studies No. 40, 1977), pp. 1-75.

Talmon, S., 'The Calendar Reckoning of the Sect from the Judaean Desert', in *Scripta Hierosolymitana. IV. Aspects of the Dead Sea Scrolls* (ed. C. Rabin and Y. Yadin; Jerusalem: Publications of the Hebrew University, 1958).

—'Addendum to Max Weber', in *King and Cult* (1979).

—*King, Cult and Calendar in Ancient Israel* (Jerusalem: Magnes Press, 1986).

Turner, V.W., *The Anthropology of Performance* (New York: P & J Publications, 1986).

Van der Waerden, B.L., *Science Awakening* (Holland: P. Noordhoff, 1954), pp. 93-4.

Weber, M., *Ancient Judaism* (New York: Free Press, 1952).

Wenham, G., *Numbers, An Introduction and Commentary* (TOTC; Leicester: Intervarsity Press, 1981).

Whaler, J., *Counterpoint and Symbol: An Inquiry into the Rhythm of Milton's Epic Style* (Anglistica, 6; Copenhagen: Rosenkilde & Bagger, 1956).

Wildavsky, A., *Assimilation and Separation, Joseph the Administrator and the Politics of Religion in Biblical Israel* (New Brunswick,: Transaction Publishers, 1993).

—*The Nursing Father, Moses as a Political Leader* (Mobile: Alabama University Press, 1984).

Williamson, H.G.M., *Israel in the Book of Chronicles* (Cambridge: Cambridge University Press, 1977), ch. vii.

—*Ezra and Nehemiah* (OTG; Sheffield: JSOT Press, 1987).

Wittgenstein, L., *Remarks on Frazer's Golden Bough* (ed. R. Rees; New Jersey: Humanities Press, 1979).

Wu, H.L., 'The Concept of Parallelism: Jin Shengtan's Critical Discourse on "The Water Margin"', in *Poetics East and West* (ed. M. Dolezelova-Velingerova; Monograph Series of Toronto Semiotics, 4, 1988–89), pp. 169-79.

INDEXES

INDEX OF BIBLICAL REFERENCES

OLD TESTAMENT

JOURNAL FOR THE STUDY OF THE OLD TESTAMENT

Supplement Series